# Ukraine's Orange Revolution

# Ukraine's Orange Revolution

Andrew Wilson

Yale University Press
New Haven and London

For information about this and other Yale University Press publications, please contact:
U.S. Office: sales.press@yale.edu   yalebooks.com
Europe Office: sales@yaleup.co.uk   www.yalebooks.co.uk

Set in Sabon by J&L Composition, Filey, North Yorkshire
Printed in Great Britain by St Edmundsbury Press Ltd, Bury St Edmunds

ISBN 0 300 11290 4

Library of Congress Control Number: 2005933591

A catalogue record for this book is available from the British Library

10 9 8 7 6 5 4 3 2 1

# Contents

# Illustrations

## Plates

Figure                                           *page*

Maps

Tables

# Acknowledgements

The story of the Orange Revolution has all the ingredients of a certain type of novel once thought out of fashion: corruption, political manipulation, murder, spies, secret tapes, secret dinners with members of the secret services, poison and power. It is also the story of a dramatic popular uprising, a belated rebellion thirteen years after the fall of Communism against an arrogant and corrupt elite in one of Europe's poorest countries. I hope to have bought some of this to life, but any book written so soon after the event will be provisional in many of its judgements. It will, it is hoped, be followed by many more.

Thanks are due to my parents, to Timothy Taylor, and at Yale to Robert Baldock, Candida Brazil, Ewan Thompson and Stephen Kent. I am particularly grateful to Sarah Whitmore, who read an early draft and supplied many of the pictures, and to Michael Hobbs for his insightful comments.

# Abbreviations

| | |
|---|---|
| CEC | Central Election Commission |
| FEP | Foundation for Effective Politics, Russia's leading 'political technology' company |
| IRI | International Republican Institute, USA |
| IUD | Industrial Union of the Donbas |
| KIIS | Kiev International Institute of Sociology, Ukraine's leading independent poll-takers |
| NBU | National Bank of Ukraine |
| NDI | National Democratic Institute, USA |
| NED | National Endowment for Democracy, USA |
| NSDC | National Security and Defence Council |
| OUN | Organisation of Ukrainian Nationalists, established 1929 |
| SBU | Security Service of Ukraine |
| SCM | System Capital Management, Rinat Akhmetov's business empire |
| SDPU(o) | Social-Democratic Party of Ukraine (united), political cover for the Kiev 'clan' |
| UAH | The Ukrainian national currency, the *hryvnia*, trading at just over five to the US dollar in 2004 |
| UESU | United Energy Systems of Ukraine, Yuliia Tymoshenko's company |
| UNA–UNSO | Ukrainian National Assembly–Ukrainian National Self-Defence Organisation, far right organisation, thoroughly infiltrated |
| UPA | Ukrainian Insurgent Army, anti-Soviet force, 1942–mid 1950s |

# Dramatis Personae

### The Opposition

Viktor Yushchenko, governor of the National Bank 1993–9, prime minister 1999–2001, head of Our Ukraine, election candidate.
Yuliia Tymoshenko, former oligarch, deputy prime minister 1999–2001.
Pora, the student movement (Yellow and Black), supposedly a collective actor with no leaders.
Vadym Hetman, Yushchenko's mentor.
Viacheslav Chornovil, former dissident, leader of the Rukh movement in the 1990s.

### Yushchenko's Staff

Roman Bezsmertnyi, chief of staff until July 2004.
Oleksandr Zinchenko, his successor.
Oleh Rybachuk, Yushchenko's chief aide as prime minister, link man with the security services (the SBU).

### Yushchenko's Business Supporters

Petro Poroshenko, chocolate king.
Davyd Zhvaniia, also financier of Pora and the Maidan.
Yevhen Chervonenko, Yushchenko's security chief.

### Tymoshenko's Staff

Oleksandr Turchynov, Tymoshenko's long-standing aide.
Mykola Syvulskyi, a financial assistant.

## The Authorities

Leonid Kuchma, president 1994–January 2005.

Viktor Yanukovych, prime minister 2002–January 2005, candidate.

Andrii Kliuiev, first deputy prime minister for the notoriously corrupt energy sector, head of Yanukovych's campaign office.

Serhii Kliuiev, fundraiser, deputy chair of Donetsk council until April 2005.

Eduard Prutnik, adviser to Yanukovych.

Volodymyr Lytvyn, head of the Presidential Administration until 2002, then head of For A United Ukraine and chair of parliament.

Mykola Bilokon, minister of the interior, 2003–4.

Mykola Azarov, head of the tax inspectorate, 1996–2002, first deputy prime minister and finance minister 2002–4, briefly prime minister in January 2005.

Ihor Smeshko, head of the SBU, September 2003–February 2005.

Volodymyr Satsiuk, deputy head of the SBU, April–December 2004.

Hryhorii Kirpa, railways minister until his death in December 2004.

Serhii Kivalov, head of the Central Election Commission (CEC).

Serhii Katkov, 'mole' on the CEC.

## The Oligarchs

Viktor Pinchuk, Dnipropetrovsk.

Serhii Tihipko, Dnipropetrovsk.

Ihor Kolomoiskyi, Dnipropetrovsk.

Rinat Akhmetov, Donetsk.

Viktor Medvedchuk, Kiev, head of the Presidential Administration, 2002–4.

Hryhorii Surkis, Kiev, owner of Dynamo Kiev.

Ihor Bakai, former oligarch, down at heel.

Oleksandr Volkov, former oligarch, turncoat.

## Their Puppets

Nataliia Vitrenko, fake 'Progressive Socialist'.

Roman Kozak, fake 'nationalist'.

Dmytro Korchynskyi, fake 'nationalist'.

## The Russians

Vladimir Putin, president.

Gleb Pavlovskii, political technologist.

Marat Gelman, political technologist.
Sergei Markov, political technologist.
Maxim 'Mad Max' Kurochkin, 'businessman'.
Boris Berezovskii, exiled oligarch.

## Other Players

Oleksandr Moroz, leader of the Socialist Party, candidate.
Petro Symonenko, leader of the Communist Party, candidate.
Anatolii Kinakh, prime minister 2001–2, candidate.
Yevhen Marchuk, head of the SBU 1991–4, prime minister 1995–6, head of the NSDC 1999–2003, minister of defence 2003–September 2004.
Hryhorii Gongadze, journalist, murdered September 2000.
Mykola Melnychenko, presidential bodyguard, fled with 'secret tapes', November 2000.
Oleksii Pukach, interior ministry thug, Gongadze's alleged killer.
Aleksander Kwaśniewski, president of Poland

Modern Ukraine

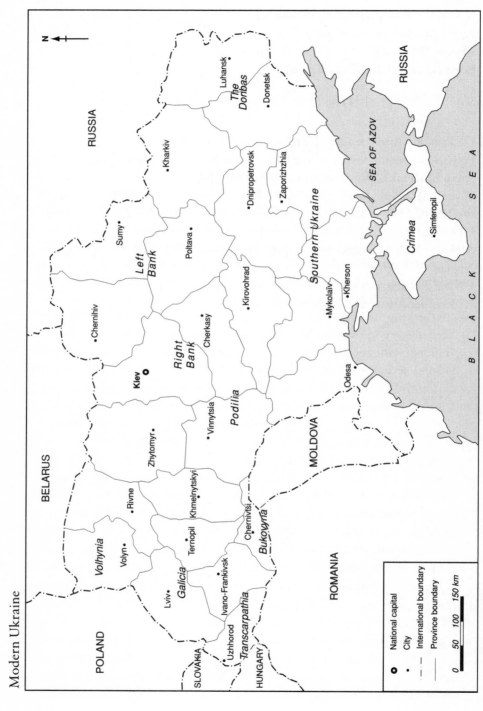

Source: Andrew Wilson, *The Ukrainians: Unexpected Nation* (New Haven and London: Yale University Press, 2000)

# 1

# How the Deed Was Done

21 November 2004 was election night in Ukraine. After a long and bitter campaign, voters now had a straight choice between the sitting prime minister, Viktor Yanukovych, and Viktor Yushchenko, his predecessor in the post from 1999 to 2001. Yanukovych was the candidate of the authorities – more or less the same authorities who had governed Ukraine since the collapse of the USSR in 1991. Yushchenko had once also been an insider, but now he was leading an opposition movement with a real chance of taking power. The first round had not gone well for Yanukovych's team, but tonight they were quietly confident. Not because they had improved their campaigning or benefited from some serious mistake by Yushchenko, but because Serhii Kivalov, head of the Central Election Commission (CEC), whose job it was to collect, count and announce the results, had supplied a secret Yanukovych team housed in the Zoriany ('Stars') cinema on, appropriately enough, Moscow Street in central Kiev, with access passwords to the CEC computer base. The 'Zoriany team' was going to count the vote instead.[1]

Liudmila Hrebeniuk, a chief consultant to the outgoing presidential administration of Leonid Kuchma, helped to oversee another system that collected information at each of Ukraine's 33,000 polling stations, and 'worked far more quickly than the CEC'. By 2:35 a.m. it was clear that turnout was high: 29,291,744 people had voted, an impressive 78.7 per cent of the population. Hrebeniuk was therefore astounded when completely different figures were announced at lunchtime on 22 November: official figures claimed a turnout of 80.7 per cent, or 30,412,994 – an extra 1.1 million votes. As one CEC member later put it rather more bluntly under oath, 'a million votes were thrown in after eight o'clock' (when the polls had closed).[2] Half of these were allocated to Yanukovych's home region of Donetsk, where turnout shot up from 83.7 per cent to 96.6 per cent, or from 3,199,983 to 3,711,763 – an extra 511,780 votes, of which 96.2 per cent were apparently cast in favour of Yanukovych.[3]

Yanukovych was declared the overall winner by just under 3 per cent – by 49.5 per cent to 46.6 per cent, or 871,402 votes; that is, by more or less the extra million. The CEC, however, had a tainted reputation. Back in 1998 it had not only fixed a previous vote, but had taken an implausible four weeks to do it. Nearly all eyes were therefore on the independent exit poll, which had been conducted by some of the country's remaining independent academics. Its massive sample of 28,000 people, with a margin of error of only 2 per cent, showed that Yushchenko had won by 53 per cent to 44 per cent.[4] A second problem for the Zoriany team was that its telephones had been tapped by the Ukrainian Secret Service (SBU). One shadow team was being shadowed by another. The tapes were passed on to Yushchenko's right-hand man, Oleh Rybachuk, who played the key role as intermediary with the SBU, paying 'expenses' where necessary.[5] (Rybachuk had studied foreign languages at Kiev University. Half of his class ended up in the KGB.) The key extracts follow.[6]

EPISODE ONE, 21 NOVEMBER, 19:05: Yurii Levenets, a local Ukrainian 'political technologist' (that is, a notorious political fixer, who had also helped corrupt the previous election in 1999), talks with an unknown 'Valerii' one hour before the polls close.

LEVENETS (ANXIOUS): Greetings! How's things?

VALERII: Not very good. We have negative results.

LEVENETS: What do you mean?

VALERII: 48.37 for the opposition, 47.64 for us [that is, the authorities had already massaged the figures in favour of Yanukovych, but not by enough].

LEVENETS: Is this for 18:00?

VALERII: We have agreed for a 3 to 3.5 per cent difference in our favour [instead]. We are preparing a table with the results per oblast; you'll have it by fax in fifteen to twenty minutes.

EPISODE TWO, 21 NOVEMBER, 22:41: Levenets phones none other than Viktor Medvedchuk, President Kuchma's notorious strong-arm chief of staff.[7] The polls have now closed. The job is almost done.

LEVENETS: My congratulations on the celebration of democracy.

MEDVEDCHUK: My congratulations, Yura [short for 'Yurii']. The friend whom we have visited yesterday [presumed to be Kivalov, the head of the CEC] is panicking; he's not getting anything.

LEVENETS: He can't be getting anything – my guys [the Zoriany team] are finishing with their work; he'll have it all momentarily, literally in fifteen to twenty minutes.

MEDVEDCHUK: But he says that something's broken down.

LEVENETS: No, everything is fine. He can't have anything right now. He doesn't have any information at all over there. It's all under my control.

MEDVEDCHUK: Thank you.

The Zoriany team were clearly in charge, rather than the CEC. They had entered the key part of the CEC computer system, the so-called 'transit database' where incoming results were collated and stored, via a fibre optic cable and altered the results (the cinema is barely half a mile from the CEC). The team therefore included some high-ranking 'technicians': Heorhii Dzekon, chair of the board at Ukrainian Telecom; Serhii Livochkin, head of its Supervisory Council and Dzekon's technical colleague Yevhen Zimin; and Serhii Katkov of the firm Soft-Tronic, one of Ukraine's largest computer system firms, who had been smuggled into a position as head of the CEC's Information Department (i.e. the computer division) before the election's first round. Eduard Prutnik, deputy head of Donetsk council when Yanukovych was its head, and now a member of the Ukrtelecom Supervisory Board, was also a key player. After the fraud that had also marked the first round (discussed in Chapter 6) the system had been disconnected and Katkov had disappeared, although he returned to the CEC once to pick up his salary.

Technical configurations had also been changed, so Kivalov had to make it easier for one part of the Zoriany team to get direct access. It is alleged that several of them walked straight in to the CEC on the night of 21 November. When another member of the technical staff, Halyna Mandrusova, who was responsible for the central database, tried to turn on the system at 10 p.m., she freaked out when it wouldn't respond. Someone else was working on it already. It then turned itself back on as mysteriously as it had turned itself off.[8]

EPISODE THREE, 22 NOVEMBER, 00:26: Serhii Kliuiev, younger brother of Andrii Kliuiev, the first deputy prime minister and the head of Yanukovych's campaign office (who once, on his birthday, got a chauffeur to crawl on his knees for a hundred dollar bill),[9] is another leading Yanukovych 'fixer' (see below). Past midnight, the technical 'team' are at work.

UNKNOWN: How's it going?

KLIUIEV: Everything is OK.
UNKNOWN: Did you get the 'digits' [codes] and the box?
KLIUIEV: No, everything works without the 'box'.
UNKNOWN: I've got it.
KLIUIEV: Everything is fine. They have everything over there.
UNKNOWN: Do you need anything else?
KLIUIEV: For now no.
UNKNOWN: OK.

The team's conversations also make it clear that the 1.1 million votes they added at the last minute were just the icing on the cake. The rest of Yanukovych's vote had also been padded with all sorts of fraud. Huge numbers of 'cookies' (fake ballot papers) had been printed in Russia, but apparently were of poor quality.

EPISODE FOUR, 18 NOVEMBER, 17:54: three days before the vote.

UNKNOWN: Have you seen at all what we have? Have you seen 'cookies' in boxes?
LEVENETS: Sure, I've seen 'cookies'.
UNKNOWN: Have you seen that it differs significantly from the 'originals'?
LEVENETS: I know. YES, YES, YES. I just cannot understand, why it differs.
UNKNOWN: It differs drastically. I mean . . . It's different everywhere. What should we do?
LEVENETS: I don't know.
UNKNOWN: The type is completely different.
LEVENETS: I know. I know. I know.

Four minutes later, at 17:58, Levenets discusses what to do with Serhii Kliuiev. All are leading members of the so-called 'Donetsk clan', the muscular business group from Yanukovych's home region in east Ukraine. The Kliuiev brothers control one of its smaller business empires, running Donbascabel (the Donetsk Cable Plant) and Donetscoke.

LEVENETS: Vasilii Mykhailovych just called; he also noticed that the 'cookies' are very different. Did you talk about this to Andrii [Kliuiev]?
SERHII KLIUIEV: No.
LEVENETS: Why not?
KLIUIEV: I don't know. This is bullshit. It can be easily discovered, especially here; it will work over there [in Russia], but not here. Damn, I don't know what to do. Should we tell Andrii?

LEVENETS: I think we should.

KLIUIEV: OK, I'll reach him on his cell phone.

LEVENETS: Try to reach him.

The Yanukovych team eventually decided to use the 'cookies' anyway, in areas where they controlled the local district election commissions. In theory, these were staffed by 'trusted persons' nominated by each of the original twenty-three candidates in the election. However, most of these were secret Yanukovych supporters (see Chapter 5). And in places such as Donetsk, the rest could simply be scared off. The Committee of Voters of Ukraine estimated that a total of 2.8 million extra votes were added to Yanukovych's score by this and other methods. The jump in turnout in some places was dramatic, to say the least.[10] The Zoriany team also destroyed votes where necessary.

EPISODE FIVE, 22 NOVEMBER, 05:30. The morning after the vote.

LEVENETS: How do you do? What's going on? How come Kiev is rising?

UNKNOWN: I have the next situation: roughly I have 18.2 per cent for our candidate and 76 per cent for Yushchenko [the established vote in the capital].

LEVENETS: Have you already summarised everything?

UNKNOWN: Yes, and I have a plan for the next step.

LEVENETS: Do you have all the protocols? [tabulations of how each local area voted].

UNKNOWN: Yes, but in the CEC they put aside seven protocols, according to my order. I have to decide now whether to cancel them or not.

. . .

LEVENETS: No problems. We are in the black. Improve our balance; we'll simply advance even more.

But that very same morning, as the Zoriany team finished their work, Kiev was indeed 'rising' in revolt. As the fraudsters slipped into the night, tens of thousands were moving towards Kiev's main square to protest.

----

Five weeks later, on 27 December, Heorhii Kirpa, boss of the Ukrainian railways, was found dead in the sauna at his luxurious home in Kiev. The immediate official story was suicide, but neighbours reported hearing several shots. Kirpa was no angel. He had fought his way to the top of a notoriously corrupt industry. His rivals had seemed dangerously prone to accidents, even explosions, after which they mysteriously no longer obstructed his career path. In office, he had raked off money from transit cargo and ticket sales via two shadowy companies, Interkontakt and Interpolis, that received a commission from every railway ticket sold. Kirpa was also in charge of prestigious projects such as the Kiev–Odesa autobahn and the new bridge across the Dnipro river in Kiev, the promised first step in a new era of luxury travel to Moscow.[11] After the Orange Revolution, it was hoped that both projects could still be built, but only if the hundreds of millions of dollars that had allegedly disappeared could first be recovered (see pages 158 and 188).

Kirpa had also been responsible for so-called 'electoral tourism'. 'Vote early, vote often' was the practice in east Ukraine; but Yanukovych's team also believed in 'Vote early, vote elsewhere', organising busloads of voters to travel the country for repeat voting. Buses could only carry so many, however. So Kirpa provided entire trains, costing Ukrainian Railways about UAH10 million. (UAH is the Ukrainian currency, the *hryvnia*. It traded in 2004 at just over five to the dollar, so Kirpa spent about $2 million on the scheme.) Before his death, he had threatened to expose the scandal, and refused to provide thirty trains with eighteen carriages each to Yanukovych's Party of the Regions for the final vote on 26 December. Moreover, shortly before the election, the Transport Ministry had taken over the former State Committee for Communications. The latter's boring name masks the fact that it helped in the technical aspects of hacking in to the CEC server. Kirpa was also reported to be thinking of switching sides. Yanukovych had allegedly physically attacked him on 7 December, knocking out two of his teeth and forcing him to be hospitalised.[12] Kirpa had a busy day before his supposedly lonely death. He had heated conversations with Donetsk kingpin Rinat Akhmetov, a key Yanukovych campaign sponsor, and Kiev 'businessman' Hryhorii Surkis, Medvedchuk's partner, and one other mystery visitor, rumoured to have been Andrii Kliuiev.

Kirpa's death followed that of Yurii Liakh, head of the Ukrainian Credit Bank, controlled by none other than Viktor Medvedchuk and another key source of illicit campaign finance. Liakh had stabbed himself repeatedly in the neck with a letter opener: obviously, this was another suicide. The old regime was now in its death throes and clearly had plenty to hide. This book attempts to tell the story of how its plans to fix the elections failed, and how the leading conspirators on 21 November were at each others' throats within a month. The dramatic turnaround that caught the world's attention was in this sense a real revolution, and it was one that was led by Ukraine's long-suffering railway travellers and taxi-drivers. Kirpa and Liakh were not the only victims on the other side. By December, it was also likely that several of the Zoriany team would end up in jail.

# 2

# The Protagonists

To begin again, nearer the beginning: what was the election about? The two main candidates, Viktor Yanukovych and Viktor Yushchenko, shared a first name, but had hardly anything else in common. The other main player in the drama was the glamorous but steely Yuliia Tymoshenko, one of eastern Europe's few prominent female politicians. The three could hardly have been more different. Yushchenko was the Great White Hope, a banker with a clean image, much admired in the West. He was also a new type of politician. Since the Gorbachev era, Ukrainian politics had been dominated by a no-brainer contest between a handful of former dissidents and writers and the former Soviet elite they were never powerful enough to replace. Yushchenko was the first real challenger who came from within the system, with an insider's knowledge of its strategic weaknesses and pressure points. Yanukovych was the system's candidate, but he was also part of its seedier underside. Tymoshenko had served more spectacularly on both sides of the fence, becoming extremely rich by trading oil and gas in the 1990s, before being catapulted into opposition. The regime feared Yushchenko's popularity, but it also feared Tymoshenko's toughness – she was the one opponent who really understood the manipulative methods the regime used to stay in power and who was prepared to play the same game. Yushchenko and Tymoshenko now formed a partnership in opposition – the relationship between them the key to its success.

## The Great *Kham*: An Orphan Amongst Hoods

Viktor Fedorovych Yanukovych was born into a poor working-class family from Belarus in the mining village of Makiivka, Donetsk in 1950.[1] His mother, Olga, a nurse, died when he was two. His father, Fedor, a metallurgy machinist, promptly remarried and though Viktor continued to live in the same house as his father (which was no more than a wooden barracks),

Fedor gave the boy over to his grandmother and ignored him. Yanukovych had to become a tough kid as he grew up. He has stated bluntly that, 'I came from a very poor family and my main dream in life was to break out of this poverty'.[2]

His chosen escape route was joining a local gang and terrorising the neighbourhood. The young Yanukovych was sent to a prison for teenagers in 1968, after a three-year conviction in 1967 for robbery with force cut short his enrolment in a local technical school. However, a fortuitous amnesty for the anniversary of the 1917 Revolution meant he was out after only six months. (Ironically, the veteran Ukrainian dissident Viacheslav Chornovil was released at the same time, halfway through one of his four sentences.) Yanukovych had another spell in jail for inflicting serious bodily harm, supposedly during an armed robbery two years later. His criminal record was cleared (and cleansed) in 1978, but various documents thought to have been destroyed surfaced in Moscow in 2004.[3] Other allegations refer to his tearing earrings from women's ears and even rape, and it is rumoured that his second conviction was actually for manslaughter.

Once out of prison, Yanukovych had various jobs, including stints in a gas workshop, as a car mechanic and general mechanic, until he worked his way up to a post looking after cars at Ordzhonikidze Coal. The ease of his subsequent admission to Donetsk Polytechnic in 1974 is often attributed to his links with the KGB, although there is no direct evidence for this. More telling is the fact that the car-mad Yanukovych attended the Monte Carlo rally the same year, when he would obviously have been vetted. As yet, he seems to have been of only limited use to the authorities, however. Like Yushchenko, in fact, like nearly everybody making a career in the USSR, Yanukovych prospered once he found the right patron, who in his case was the local hero kosmonaut Georgii Beregovoi (1921–95), who spent four days in space in 1968 – when Yanukovych was in prison – at the grand age of forty-seven. In 1978, Beregovoi helped with the matter of Yanukovych's old convictions, and in 1980 helped him to get his party card. Yanukovych was soon heading a series of local factories with tough-sounding names: Donbas Transit Repair, Ukrainian Coal Industrial Transport and Donetsk Auto Transport.

Economic life in the Donbas was also tough. In the late 1980s and early 1990s, the Donbas region was severely depressed. One of the key industrial heartlands of the Soviet Union, home to the Stakhanovite movement in the 1930s, was suddenly cut adrift when Ukraine became independent in 1991. Ukraine's massive mining industry employs 450,000 in 193 mines (105 of these were in Donetsk), which produced 90 million tons in 2004, about 100 tons per actual miner, compared to 400 per miner in Poland or 4,000 in the USA. The industry survives on estimated annual subsidies of $2 billion. The old guard, the so-called 'red directors', had been formidable lobbyists in Moscow, but now struggled to play the same game in Kiev. In the summer of 1993 they used the crudest of methods, inciting a strike wave as a means of barging into government. The strikes' secret sponsor, Yukhym Zviahilskyi, who had headed the largest mine at Zasiadko since 1979, became acting prime minister. The Ukrainian government was terrified of the 'separatist' political demands raised by the miners in a region where almost everybody speaks Russian, and was happy to keep the subsidies flowing. Increasingly, however, the likes of Zviahilskyi saw no need to pass them on. Moreover, in 1994 Zviahilskyi was accused by the Ukrainian procurator general, Vladyslav Datsiuk, of helping the dumping abroad of 200,000 tons of aviation fuel at rock-bottom prices, for a profit of $25 million. He also introduced a crazy dual exchange rate scheme, in which all Ukrainian enterprises were obliged to surrender 50 per cent of their foreign earnings at an artificially low exchange rate fixed by the state – and most of the money went to banks controlled by Zviahilskyi's cronies. His political protection was good, however. In March 1993, at Zviahilskyi's request, the then prime minister, Leonid Kuchma, had authorised the release of DM25 million from Ukraine's then extremely limited foreign exchange reserves to the cast-alloy company Donkavamet, to redeem stock owed to the German company Varex. DM12 million ($5.3 million) ended up financing Kuchma's victorious presidential election campaign in 1994.[4] Zviahilskyi temporarily fled to Israel in 1994, but, once he was president, Kuchma agreed to his return in 1997, to face no charges, as a gesture to the Donetsk clan in advance of the next round of elections. Zviahilskyi settled back to a quiet life back at Zasiadko, in Donbas politics, and on the board of the Jewish Confederation of Ukraine.

The 'red directors' in their Soviet sinecures, however, were increasingly challenged by the various local mafias that began to develop in the Donbas, given the relative scarcity of capital for setting up legitimate businesses. Most notorious was Akhat Bragin, 'Alik the Greek', whose first turf victory was the takeover of Oktiabrsk market in 1988. He then built up the trading company Liuks, which specialised in the then hard to find 'luxury' items (I was unknowingly guilty of supporting its Kiev branch in the early 1990s, when it sold the only drinkable alcohol available), followed by the Dongorbank (Donetsk City Bank), and, the jewel in his crown, the Shakhtar Donetsk football team in 1995. Like Dynamo Kiev and other east European teams, Shakhtar became a mini-empire in itself, owning a hotel and newspaper and becoming a conduit for alleged money laundering. Bragin's eventual successors spent $10 million on a state-of-the-art training complex, and began splashing out on foreign players such as the Nigerian Julius Aghahowa ($7 million) and coaches, such as Nevio Scala from Italy, Bernd Schuster from Germany and the Romanian Mircea Lucescu. A new 50,000-seater stadium is also promised; it will be built by 2007 and will rival any in Europe. The result was Shakhtar's first league title in 2002 and regular spots in the lucrative Champions' League. Meanwhile, Bragin's men continued with more traditional activities, wiping out all the 'old generation' gang leaders in 1994, including Viacheslav Frolov, Eduard Brahinskyi, Mykhailo Dvornyi, Anatolii Dutko and others. Once their local monopoly was established, rival mobs from elsewhere were dealt with in a similar fashion. The Dolidze brothers from Georgia, Akop Akopian from Armenia, and the Dzhamalov brothers from Dagestan,[5] all came a cropper when they stepped on the wrong turf.

Phase two for the new Donetsk clan was to move into energy supply. In 1995, the Industrial Union of the Donbas was established (which has a 'respectable' web site, www.isd.dn.ua). Its purpose was ostensibly to act as a coordinating lobby for local businesses, but its real aim was to corner the market for supplying gas to those enterprises, and asset-strip those who couldn't afford to pay hard cash in return. Unfortunately, this move coincided with the premiership of Pavlo Lazarenko (see pages 39–40), who came from the rival region of Dnipropetrovsk and sought a national monopoly for his own United Energy Systems of Ukraine. A series of shocking murders brought the Donbas clan down to earth. Bragin was killed by a massive bomb in Shakhtar's stadium in October 1995, that also did for his chief bodyguard, retired KGB Colonel Viktor Dvoinykh, and four others. In November 1996, Bragin's business partner, the former regional governor Yevhen Shcherban, owner of the Aton energy and metal trading concern, was gunned down in broad daylight at Donetsk airport by assassins in police uniforms hiding under the plane wings. Shcherban's wife also died. His son only survived by hiding under the waiting limousine. Others who died at this time included Oleksandr Momot, head of the Industrial Union of the Donbas (IUD), and, in Kiev, Oleksandr Shvedchenko, former governor of the region, and the then director of the Russian gas company Itera-Ukraine.

Phase three in the modern economic life of the Donbas was quieter and less dramatic, but ultimately much more profitable. It also marked the ascendancy of a younger generation, which used mafia methods to push aside the 'red directors' of the IUD, led by a younger member of Bragin's 'Tatar' clan, his alleged enforcer Rinat Akhmetov (born 1966),[6] whom some rumours associate with the death of Bragin and an attempted murder in 1988. By now, the IUD had established an effective lobby for milking coal subsidies – but there was not much money to be made in coal. Forced to concentrate on husbanding their own resources, local businessmen-politicians such as Akhmetov developed two highly lucrative 'closed-cycle' schemes. Most of the local coal mines were still nominally owned by the state. Most lost huge amounts of money, but were heavily subsidised by Kiev, which, since the 1993 strikes, had backed away from confronting the potent mix of economic, political and language problems in the region. Akhmetov's group had won power over the mines through its monopoly of investment capital, but did not want to exercise control. It just wanted the cheap coal. The scam worked as follows: once 'the whole chain of production from the mining of coal to the export of metallurgical products [was] in single hands, it was possible [for Akhmetov *et al.*] to . . . divert the state subsidies abroad in the form of profits for metal exports and recovered VAT.'[7] In plainer English, the steel factories now made big money from exports, because their raw materials were astoundingly cheap – especially if the new owners forgot to pay the workforce as well. Significantly, the only exception to this general pattern, the Pavlohraduhol (Pavlohrad Coal) association, made up of ten mines and two coal-enrichment plants, which was bought by Akhmetov's group in early 2004, was both profitable (making $65.4 million in 2004) and based outside the Donbas, near Dnipropetrovsk. It therefore operated differently. Akhmetov even paid well.

Businesses linked to Akhmetov, in other words, got very rich through hard currency surpluses, but only at the cost of driving the local mining industry further into the ground. A second scam involved using the regional financial-industrial groups and the regional administration to acquire shares in the energy generating and distribution companies to provide another cheap input for the local metal industry (although this repeatedly led to anti-dumping measures being taken against Ukraine). A final scam was to have much of the region declared a 'Free Economic Zone', with minimal taxes.

By the early 2000s the Akhmetov business empire therefore had four main parts: System Capital Management group (SCM), Ukraine's biggest company, which controlled iron and steel production; the ARS joint stock company (supposedly Alik Rinat and Samson, another local tough guy), which coordinated mining and the supply of coke; Ukrvuhillyamash ('Ukrainian Coal Machinery'), which supplied local pits with mining equipment; and the Concern Enerho conglomerate, another regional energy supplier. Other groups moving into the Akhmetov orbit included

Oleksandr Leschynskyi's UkrInterProdukt, the biggest player in the Ukrainian food industry, allowing SCM to diversify to an extent. Significantly, Akhmetov's empire only operated a little in Russia, despite interests in the machine-building plants just over the border at Kamenka and Shakhtynsk. Despite being the most Russophone region in Ukraine, after Crimea, the Donbas region was very self-focused in one sense, and oriented towards global exports in another. The neighbouring Kharkiv region, by contrast, has many machine-building industries that are much keener on maintaining close industrial cooperation with Russia. Historically Donetsk always resented control from outside – whether from Moscow, St Petersburg or Kiev – even in 1917. Outsiders were always viewed with suspicion – in 1905, radical agitators who sought to stir up local strikes 'were seized and thrown alive into the hot slag and blast furnaces'.[8] On the back of massive demand from China, steel made up 40 per cent of Ukrainian exports by 2003, and accounted for the lion's share of the 26 per cent surge in exports that year.

In the mid-1990s, Viktor Yanukovych rose rapidly through the ranks of the Donetsk regional administration. By May 1997, he was its head, mainly because his methods were tough, and he had achieved a good division of labour with Akhmetov. Yanukovych made his name locally with the purge of Lazarenko supporters and others in 1997, after Lazarenko lost office in Kiev, and by providing political cover for Akhmetov's takeover of all local rackets. Nationally, he came to prominence with the increasing importance of the Donbas in Ukrainian politics, and with President Kuchma's increasing dependence on the power of the local clan. After flirting with separatism in 1993–4, the local machine began to organise its own backyard politically as well as economically. After an infamous visit in 1998, Kuchma promised to leave the clan to its own devices if it delivered him the vote. Previously, the large but impoverished local working class had voted for the Communist nostalgia ticket at most elections in the 1990s. They won twenty-two out of forty-seven seats in 1994; and, in the mixed system used in 1998, seven out of twenty-three local seats and 39 per cent of the local party list vote. First, the clan set up fake left parties of their own to siphon off Communist votes; then Yanukovych used 'administrative resources' to build up an all-powerful local machine, dubbed the Party of the Regions, an unintentionally ironic reference to its overwhelming dominance of one region (only). Locally, everyone just called it 'The Party'. As in Soviet times, there was no danger of anyone not knowing whom you meant. In 2002, this won 37 per cent of the vote, compared to a national average for the government party of 11.8 per cent. Kuchma was impressed with the 52.9 per cent vote the Party organised for him in the 1999 election, which ensured Yanukovych's move to Kiev. In the late 1990s, the locals liked to say 'In Kiev they make politics, in Donetsk money', but the Donetsk clan was now needed in national politics, and there was money to be made in Kiev.

When politicians are called 'tough', it is usually a metaphor. Yanukovych's reputation for verbal and physical violence, however, is not just a historical matter. His nickname in prison was *kham* (a boorish villain or thug) and his impulsive character was more like Sonny than Michael Corleone. In 2004, while out campaigning in west Ukraine, Yanukovych was forcibly questioned by an elderly man who opposed Russian as a second state language. Yanukovych's aside to an aide, 'Get him the fuck out of here', was all too audible. On secret tapes made in 2000, he threatened that non-obedient journalists 'will have their heads smashed against the wall'. One campaigning editor from Donetsk, Ihor Aleksandrov, had his head smashed not long after – not against the wall, but by baseball bats.[9] During the 2004 campaign, Yanukovych was also privately rumoured to have come to blows with several prominent politicians on his own side, and his regular shouting matches with the likes of the head of the Security Services did little to help the elite's unity in the face of a strong opposition challenge.

Yanukovych represented that part of the Ukrainian elite which preferred to use such methods. Chapters 3 and 4 will show why some establishment politicians and businessmen did this, and what they had to hide. Not everyone behaved like this, however. After over a decade of orgiastic corruption, those parts of the business elite that had already made their fortunes through corrupt privatisations and now had going concerns that would benefit from secure property rights wanted to become legitimate. The contradiction would ultimately undermine Yanukovych's campaign.

### A Banker Amongst Thieves

Viktor Andriiovych Yushchenko was born in 1954, in a small village in Sumy in the north-west of Ukraine near the Russian border; ironically, his birthplace was not far from the village of Chaikine in Chernihiv, where President Leonid Kuchma had been born in 1938. Yushchenko's parents were both village teachers; his father, Andrii, taught foreign languages and his mother, Barbara, mathematics. Andrii Yushchenko served in the Red Army and was taken prisoner, but escaped from seven camps, including Auschwitz, Buchenwald and Dachau (he died in 1992). According to Stalin's warped logic, capture was surrender, and any time spent outside the USSR was grounds for intense suspicion. Many of those who returned to the Soviet

Union were shot, and others were shot before they could return, so young Viktor was doubly lucky even to be born.

Yushchenko could, however, have grown up a Soviet patriot. It is worth emphasising that he is not from west Ukraine, the regions formerly under Poland and the Habsburg Empire, but from Sumy, which has been closely tied to Russia since the seventeenth century, some parts since 1503. Yushchenko is a country boy. He speaks with an accent that involves some *surzhyk* (the local admixture of Russian and Ukrainian); his often perilous hobby is bee-keeping. Ukraine has three main churches: the Greek Catholics in the west and the two branches of the Orthodox Church elsewhere. Perhaps surprisingly, Yushchenko belongs to the one that is still loyal to Moscow. On the other hand, he heard terrible stories in his youth of the Great Famine of 1932–3, caused by Stalin's collectivisation and grain-requisitioning policies, when rural regions such as Sumy were ravaged by some of the highest death rates, estimated at between 15 and 20 per cent of the local population – some four hundred souls in Yushchenko's immediate region.[10] Other happier stories celebrated the traditions of Yushchenko's home village, Khoruzhivka, as a winter outpost for Ukrainian cossacks in the seventeenth and eighteenth centuries. Yushchenko was also an economics student in Ternopil, west Ukraine, in the early 1970s, a period that he says made him 'more Ukrainian'.

Yushchenko was soon upwardly mobile. After army service in 1975–6 and some desk jobs back in Sumy, he moved to Kiev in 1986, joining up with his first patron, Vadym Hetman, at the USSR Agroprombank. The bank was a Soviet giant, responsible for funding the collective farm system, but once *perestroika* began its local branches were converted into a Ukrainian bank, Ukraïna, in November 1990. Some allege that the family connections of his first wife helped Yushchenko at this time, but others vigorously deny this. Hetman's patron, in turn, was the then chairman of the Ukrainian parliament, Ivan Pliushch. Yushchenko's once slow rise was now rapid. He became the deputy head of the bank in December 1989. Hetman became the first head of the brand-new National Bank of Ukraine (NBU) in 1991, and ensured the relative unknown was appointed his successor in December 1993. Hetman cited ill-health as the reason for his resignation, but in reality he had constantly quarrelled with President Leonid Kravchuk and Prime Minister Leonid Kuchma, over inflation-boosting monetary emissions. Yushchenko was able to introduce some belated discipline. In 1993, the inflation rate had gone so far off the scale that it was difficult to calculate. One estimate had it at 5,371 per cent, another at 10,200 per cent. Yushchenko brought it down to a mere 80.2 per cent per annum by 1996, and then to an almost stable 15.9 per cent in 1997. Hetman had organised the printing of a proper currency, the *hryvnia*, in 1992, but had refused to launch it at a time when he feared it would only be devoured by hyperinflation. Until the economy stabilised, Ukraine had to make do with the joke 'coupon' – essentially monopoly money, which initially had no serial numbers or watermark. Yushchenko was able to introduce the *hryvnia* successfully in September 1996, with no panic, confiscation or inflation spike. The notes still had the words 'printed in 1992' plaintively written on them. Although the *hryvnia* took a temporary slide during the local currency crisis in 1998–9, it has largely been a stable store of value, both before then and since. Yushchenko was now unmovable; he served at the NBU for six years, at a time when other Ukrainian ministers were lucky to last one. During this period, he largely stayed out of politics, apart from a brief flirtation with the National-Democratic Party from 1996, which was then pro-market, but also pro-Kuchma.

Yushchenko's second wife, Katherine Yushchenko-Chumachenko, is from the Ukrainian diaspora. Her parents met in Nazi Germany, where they were both *ostarbeiters* (slave labour from eastern Europe), but found their way to Chicago, where Katherine was born in 1961. After working as the Washington representative of the Ukrainian Congress Committee of America from 1982 to 1984 and receiving an MBA from the famously free-market University of Chicago in 1986, Chumachenko worked in the State Department and in the Reagan-era White House, where she became the administration's ethnic affairs liaison in 1988, working on 'Captive Nations' issues. Katherine (Kateryna) moved to Kiev in 1993 with KPMG consulting, who were advising Ukraine's new breed of financiers, including those at the Central Bank. It was here that she met Yushchenko, and the couple were married in 1998. Yushchenko has two children from his first marriage and three from his second, and his first grandchild was born in February 2000. His marriage to Chumachenko made him a more cosmopolitan figure than most politicians in Ukraine, but it also opened him up to some particularly vicious attacks in 2004.

The next two chapters will describe Yushchenko's move into politics after 1999. His clean image was his main asset, but it was also seen as a threat to many, so there have been at least three serious 'black PR' operations in the attempt to undermine it.[11] The most serious by far targeted Yushchenko's highly successful stint at the National Bank.[12] This focused on the period before the 1998 regional currency meltdowns, when the NBU allegedly transferred $613 million of IMF funding through Credit Suisse First Boston to 'speculative', or just plain risky, accounts. Part of the money, $275 million, was used to buy the government's own treasury bills over the winter of 1997–8, creating a false market in domestic debt. The National Bank also double-counted $150 million via a round tripping operation through various accounts (to Cyprus and back), to inflate its perilously low foreign exchange reserves and therefore qualify for further credits. The NBU later agreed to an audit by PricewaterhouseCoopers, who found no actual appropriation of monies, but stated that the 'NBU's reserves were potentially overstated by an amount that varied from US$391 million in September 1997 to US$713 million in December 1997'.[13] In other words, the NBU was guilty of extremely creative accounting. The IMF stopped funding Ukraine, despite Yushchenko's apology. The NBU's inelegant defence is that they did what they had to do to survive in the conditions of the time.

The second smear campaign concerned the Gradobank affair. In the early 1990s, after the USSR broke up, Germany agreed to make separate payments to Ukrainian *ostarbeiters* of $178 million, and between 1994 and 1997 slightly over half of this was administered through one of Ukraine's more obscure new banks, Gradobank. However, $38 million was embezzled and diverted to a front company, Centurion Industrial Group, based in Hong Kong. The duo responsible, bank president and parliamentary deputy Viktor Zherditskyi and Ihor Didenko, later boss of the notorious Oil and Gas of Ukraine, were arrested in October 2000 and July 2001, respectively, the latter, entirely coincidentally no doubt, at the same time as the founding conference of Yushchenko's political movement, Our Ukraine. The official Ukrainian media implied that Yushchenko was indirectly involved, given his duty of oversight at the National Bank, and that he had sanctioned a loan of UAH5 million to the ailing bank in 1998. The loan was secured against a promised sale of the bank's art collection. Although the bank was small, it served the post-Soviet *nouveaux riches*, and therefore owned a Picasso, but the sale never took place. Yushchenko's liberal colleague Viktor Pynzenyk, who was in government as a deputy premier in 1994, was supposedly also guilty of (a lack of) oversight; but there is little more than insinuation in any of this. Given their family histories, the slur was particularly offensive to Yushchenko and his wife.

The third PR offensive was the attempt to rewrite the various scandals around the Ukraïna Bank, which went bankrupt in July 2001. Money from the bank supposedly funded the studies of Yushchenko's oldest daughter, Vitalina, at Kiev University. Vitalina also allegedly took a number of banking courses, costing about $3,500, in Ukraine at the bank's expense. In addition, Yushchenko's brother Petro allegedly failed to repay a $35,000 loan from the bank, and also received shares in a sister bank, First Investment

Bank. However, despite also becoming a parliamentary deputy for Yushchenko's political bloc, Our Ukraine, in 2002, Petro was no equal to Marko Milošević, Mark Thatcher, Billy Carter, or even Tony Blair's hell-raising father-in-law, actor Tony Booth in the damaging or embarrassing relative stakes. (Petro Yushchenko is the older brother.) Amongst Yushchenko's other 'family', Serhii Buriak, the founder of Brokbiznesbank, is godfather to one of Yushchenko's children, but was in the clan 'party' Labour Ukraine, along with his brother Oleksandr (who defected from Yushchenko's party, Our Ukraine). Little has been made of this, however, as Brokbiznesbank is actually close to the Communists, who are, in turn, close to the authorities.

Again, the Ukraïna affair was another blatant case of the pot calling the kettle black. By the late 1990s, the bank's funds were controlled by President Kuchma's associates, who were queuing up to leech them in characteristic fashion. The head of the supervisory board, Volodymyr Satsiuk, and his deputy, Oleksandr Volkov, used them to fund Kuchma's 1999 presidential campaign, and Kuchma's wife, Liudmila, dipped in for money to finance the $40 million overspend at, appropriately, the Ukraïna palace, Kiev's new concert venue for the *nouveaux riches*. The bank transferred $50 million 'at Putin's request', to help pay for Russia's 2000 election.[14] Oleksandr Tkachenko, chair of parliament from 1998 to 2000, also had his nose in the trough. He and Satsiuk transferred many of its resources to their company, Ukrros.

Yushchenko may not be completely innocent of involvement in these scandals, but he does seem never to have had his own hand in the till. With the important exception of the NBU case, the PR campaign against him amounted to vague insinuations about circles close to Yushchenko, including the patrons of Yushchenko's patron, contacts of Yushchenko's contacts and so on, as is also the case with other vague and unsubstantiated allegations that Hetman and/or Pliushch had appropriated agricultural credits in the early 1990s. The important difference was that there was no Hetman or Yushchenko 'clan' as such. Unlike the Donetsk clan or the Dnipropetrovsk clan or the Kiev clan (see Chapter 3), Hetman and Yushchenko did not rob the state. They did not enrich themselves with rigged privatisations. They did not use their ill-gotten gains to corrupt the political process. Both men belonged to a team of would-be professionals, uneasily situated between Ukraine's post-Soviet class of robber barons and the nationalists, who were pushing for a monetary break with Russia. In April 1998, Vadym Hetman was gunned down in the lift outside his flat, with five shots to the body and a final shot to the head. There were clearly greater misdeeds elsewhere.

## Yuliia

Yuliia Volodymyrivna Tymoshenko, the youngest of our three protagonists, was born in 1960 in the city of Dnipropetrovsk, Donetsk's long-term rival as the unofficial capital of Ukraine's industrial east.[15] Tymoshenko is not just comparatively young, but has also used her undoubted glamour as a political asset in a way that would not work in the West. To the Ukrainian, and increasingly to the foreign, press, even the hostile press, she is usually just 'Yuliia' – a priceless asset in itself – aka the 'Gas Princess', the 'Ukrainian Princess' or 'Lady Yu', and ultimately the 'Joan of Arc' or 'La Passionara' of the Orange Revolution. The political movement she set up for the parliamentary elections in 2002, the 'Bloc of Yuliia Tymoshenko', where she emerged as a resounding success with 7.3 per cent of the vote, was not only named after her, but was deliberately designed to produce the acronym BYuT or BYuTy (pronounced as 'beauty').

She has always dressed well and expensively. In a stormy TV debate on how to replenish the state budget in March 2002, faux-left winger Nataliia Vitrenko icily remarked that Tymoshenko's '$30,000' earrings would make a good start. But Ukraine is not the West. Post-Communist societies value consumption, and are often happy to forget about what pays for it. Tymoshenko has also adopted a trademark hairstyle. Version one, with folkish braids arranged in side-buns made her look not unlike Star Wars' Princess Leia. Version two, a Heidi-like arrangement, with the braid now crowning the head, running from one ear to the other, was more distinctive. As a hairstyle, it would never top a 'Rachel' from *Friends* , but after 2004, it was much in demand the world over (see plate 9).

Tymoshenko is also tough. The different sides to her character could be taken straight out of a play by Shakespeare or Goethe. Like Yanukovych, she was deserted by her father at the age of two, and was brought up in relative poverty in a Khrushchev-era apartment building mainly inhabited by local taxi-drivers, where she played football with the local boys.[16] Her paternal maiden name is supposedly Grigian and her maternal name is Telegina, but she is understandably coy about this. She found a traditional Soviet way out of hardship, marrying young, at nineteen, to Oleksandr Tymoshenko, after he reportedly rang her flat by mistake, but stayed on the line and asked her out. Accident or not, the marriage was fortuitous. Oleksandr's father, Hennadii Tymoshenko, was a powerful figure in the local Communist Party, so Yuliia soon gained promotion in her first job as an engineer-economist. The marriage didn't last long. Oleksandr was the first in a series of men left by the wayside.

The couple's only child, Yevheniia, was born within a year, but her parents have not cohabited for ten years.

Tymoshenko's career proper began as a typical *komsomol* cooperative entrepreneur in 1988 (see pages 32–3), running a youth centre, Terminal, whose actual business was using imported VCRs provided by her father-in-law, whose party duties included looking after the local cinemas, to run off pirate copies of Western videos such as *Rambo*.[17] Oleksandr Turchynov, who would serve as Tymoshenko's political right hand for the next fifteen years, was then a twenty-five-year-old *komsomol* agitprop specialist, who also worked for Terminal. In May 1991 the extended Tymoshenko clan moved into the bigger time, using its capital to set up the Ukrainian Oil Corporation (in Ukrainian, KUB). KUB also benefited from offshore capital from Cyprus of unknown origin, and was registered as a Ukrainian–Cypriot joint company, 85 per cent of whose shares belonged to the shadowy Somolli Enterprises Ltd, which was controlled by the family's financial mentor Oleksandr Hravets (now a resident of Israel), although Yuliia Tymoshenko had 5 per cent of the shares. KUB began to make serious money in 1992–4. Its 'business model' was based on its monopsony control of agricultural produce in Dnipropetrovsk, obtaining produce by barter for its petrol and selling it at a high mark-up for hard cash.[18] It could not have obtained this position without good political contacts, namely the future prime minister Pavlo Lazarenko, then head of the local Agro-Industrial Complex (an old Communist Party sinecure). At the same time, Hennadii Tymoshenko ran another international company, Sial, whose main business was natural stone mining, with a quarter share in the lucrative red granite quarry at Totovske, then turning over an estimated $84 million a year.

This was still small beer, however. Yuliia Tymoshenko was soon able to lever herself into public prominence by skilfully exploiting oligarchs who were then further up the feeding chain. The first of these was another young *komsomol* entrepreneur from Dnipropetrovsk, Viktor Pinchuk, with whom Tymoshenko set up a joint corporation named Sodruzhestvo ('Friendship' or 'Community'), to exploit Pinchuk's Moscow contacts and set herself up in the energy import business. Pinchuk left for unknown reasons in 1995 – subsequent relations between the two have not been particularly friendly – and in November 1995 Sodruzhestvo, now led by Hravets, Hennadii and Yuliia Tymoshenko, became United Energy Systems of Ukraine (UESU). Yuliia Tymoshenko, then aged thirty-six, was the company's general director. Pinchuk now heads the Interpipe business empire, producing metal pipe, and is one of Ukraine's, indeed one of Europe's, richest men. In 1999, he married President Kuchma's daughter, Yelena. His political party, Labour

Ukraine, Trudova Ukraïna, was nicknamed *Trubova Ukraïna* because *truba* is the Ukrainian for 'pipe'.

United Energy Systems' time in the sun was brief, but spectacular. At the time, the burden of Russian energy imports had almost bankrupted the Ukrainian state, which therefore sought to set up a series of regional energy wholesalers to shoulder the burden instead. UESU won the right to supply the thirsty local industry in several oblasts around Dnipropetrovsk (the others being Kirovohrad, Poltava, Cherkasy, Mykolaïv, Sumy and Donetsk). It was therefore in competition with the Donbas clan to the east (see page 10) and the Republic group, controlled by two other oligarchs, Ihor Sharov and Ihor Bakai, to the west (see pages 46 and 57). UESU had the best political connections, however. Significantly, it won its initial concessions when Yevhen Marchuk was prime minister (1995–6), *before* his successor, none other than Pavlo Lazarenko, jumped on board (1996–7). By mid-1997, UESU was distributing 800 billion cubic metres of gas a year. Energy imports were still heavily subsidised, with Ukrainian and Russian oligarchs splitting the difference to earn huge profits on the side (see pages 45–6). UESU was therefore able to build up an empire in double-quick time, becoming almost a 'state within a state', including the airline SES-Avia, the Slovianskyi ('Slavic') and Pivdencom ('Southern Industrial') banks, and over twenty industrial affiliates – like KUB, it basically focused on exploiting energy supply to asset-strip desperate local factories. According to several guesstimates, UESU enjoyed annual revenues of $10 billion to $11 billion – 20 to 25 per cent of Ukraine's then GDP – and paid $11,000 in tax.[19]

The good times did not last, however. Explanations for this vary, but the golden years of UESU's economic ascendancy were also the years when the political influence of the Dnipropetrovsk clan, including not just Tymoshenko, but also the prime minister, Lazarenko, and President Kuchma, was at a maximum in Kiev. Who fed whom in the relationship was far from clear, and it was equally unclear whether UESU's riches primarily benefited Tymoshenko or Lazarenko, or served as a general honey-pot for all the top Dnipropetrovsk clan. Its influence was much criticised abroad, as it began to seem that the whole of Ukraine was falling under its lopsided control, as was Lazarenko's allegedly gargantuan corruption (see pages 39–40). In July 1997, Lazarenko resigned, swiftly followed by other clan members such as the procurator Hryhorii Vorsinov (who was notorious for not prosecuting Lazarenko) and the energy minister Yurii Bochkarov, suddenly depriving Tymoshenko of her political protection.

Tymoshenko's second problem was her relations with the Russian energy giant Gazprom. In March 1997 she had written to none other than Bill

Clinton to complain about its abuse of its monopoly, but Gazprom was the devil most Ukrainian politicians knew and grew rich from. Gazprom's then boss, Rem Viakhirev, whom Tymoshenko had once charmed in a mini-skirt and thigh-high boots, was on the way out, and in 2001 would be replaced by Aleksei Miller, with whom Tymoshenko had no similar 'understanding'. The two factors combined to persuade Kuchma to transfer UESU's local monopoly to a new company, Oil and Gas of Ukraine, under Ihor Bakai. Feeling the heat, Tymoshenko began to build a political base, standing for parliament in a by-election in Kirovohrad and winning 91.1 per cent of the vote. Tymoshenko paid off all pension and wage arrears in the constituency, using a 'commercial loan' – her official salary was then UAH13,000, only $7,200. Then she built up the largely dormant Hromada Party, which was controlled by her old ally Oleksandr Turchynov, into a mass organisation with 300,000 members. Lazarenko barged in as leader, but only at the party conference in October 1997. (Hromada was basically an east Ukrainian party, which was strongest in Dnipropetrovsk, although it took its name, meaning 'Society', from the political clubs set up by the Ukrainian intelligentsia in the nineteenth century.)

Tymoshenko had showed her mettle. Hromada set itself up as the first 'dissident' oligarchs' party. Tymoshenko even headed its 'shadow cabinet'. However, its political opposition to the president cost UESU dear. It was hit with a tax demand for UAH1.4 billion (then $750 million), a $42 million debt to Ukrhazprom, and stripped of its lucrative quarter share in the Khartsyzskyi pipe factory. In September 1998 Tymoshenko's colleague Mykola Syvulskyi, a former deputy finance minister, was arrested. The authorities claimed he had illegitimately channelled funds from Ukrhazprom to UESU, while Tymoshenko said it was because he was organising Hromada's campaign to impeach Kuchma. By November 1998, Tymoshenko was willing to sue for peace – although with the economy mired in recession and an election in the offing (1999) Kuchma was also then in a weak position and needing to make a deal. At a famous semi-secret meeting 'for tea' (not Kuchma's normal drink of choice), Tymoshenko agreed to leave Lazarenko and Hromada – this was just *before* Lazarenko was arrested in Switzerland – in return for being allowed to build up a new party of her own, called Fatherland, which soon held the balance of power in parliament. Tymoshenko could clearly play it as tough in politics as in business. Her remaining business interests were temporarily secure, and she was increasingly spoken of as a candidate for government. On the other hand, when rumours surfaced that she was backing the socialist party leader Oleksandr Moroz for the presidency in 1999, Slovianskyi Bank came under political pressure. Clearly, Tymoshenko now had to become a top-rank politician herself in order to survive. However, it was not yet clear with whom she would ally herself. Before Yushchenko became a candidate for prime minister in December 1999, Tymoshenko was backing another term for his rival Valerii Pustovoitenko (who had served as prime minister after Lazarenko, 1997–9) as the best means of keeping her remaining UESU interests alive.[20] Once Yushchenko declared his interest however, Tymoshenko joined his side. She also began learning Ukrainian, and reinventing herself as a patron of national and even nationalist causes.

### Criminality or *Kompromat*?

Accusations of corruption involving Tymsohenko are numerous. As early as 1995–6, she was twice accused of 'failing to declare' large sums of money at customs. The first case involved $100,000 at Moscow Vnukovo airport in July 1995, and the second concerned $26,000 in her luggage at Zaporizhzhia airport in east Ukraine in 1996. These charges were dropped in 2001, if only because the rules for money movement had changed.

In March 2000, the pressure on Slovianskyi Bank, then Ukraine's biggest commercial bank, with profits of UAH83.3 million (then about $20 million) in 1999 and assets of UAH556.1 million (just over $130 million) began to tell. Bank chair Borys Feldman, another Dnipropetrovsk native close to Tymoshenko, was arrested for failing to pay tax on a loan (not actually a criminal offence). Kuchma was caught on tape (see pages 51–2) in May 2000 urging the chief tax inspector, Mykola Azarov, to deal with Feldman: 'You sit him down [in a cell] with criminals, let. . .'. Kuchma felt able to trail off because Azarov obviously knew what his boss had in mind. The case was moved to east Ukraine. In August, Azarov reported that, 'We've already agreed with the Luhansk court . . . where the possibilities for influence are organised enough' and the judge has agreed to add whatever charges Azarov deems necessary.[21]

In February 2001, Tymoshenko was accused of transferring (or laundering) a total of $1.21 billion through Slovianskyi to the Latvian bank Aizkraukles, and on to the 'First Trading Bank' registered on the always financially active Pacific island of Nauru.[22] In April 2002, Feldman was duly sentenced by the Luhansk court to nine years, although the conviction was overturned by the Supreme Court in May 2004. The charges against Tymoshenko also failed to stick, and in 2002 the government returned more directly to the UESU affair. Slovianskyi had, of course, collapsed back in 2000.

In the summer of 2002, Tymoshenko's father-in-law, Hennadii Tymoshenko, the former UESU president, company director Yevhen Shaho and former UESU accountants Lidiia Sokolchenko and Antonina Boliura, were charged with illegally acquiring $2.25 billion through sales of Russian natural gas in Ukraine. The four were arrested in Turkey in June and extradited in October 2002, but a Kiev court threw out all charges in May 2003, only for that decision to be reversed again in October. Also in October, the parliamentary Rules Committee turned down the first of several requests to lift Tymoshenko's immunity.

Finally in September 2004, Russian prosecutors dusted off an old case and demanded her extradition on charges of bribing five Russian officials in 1996, including defence ministry finance chief Georgii Oleinik, under house arrest since December 2000, and deputy finance minister Andrei Vavilov, whose dismissal in April 1997 didn't stop him becoming chair of Severnaia Neft ('Northern Oil'). According to the *Moscow Times*, the complicated scheme worked as follows: Gazprom borrowed $450 million from Imperial Bank and the National Reserve Bank to pay taxes. The money was forwarded to the defence ministry via Vavilov, which then paid United Energy International, a UK-based company linked to Lazarenko and Tymoshenko, for associated Ukrainian companies to deliver equivalent 'material-technical valuables' in lieu of Ukraine's energy debt.[23] One side says they never arrived, at least not in the quantity promised; another that Gazprom forwarded military uniforms supplied by a UESU company to the defence ministry against tax. Ultimately, the charges come down to the accusation that Tymoshenko may have bribed defence officials to exaggerate the value of the supply contracts by $80 million.

A request was sent to Interpol to issue an international warrant for Tymoshenko's arrest because she had failed to come to Moscow in September for questioning. The warrant for Tymoshenko was posted on Interpol's site, but lifted on 8 December 2004, pending further information. In the wake of the Orange Revolution the Ukrainian authorities dropped all charges against Tymoshenko and her associates on 28 January 2005, for 'lack of evidence'. The Russian authorities did not. Mixed signals included a promise that she would not actually be arrested as soon as she stepped foot on Russian soil, but various statements indicating the investigation was still open led to her cancelling her first visit to Moscow after the Orange Revolution in April 2005.

It is far from clear how much of Tymoshenko's former business empire survived the late Kuchma era. However, it is certain that she ceased to be a key economic player at the very time when Ukraine's privatisation programme was getting started. Nowadays, she may well live off dividends and interest from her former riches, which are allegedly based in Cyprus or Lebanon, possibly channelled through the shell of UESU, which still has about 3 per cent of the energy market in Ukraine. She is also said to control the paper *Vechernie vesti* ('Evening News'), which her website links to (www.tymoshenko.com.ua).

----

The figures of Yanukovych, Yushchenko and Tymoshenko encapsulated the changing nature of Ukrainian politics, economy and society at the time of the 2004 election. Unlike previous Ukrainian elections, which all too often were dummy contests between the unelectable and the unmovable, all three stood on the tectonic plates between 'government' and 'opposition' that were now beginning to shift. Viktor Yushchenko promised a big clean-up in Ukraine's political and business culture, but was close enough to the heart of the old system to make this promise sound less threatening. Viktor Yanukovych represented many of the worst aspects of Ukraine's new robber capitalism, about which some of the elite already had their doubts. Once she turned into a politician, Yuliia Tymoshenko would use her experience of Ukraine's murky business world to stop others following in her path. Having been an enthusiastic poacher, she would become a particularly zealous game-keeper. After sketching in some wider historical background, the next two chapters will pick up their careers again, going back to around 1999.

# 3

# A Short History of Ukraine:
# What was at Stake in the Election?

Yanukovych, Yushchenko and Tymoshenko also stood on different sides of deep historical divides. Ukraine is not Russia, but the two nations are kin. Their closely intertwined history has left strong tidemarks in both Ukrainian and Russian society. Most Ukrainians can and will speak Russian, but not all do, as President Putin inadvisedly blurted out in 2004. The difference between the two countries being sibling nations rather than two parts of the same divided nation is crucial. Siblings might be expected to have a love–hate relationship.

The three modern east Slavic nations, Ukraine, Russia and Belarus, were once collectively known as the Rus´ (*Рycь*), although the three have fought over the name for centuries. One lot of Rus´ eventually became the Russians; another lot became the Little Rus´ (*malorusy, rusyny* or Ruthenians), but eventually decided to call themselves Ukrainians to avoid confusion, while most Belorussians (White Russians, the Russian spelling) now prefer to be called the Belarusians, or the White Rus´ (Belarusian spelling). From its beginnings in the eighth century until the Mongol invasion in 1237–40, the united kingdom of the Rus´ was the dominant power in eastern Europe. The Byzantine Empire to the immediate south was then at the height of its power, so the Rus´ took a much more central place in the political and cultural geography of Europe, including further to the west. Viktor Yushchenko is fond of repeating the story of Anna, the daughter of Yarolsav the Wise, Prince of Kiev and ruler of Rus´ from 1019 to 1054, who married Henry I, the Capetian King of France (1031–60) at Rheims in 1049. She provided the lavish Slavic Gospel subsequently used at French coronations, although Henry, who was on his third wife, could not read it, and further lowered the tone by signing an 'x' alongside Anna's name.

Some Ukrainian historians accept the idea of the common origin of the east Slavic nations, but insist that their subsequent development was entirely separate. Their more radical colleagues, however, argue that the territories north-west of Kiev, that now make up modern Russia, were marginal to the history of Rus´; or that medieval Muscovy's authoritarian political culture developed later, under Mongol influence, and was alien to the original traditions of Rus´. Similarly, the national camp in Belarusian historiography likes to depict Rus´ as a loose federation at best, and the various local principalities, Turaw, Novaharadok, and above all Polatsk, as half-in, half-out of Rus´. Some modern Russian historians are open to the idea of diversity in Rus´, but the version of history still taught in most Russian schools is that the Ukrainian capital, Kiev, is 'the mother of all Russian cities' and is therefore only technically 'abroad'. The compromise version of history now taught in most Ukrainian schools combines a Kievocentric view of Rus´, with general homilies to the original unity of the eastern Slavs.

What happened after the Mongol invasion in 1240 is also the subject of much dispute. The dramatic changes in political borders cannot be gainsaid. The original lands of Rus´ were now divided between Poland, Lithuania, Hungary and the Mongol suzerainty over Vladimir and Muscovy, while Novgorod remained quasi-independent. Muscovy eventually emerged as a power in its own right, but several other principalities could have done so in its stead. More importantly, the extent to which a loose cultural unity survived over four centuries of political division is debatable. To talk of the lands that eventually became 'Russia' winning control of lands between 1654 and 1795 that had by then become 'Ruthenia' (the east Slavic territories of the Polish Commonwealth) as simply 'reunion' is therefore strange; although many Russians still cling to this view. The years of radical disunity were as long as the years of relative unity.

Divorced from Moscow, the lands around Kiev maintained much of their legal autonomy until 1569. The social structure dominated by the old Rus´ nobility remained intact, as did the local Orthodox religion established in Kiev in 988, although since 1240 (the bishops moved north in 1299) there had often been rival hierarchies in Moscow and Kiev, or in the would-be Belarusian cities of Vilna (Vilnius) or Novaharadok. This competition was episodic until the fall of Constantinople in 1453, but permanent thereafter. In 1569, however, the Union of Lublin transferred most of the region from the control of laissez-faire Lithuania to Counter-Reformation Poland, bringing the triple threat of Polonisation (assimilation to Polish language and culture), Catholicisation and the enserfment of the peasantry. Some locals compromised, particularly the old nobility, and helped set up the Uniate, later the Greek Catholic, Church at the Union of Brest in 1596, which retained the old liturgy, but was placed under the Pope's authority.

Others fought back. Kievan churchmen used the methods of their opponents to promote an Orthodox revival, creating in the process a synthesis of Orthodox and quasi-Protestant, quasi-Trentine religion that now distinguished the Orthodox of Kiev from the still orthodox Orthodox in Moscow. Another faction appealed to the protection of Moscow against the Poles – but on the grounds of faith rather than ethnicity. Placing themselves between these two options were the cossacks, who were most alarmed by the third threat of enserfment. They were always violently anti-Catholic but, while fighting in defence of the Kiev bishops, were also usually pro-Moscow.

After the Great Rebellion of 1648, the cossacks' estranged noble leader, Bohdan Khmelnytskyi, forcibly established a quasi-state dubbed the 'Hetmanate' out of a weakened Poland. With all of his putative allies proving unreliable, Khmelnytskyi fought the war with Poland to a draw, and accepted the suzerainty of Russian Tsar Aleksei Mikhailovich at the Treaty of Pereiaslav in 1654. However, the Hetmanate survived until 1785, as did a 'Ukrainian Baroque' culture that was originally much more European than anything then in the north. The Kievan Church lost its independence in 1685–6, but only after it had helped influence Russia's own project of religious modernisation that helped produce the schism between 'old' and new believers under Patriarch Nikon in 1667. Russia resumed its territorial expansion in the region in the eighteenth century, with the three partitions of Poland between 1772 and 1795 (Russia mainly got the 'Ruthenian' parts), and the conquest of the Black Sea coast and Crimea from the Crimean Tatars and Ottoman Turks, in 1768–74 and 1787–92.

The westernmost Ruthenian territories passed to the Habsburg Empire in the 1770s, however, in addition to the region of Transcarpathia, which had long been under the Hungarian crown. Relatively tolerant Austrian rule, and the intensity of the local competition with the Poles, allowed the west Ruthenians to develop a strong sense of distinct identity by 1914, and, during the course of the nineteenth century, to settle on the name 'Ukrainian'. The 'Greek' part of the locally predominant Greek Catholic religion became more important, as most local Ukrainians now lived surrounded by Roman Catholic Poles. In the era of 'enlightened despotism', the west Ukrainians revered Joseph II of Austria (1780–90). Catherine the Great's (1762–96) rule over the rest of Ukraine, however, was more despotic than enlightened. Her rule brought about the assimilation of the Hetmanate nobility, the enserfment of the cossacks, and the abolition of the vestiges of legal autonomy. Ukrainian culture enjoyed a further half-century of residual tolerance, but the formation of the first Ukrainian political group in the 1840s, the Society of SS. Cyril and Methodius, followed by the tiny Hromada ('Community') societies in the 1860s, and the more serious threat of the Polish Rebellion, from 1863–4, led to political and linguistic repression.

The Ukrainian national movement that belatedly developed under semi-clandestine conditions during the latter phases of imperial rule, mainly after political restraints were relaxed in the wake of the 1905 revolution, was therefore ill-prepared to make the most of the opportunities that arose after 1917. The tiny intelligentsia attempted to lead the illiterate peasantry, but the latter's primary interest was in the land, and their support for the Ukrainian People's Republic that declared independence in January 1918 proved ephemeral. The invading Central Powers (now mainly Germany, as Austria-Hungary was already weak) backed a rival Hetmanate state under nobleman Pavlo Skoropadskyi for eight months in 1918, but their defeat on the Western front led to its instant collapse. The withdrawal of the Germans allowed the leaders of the Ukrainian People's Republic to try again, and the west Ukrainians to set up their own Republic (the two were symbolically united in January 1919); but both were engulfed by the rival options and growing anarchy that emerged later in 1919. The Bolsheviks established their own Ukrainian Soviet Socialist Republic, and although the west Ukrainians fought against the Poles and Romanians, they lost to both, so that their territories went to Warsaw and Bucharest. Transcarpathia was peaceably incorporated into the new Czechoslovakia.

### The Soviet Era

Nevertheless, the establishment of Bolshevik rule in Ukraine proved suffi-ciently difficult (it took three attempts, and the local Soviet government was not militarily secure until November 1921; it joined the USSR via the Union Treaty of December 1922) for Lenin to sanction both concessions to the peasantry (the New Economic Policy, or NEP) and a degree of Ukrainianisation. The 1920s were therefore a golden age of sorts for Ukraine, producing a cultural revival strong enough to challenge Russia's century-old monopoly of high culture, a thriving local economy based on peasant agriculture and cottage industry and a brief revival of Church inde-pendence in 1921–30. Stalin's consolidation of power soon brought all three to an end. The Ukrainian intelligentsia's call, 'Away from Moscow', and the perceived threat to Soviet control of Ukraine from Germany and Poland produced a brutal clampdown from 1929–30, a halt to further Ukrain-ianisation in 1933, and, worst of all, the Great Famine of 1932–3, in which an estimated five to seven million perished. Ukraine was the centre of resist-ance to the disastrous agricultural collectivisation policies introduced in

1929 and was the heartland of *kulak* farming that Stalin was determined to 'liquidate'. The simultaneous forcible solution of the national question with the onset of starvation has led many Ukrainians to label the Famine as genocide, and a Ukrainian Holocaust.

The Famine was followed by the Great Purges across the USSR in the mid-1930s. These came on top of the local purges that Ukraine had already suffered in the late 1920s and early 1930s. There was therefore no repeat of the 1917–18 national movement in 1941, when the Germans invaded the USSR, despite the passive welcome that was given by those Ukranians who expected a rerun of the Junker administration of 1918. Many local police pragmatically collaborated, as did many, initially in the Organisation of Ukrainian Nationalists (OUN), set up in 1929, albeit for more ideological reasons.

Erich Koch's rule in *Reichskommissariat* Ukraine was so brutal, however, that the Soviets were generally seen as the lesser evil by 1943–4. Millions of those Ukrainians who fought in the Red Army also accepted the idea of danger to what they saw as a common fatherland of sorts. West Ukraine, however, was part of *Generalgouvernement* Poland, where a Ukrainian insurgent army (known by its Ukrainian acronym, UPA) was established in 1943, and fought against all sides – including 'moderates' or 'collaborationists' on its own side and other Ukranians in the Red Army – until the early 1950s.

Making permanent the annexation of (most of) west Ukraine, which had first been occupied temporarily after the Nazi-Soviet pact in 1939–41 and then permanently after 1945, was therefore a difficult task, particularly as it was undertaken by the Soviet authorities rather than the nationalists. The addition of the west made Soviet Ukraine more Ukrainian, but west Ukraine often felt like occupied territory. The western city of Lviv, but also Kiev in central Ukraine, were the main centres of the dissident movement that grew up amongst a new generation of cultural intelligentsia in the 1960s. There was no equivalent movement in the new Soviet cities of the east and south, however, although there were a handful of isolated exceptions and plenty of general working-class discontent. The dissident movement was in any case suppressed in three arrest waves: in 1965–6, 1972–3 and 1976–80. By the time of the Moscow Olympics in 1980 (some of the early football matches were held in Kiev, which therefore has its own Olympic stadium), Yurii Andropov at the KGB had ensured there was no longer a dissident 'problem' as such.

Soviet rule, moreover, decisively altered Ukraine's general demographics. Ukraine became less multicultural, with the previously large Polish, German and Jewish minorities succumbing to forced migration and the Holocaust.

Conversely, the number of Russians increased, reaching 21 per cent of the population by 1989. Ukraine became 50 per cent urban by the 1960s, but more than half the urban population was now in the melting-pot of cities of the east and south, which were heavily Sovietised and usually Russian language-speaking, if also partly Ukrainian. In fact, the whole of Soviet Ukraine was only partly Ukrainian in various degrees. Many thought of themselves as somehow both Ukrainian and Russian, or Ukrainian and Soviet.

Ukraine therefore initially made only a sluggish response to the new opportunities of the Gorbachev era, particularly as the elderly Brezhnevite, Volodymyr Shcherbytskyi, remained in power in Kiev until September 1989. The Chernobyl disaster in April 1986 provoked snowballing protest, but mainly as a symbol of Moscow's remote and often ineffective control. A proper opposition movement, Rukh (simply named after the Ukrainian word for 'movement'), was only organised when Shcherbytskyi was on his death-bed (though one version of events has it that he was forced out of office and committed suicide). When the first real competitive elections were held for the Ukrainian parliament (known as the 'Supreme Council', *Verkhovna Rada*) in March 1990, Rukh won 108 out of 450 seats, while the more moderate Democratic Platform had twenty-eight. Most of the rest, originally 385, were Communists, although after a spate of defections they were known as the 'group of 239'.

The approximate quarter strength for the anti-Communist opposition represented deep historical divisions. The former Habsburg territories in the west and the Ukrainian intelligentsia backed Rukh. Voters in the country-side were still in thrall to the collective farm system and dutifully backed their nominally 'Communist' bosses. The urban population of the south and east remained characteristically Soviet, combining passive support for the powers-that-be with occasional anti-Communist populism, but it was broadly indifferent to any national message from Kiev or from west Ukraine, if only because, unlike in 1654 or 1941, there was no external Polish or German threat to motivate them. Ukraine therefore had a stronger national opposition movement than central Asia or Belarus, but it was much weaker than similar movements in the Baltic republics, or the nationalist strongholds of Georgia and Armenia. Ukraine was also unlike Moldova, where a strong Popular Front was counterbalanced by the Sovietised population east of the river Dnistr, which was agitated by the spectre of unification with Romania.

A similar picture unfolded with Gorbachev's referendum on preserving the USSR in March 1991. The six most radical Soviet republics (the Baltic three, Georgia, Armenia and Moldova) boycotted the vote. Ukraine did not, and 70.5 per cent voted in favour. In the west only, in the three oblasts of Galicia, the former Habsburg heartland, a vote on independence was held, and backed by 88 per cent. However, the wily chairman of parliament, Leonid Kravchuk, inserted a third national question on support for Ukrainian sovereignty within a looser 'Union of Sovereign States', which 80.2 per cent backed across Ukraine. Ukraine was therefore half-in, half-out of the negotiations to create a new Union Treaty and a looser USSR, which were forestalled by Party conservatives who staged a coup in August 1991. Ukraine was not actually due to attend the aborted signing ceremony on Monday 19 August, the first day of the coup.

On the other hand, Kravchuk and most of the Ukrainian establishment equivocated during the coup. On all-Soviet TV, Kravchuk declared that, 'what has happened, was bound to happen'. On Ukrainian TV, he pointed out that 'no emergency situation has been declared' locally, but his main stress was on the need to 'avoid destabilising the situation . . . we will all act in order to avoid spilling innocent blood'.[1] Other Ukrainian leaders, particularly the local Communist party apparat, actively supported the coup.

Its eventual collapse after two days had little to do with events in Kiev. Nevertheless, the coup's failure provided Rukh with a glorious opportunity. The Communists swung behind independence to save their own skins. As Party leader Stanislav Hurenko eloquently put it in private, 'we must vote for independence, because, if we don't, we'll find ourselves up to our ears in shit'.[2] At a special session of parliament on 24 August 1991, a Declaration of Independence was passed by 346 votes to one. The Communist Party was banned on 31 August, but all attempts to exclude former Communists from power were roundly defeated.

With no serious political force now opposed to it, the Rada's vote for independence was confirmed by a popular referendum on 1 December, with 90.3 per cent in favour. Ukraine's first ever president was elected on the same day (technically, the historian Mykhailo Hrushevskyi had also served as president of the Ukrainian People's Republic in 1917–18, but he was elected by the parliament, not the people). The 'romantic nationalism' and princi-pled anti-Communism of former dissident Viacheslav Chornovil won him 23.3 per cent of the vote – essentially replicating Rukh's support at earlier elections in March 1990 and March 1991. Chornovil had been sentenced four times by Soviet courts and served a total of almost fourteen years; his main opponent Leonid Kravchuk, only three years older, had served in the Party *apparat* since 1960, from 1970 in the agitation and propaganda department of the Central Committee. From 1988, he headed the ideology department. Nevertheless, Kravchuk won a sweeping victory with 61.6 per cent of the vote, by adapting the 'safety first' theme of his comments during the August coup (while denying his actual words) to sell a conservative version of alternative Ukraine, in which the Soviet social system could coexist with a fudged vision of sovereign-but-still-Russia-friendly Ukraine, *and* in which Ukraine would be better off economically. Kravchuk won everywhere in the east and south and in the central Ukrainian countryside, while Chornovil's vote was concentrated in the west.

### The Roots of Corruption

The political story is the one that is normally told, but Ukraine also began to develop a serious corruption problem in the late Soviet era. Most of the bigger sums were laundered by the Communist Party *apparat* in Moscow, but many leading Ukrainians took part, and began to develop their own local opportunities in 1990–1. As of 1 June 1990, the Communist Party of Ukraine had 567 million roubles in cash; the Central Committee in Kiev had 86 million in physical assets and regional party organisations a further 190.6 million (in total $562 million, assuming the then official exchange rate of 1.5 roubles to the dollar – the market rate was ten times higher or more, but many official assets were shimmied aboard at the 'official' rate).[3] At least 40 million roubles disappeared via Ukrinbank. None of the cash was recovered when the Party was banned in August 1991, and only the most immovable of physical assets, party buildings in the main, were nationalised. The local assets of the Orthodox Church disappeared down a similar black hole.

Everywhere, former Communists became 'red entrepreneurs' – even though most had no entrepreneurial skill. Party property in Kiev set up the career of the 'Magnificent Seven' business-mafia group, who later decided to trade under the more consumer-friendly but bizarrely inappropriate brand name of the 'Social-Democratic Party of Ukraine (united)', commonly known as the SDPU(o). In Crimea, Party funds – reportedly 810 million devalued roubles in no- or low-interest loans – were used to set up the import–export business Impeks and its partner bank, Intersot, a Soviet-Swiss joint venture. The funds were also invested in the car factory Krymovatogaz, and used to build a local aquapark.[4] Impeks allegedly funded Crimean separatists in 1994.

As elsewhere in the USSR, *komsomol* businesses also flourished in the Gorbachev era, such as the Youth Housing Cooperatives that met key shortages of labour and supply. Even more lucrative were the 'Youth Science and Technology Development Centres' set up by official decree in 1987, that soon morphed into traders in all kinds of deficit goods, especially coveted consumer items, which were resold for vast profit if they were of Western origin, and tended to be cheap and cheerful domestic copies if they were not. Many *komsomol* entrepreneurs were genuinely entrepreneurial and even those who were not were able to use their political connections and monopoly positions to grow rich in the distorted half-reformed economy of the time. And soon *komsomol* money begat *komsomol* banks, such as Privatbank in Dnipropetrovsk, which was accused in 2001 by independent deputies of laundering $150 million, mainly through Latvian partners. As proof, the deputies cited a memo sat on by President Kuchma in 1996.[5]

## Internal Divisions: Myth and Reality

Given the internal divisions that apparently dominated the 2004 election, how fragile, indeed how artificial an entity, is modern Ukraine? An independent Ukrainian state has only existed in its exact current borders since the collapse of the Soviet Union in 1991. However, similar versions existed-from 1648–1785 and from 1917–20. The country has several potential internal fault lines, but fortunately these are distinct, and do not coincide in such a way as to split the country neatly in two. They don't have too much of a history, either. A historical divide might set the westernmost 10 per cent of the country that was part of the Habsburg Empire between 1772 and 1918 against the rest. Religious divides within Ukraine are more complex: most of the west is Greek Catholic, and most of the rest is Orthodox, but there are two main rival branches within the Orthodox Church, one of which is loyal to Kiev and one of which follows Moscow; and religious fervour is largely absent from the heavily Sovietised eastern regions. Following the traditions of the seventeenth century, the Kievan Church is more ecumenical and less messianic than its rival, which is institutionally still a part of the Russian Church, based in Moscow. The Kievan Church uses Ukrainian, while the Moscow Church uses Church Slavonic for the liturgy and, normally, Russian for sermons.

Linguistic and cultural divides are also complicated. The ethnic Russian minority is not as large as it used to be, and was down to 17 per cent in the census of 2001, but there is a much larger 'Russian-speaking' population, although it is difficult to say exactly how large it is. Nearly all Ukrainians can speak both Ukrainian and Russian; smaller numbers of Russians are effectively bilingual, because their language predominated under the USSR and they didn't have to make the effort. The languages are close, however – not as close as is often claimed, but certainly closer than, say,

English and Welsh, though the literary standards of each are very different, because nineteenth-century language planners made them so. There is more gradation on the level of dialect. Ukrainianised Russian gradually becomes Russianised Ukranian somewhere between Moscow and Kiev. Many people constantly mix both language and dialect – there is even a quasi-official mixture of both known as *surzhyk*. The attempt to spread the use of literary Ukrainian after 1991 had only limited success. A *modus vivendi* of sorts has therefore emerged since the mid-1990s, although it is not one that Ukrainian nationalists like, as the basic compromise is that Ukrainian is the sole state language, but its use is not particularly vigorously enforced.

Regionally, the country is divided into twenty-five oblasts and one 'Republic' (see the map on page xiv), Crimea, but the breakdown is more easily understood in terms of west, centre, east and south. Each of these areas has a distinct history, of which the most important aspects are summarised below. For instance, the three oblasts of Lviv, Ternopil and Ivano–Frankivsk make up the historical Habsburg region of Galicia (technically, this is east Galicia, and west Galicia, centred around Kraków, is now in Poland). To the north is Volhynia, which is traditionally linked to Galicia, and a principality of Galicia and Volhynia flourished as one of the main successor states to Rus´ from 1199 to 1349. The historical link with Hungary (formed through occupation by the Hungarian King Bela III in 1189 and through the claims reiterated in the Treaty of Spish in 1214) justified the Habsburgs' (re)creation of the Kingdom of Galicia and Lodomeria in 1772, but Volhynia proper then passed to the Romanovs. (Lodomeria is a Latinised version of Volodymyr–Volynskyi, a reference to Volodymyr the Great founding the city in Volhynia in 988.) Thanks to the abolition of the Greek Catholic Church under Nicholas 1 in 1839, Volhynia is now largely Orthodox in religion. The two territories were linked again as part of inter-war Poland, although Warsaw tried to keep them apart with the so-called 'Sokil line'.

In the south-west, Chernivtsi is the capital city of the northern half of the historical province of Bukovyna, the name of which means 'Land of Beech Trees'. It, too, has historical links with Galicia, but is also mainly Orthodox and has retained an ethnic diversity that Galicia has lost. It was part of Greater Romania between 1918 and 1940, and is still coveted by many Romanian nationalists today.

Transcarpathia is 'over' the Carpathian mountains, if you are in Lviv or Kiev. It is therefore Ukraine's most geographically distinct region. It was part of the kingdom of Hungary from the middle of the eleventh century until 1918, and was then amalgamated into interwar Czechoslovakia.

Despite the formation of a 'Carpatho–Ukraine' mini-state after Hitler dismembered Czechoslovakia in 1938–9, it is often claimed that the local population forms a distinct 'Rusyn' nationality. From a local point of view, the region is Subcarpathia. Most locals also belong to a separate branch of the Greek Catholic Church centred in Mukachevo rather than Lviv, or are Orthodox.

Central Ukraine is now relatively ethnically homogenous, but there is a historical difference between the territories east (the Left Bank) and west (Right Bank) of the mighty river Dnipro. The Left Bank overlapped with the territory of the Hetmanate after 1648, and was linked to Russia in 1654. On the other hand, the local cossack elite became a nobility of sorts in the eighteenth century. It was largely assimilated into Russian culture in the nineteenth century, but some vestiges remained. Pavlo Skoropadskyi, for example, who led the 'Hetmanate' version of independent Ukraine in 1918, was a descendant of Ivan Skoropadskyi, who served as Hetman from 1709 to 1722. By contrast, the Right Bank was only added to the Russian Empire in 1793–5. Polish landlords, Ukrainian peasants and Jewish middlemen remained the local norm until the twentieth century.

The centre and west of Ukraine are the historical heartland of the country, and are home to settled agriculture and the protective forest zone. To the south is the steppe, which Ukrainians and their ancestors settled in quieter times, but abandoned in times of conflict. Hence its nickname of the *dike pole* or 'wild field'. Modern oblast boundaries do not coincide precisely with the historical border between central Ukraine and the steppe. The cossacks' military headquarters at Zaporizhzhia, the *Sich*, was deliberately situated to the east, so as to be out of Polish reach. Moreover, the area of cossack settlement in the sixteenth to eighteenth centuries straddled the modern Russo-Ukrainian border, particularly the area known as *Slobidska* or 'Free' Ukraine, which centred on Kharkiv. The steppe region can itself be roughly divided into three. East Ukraine is the industrial heart of Ukraine, though its two big cities, the steel- and chemical-producing Dnipropetrovsk and the mining capital of Donetsk, have a long rivalry. The coal-mining region of the Donets river basin is known as the Donbas (Don-basin). South Ukraine, the northern Black Sea coast, has been a battleground for millennia, fought over by Ukrainians from the north, Greeks, Venetians and Ottomans from the south, and invaders such as the Huns, Polovtsians and Mongols from the east. The eighteenth-century conquest of the region by Russian and Cossack forces was but a further stage in this cycle. The Imperial name of 'New Russia', which was given to the region, and its nickname of the 'European California', reflected its image of a land of opportunity and multi-ethnic settlement.

Crimea has an even more chequered past. One branch of the Mongol Golden Horde mingled with diverse local elements to create the Crimean Tatar Khanate in the 1440s, which, despite ceding sovereignty of the southern coast to the Ottomans in 1475, remained quasi-independent until Russian annexation in 1783. (Many Crimean Tatars prefer to be called simply 'Crimeans', or *kyrymly*.) Deported *en masse* to central Asia in 1944, about 260,000 have returned since 1989. Crimea is the one Ukrainian region with an ethnic Russian majority (58.5 per cent, compared to 24.4 per cent Ukrainian and 12.1 per cent Crimean Tatar), and the peninsula is historically and militarily (as was shown by the Crimean War in 1854–6, and the second siege of Sevastopol by the Germans for 250 days in 1941–2)[6] important to Russian nationalists. In fact, it is still home to the Russian Black Sea Fleet. A Republic of Crimea was established within Ukraine after a referendum in January 1991, and although many of its powers were reduced in 1995–6, Crimea still has a separate government.

Internal divisions are therefore considerable but complex. There is no simple 'east versus west' within Ukraine. Differences of language, religion and regional history vary enormously in their potential saliency. Nevertheless, they cannot be wished away. A more united country would have had a very different political trajectory in the 1990s. It was itself a sign of division that one part of the country, the ultra-cynical post-Soviet business and political elite based largely in the east and south, was prepared to exploit these divisions in 2004. It was Viktor Yushchenko's greastest initial achievement that he worked so hard to overcome them.

### Independence, But No Revolution

In December 1991, when Ukraine became independent, it hit the headlines around the world. However, the 'national-democratic' opposition found it very difficult to displace the former Communists from power in the 1990s, largely because of the regional problem that limited their support base. Trapped in a minority, the opposition fell victim to internal squabbling and the authorities' divide-and-rule tactics (see pages 42–3). Part of the opposition also simply gave up. Many of Rukh's leaders were happy to support the old guard now that Ukraine was independent. With someone like Leonid Kravchuk, rather than a former dissident such as Václav Havel or Lech Wałęsa, at the helm, politics retained a neo-Soviet style. Kravchuk operated through elite bargaining, and set out to coopt or divide opponents (Rukh split after its third congress in spring 1992, not without some prompting from Kravchuk). A natural populist, Kravchuk passed up several opportunities to act more radically. Parliament was not dissolved, although a more reform-minded assembly would surely have been the voters' verdict in 1992. Kravchuk also failed to take advantage of the ban on the Communist Party, which re-emerged as Ukraine's largest political movement after the ban was renegotiated in 1993 (it would retain this status until 2002). Like Boris Yeltsin, Kravchuk was averse to setting up a presidential party to act as an agent of power. Crucially, there was no economic reform. Ukraine joined the World Bank and IMF in 1992, but Kravchuk's fig-leaf liberal economics minister, Volodymyr Lanovyi, only survived until July 1992.

Ukraine missed the chance of a political relaunch when Leonid Kuchma became prime minister in October 1992. Kuchma tried to set up a coalition government, but included too few real liberals and Rukh-ites. He obtained emergency powers to enact economic reform by decree for six months, but frittered the opportunity away. Perhaps none of this is surprising, as Kuchma was a typical 'red director', who already had links with the mobster Boris Birshtein and his firm Seabeco, who had allegedly pushed the previously obscure Kuchma forward to promote the shadowy trading company Ukraïna, set up with most of the other leading east Ukrainian 'red directors' to divert export surpluses into their own pockets. Kuchma's term ended controversially, with a mass wave of strikes in east Ukraine in June 1993. Kravchuk then missed another chance, by appointing Yukhym Zviahilskyi, the mayor of Donetsk as Kuchma's replacement, who was selected solely to clean up the political problems of the summer strikes, but who brought corruption rather than regional compromise to Kiev.

These were all political choices, which could have been made differently, though it can be accepted in part that Ukraine's overall starting position was not good. Given the sheer speed of the Soviet collapse, Ukraine became independent without a basic state infrastructure. An army, an administration, borders, and a currency all had to be built from scratch. A famous Deutsche Bank report that argued in 1991 that Ukraine had the best economic potential of any of the then Soviet republics, was based mainly on Ukraine's resource profile, human capital and export potential, rather than on its likely macroeconomic trajectory. Ukraine was also limited in its choice of leaders.[7] Rukh represented the cultural elite, which was then more interested in national symbols than in economic reform. Kravchuk and Kuchma represented the former Communist nomenclatura, who were mainly interested in themselves. The government was therefore increasingly split into rapacious rival 'clans'. In 1994, Seabeco backed Kuchma, while another Mafia firm, Nordex, linked to the Russian Solntsevo gang and the controversial 'businessmen' Grigorii Loutchanskii and Semion

Mogilevich, backed Kravchuk.[8] Unfortunately for Kravchuk, Seabeco was the richer of the two. Mogilevich supposedly switched sides easily enough, however.[9]

## Kuchma Becomes President

Kravchuk had no economic record to stand on when he faced re-election in 1994, especially given the promises of prosperity he had made in 1991. The GDP fell by a scarcely credible 9.9 per cent in 1992, by another 14.2 per cent in 1993, and by 22.9 per cent in 1994. Inflation in 1993 on one calculation was 10,200 per cent. Indeed Kravchuk, who was elected for five years in December 1991, had been forced into early elections by the economic crisis. He therefore chose to emphasise his achievements in 'state-building', and deliberately polarised the election on the national issue, painting his opponent, Leonid Kuchma, as a dangerous Russophile who would sell out the independence so recently won. Hence the initial shock when Kravchuk lost, by 45.1 per cent to 52.1 per cent in the second round. Kuchma won every oblast east of the river Dnipro, plus Kirovohrad, while Kravchuk won every oblast further west.

Kuchma was many things, but he was not simplistically pro-Russian. He understood that the centre of electoral gravity within Ukraine's complex regional politics better than Kravchuk; it was geographically closer to his home region of Dnipropetrovsk, and culturally closer to Russian-speaking Ukrainians such as himself. Like Kravchuk, he was what Ukrainians call a *derzhavnik* ('statist'), but one who saw the state primarily as a vehicle of power, rather than, culturally, as 'an icon to which one prays', in the words of his inauguration address. In 1994, he also skilfully combined two views of a way out of Ukraine's economic crisis, playing both to populist sentiment in the east (hence his vague talk condemning Ukraine's alleged economic 'isolation' from Russia) and to the 'red directors' that he himself represented. Kuchma had served as factory director for the giant missile factory that built Soviet ICBMs in Dnipropetrovsk, and as boss of the Ukrainian (red) directors' union since he had been ousted as prime minister in 1993.

At the time, Kuchma's many faces were an electoral asset. His campaign slogan promising 'Deeds not words' convinced many in the West that he would be an improvement on the prolix Kravchuk, especially after he swiftly brought the country back from the economic brink by launching Ukraine's first real economic reform programme in October 1994. However, it was not long before problems that had plagued the Kravchuk era began to resurface. Kuchma's choice of prime ministers was a warning sign: first, he left in office a dinosaur from the Gosplan era, Vitalii Masol; and secondly, he chose Ukraine's former security chief, Yevhen Marchuk, who had been widely accused of initial collaboration with the Moscow junta in August 1991. His third selection, in May 1996, was a colleague from Dnipropetrovsk, Pavlo Lazarenko.

Lazarenko's colourful past was already known to many. Hryhorii Omelchenko of the parliamentary 'Anti-Mafia' group, had provided Kuchma with details of his shady dealings on no less than three occasions: in December 1994, April 1995 and January 1997. The last report had, however, ended up on Lazarenko's desk the very same day, thanks to its timely interception by the procurator, Hryhorii Vorsinov, an old friend of his from Dnipropetrovsk. Lazarenko had also just paid Kuchma a bribe of $3.7 million, as starter capital for a then unknown mobile phone company called Kyïvstar. As it employed Kuchma's daughter and brother-in-law, Kyïvstar was a surprise winner alongside two Russian-backed companies in the March 1997 auction for GSM-900 frequencies in Ukraine, causing Motorola to quit Ukraine in disgust.

Once installed as prime minister, however, Lazarenko had bigger things in mind. UESU, the company he had helped Yuliia Tymoshenko set up, was granted a monopoly on the distribution of Russian energy imports in the industrial centres around Dnipropetrovsk, which constituted the most lucrative third of Ukraine (see page 20), and a five-year tax holiday under the 1992 Joint Venture Law. Much of UESU's subsequent income was transferred to two other companies linked to Lazarenko – United Energy International Ltd and the Cyprus-based Somolli Enterprises Ltd., from which $101 million was moved in 1996 to other accounts in Switzerland controlled by Lazarenko's colleague, Petro Kiritchenko. From here, Lazarenko withdrew two bearer cheques for $48 million, which ended up in the EuroFed Credit Bank in Antigua. Finally, Lazarenko moved $114 million to various banks in the US, mainly in California, where Lazarenko owned a lavish San Francisco mansion with five swimming pools that had once belonged to the Hollywood actor Eddie Murphy.

It was also alleged that much of UESU's 'income', $72 million out of the money transferred to Somolli Enterprises, was in fact obtained by extortion from other Ukrainian factories.[10] Lazarenko was also engaged in a long and bitter war with a rival group, the newly-formed IUD (see pages 10–11), to expand his energy monopoly. In July 1996, he claimed members of the group tried to assassinate him, when a huge bomb exploded near his motorcade on his way to Kiev airport to fly to Donetsk. In 2002, it was alleged in turn that he had paid the Donetsk-based Kushnir gang $2 million for the murder of IUD leader Yevhen Shcherban in 1996.

Lazarenko was forced out of office in July 1997, citing an undisclosed 'illness'. In December 1998, he was caught entering Switzerland on a Panamanian passport and arrested. He posted bail of $3 million and returned to Ukraine, but fled again in February 1999, when parliament voted 337–0 to lift his immunity. This time, he went to the USA (via Greece), where his claim for asylum instead became a public trial in 2004. Kiritchenko was the prosecution's star witness, but Lazarenko hired a string of expensive lawyers, whose first victory was to accept a staggering bail of $86 million, which, as this was mainly the money now frozen in Antigua, was no loss. More importantly, they claimed Lazarenko was a political victim, all of whose activities had conformed with the fuzzy status of Ukrainian law at the time, and were in any case out of US jurisdiction. Kiritchenko was too obviously a partner-in-crime, if crime it was, and in May the judge threw out twenty-four of fifty-three counts. The jury, however, rebelled at the general atmosphere of sleaze and returned twenty-nine guilty verdicts on all the remaining charges. Lazarenko faced a possible fifteen years in prison, but in May 2005 the judge overruled the jury on fifteen charges, leaving only $10 million to clear up. According to Judge Jenkins, 'jurors simply threw up their hands rather than work their way through the hard task of distinguishing clean from allegedly dirty money'. Lazarenko also received an eighteen-month suspended sentence and a 10.6m Swiss Franc fine *in absentia* from the Swiss in 2000.

Lazarenko was just one of many of what the Ukrainians soon began to call 'oligarchs', however. His schemes and scams were reworked by his successors. Once large-scale privatisation began, slightly later than in Russia in the late 1990s, it was rarely transparent or fair, and a dozen or so men and, temporarily, one woman, became plutocratically rich. By 2002, the Polish magazine *Wprost* estimated the wealth of Rinat Akhmetov, Ukraine's richest man, at $1.7 billion, that of Kuchma's son-in-law, Viktor Pinchuk, at $1.3 billion, and the presidential chief of staff Viktor Medvedchuk's opaque holdings at $800 million.[11] The three men represented the three major regional 'clans' of Donetsk, Dnipropetrovsk (where Pinchuk inherited most of Lazarenko's former empire) and Kiev. Three smaller business clans were based in Kharkiv, Odesa and Crimea. By the time *Wprost* compiled its 2004 list, five Ukrainians were included amongst Eastern Europe's fifty richest businessmen and women. Akhmetov was now valued at $3.5 billion, with his compatriot Serhii Taruta, who headed the Industrial Union of the Donbas, catching up at $1.9 billion. Pinchuk, at $2.2 billion, was matched by another Dnipropetrovsk oligarch, Ihor Kolomoiskyi of the Privat Group, who was also on $2.2 billion. Oleksandr Yaroslavskyi of Kharkiv was now a force in his own right, with $850 million. Medvedchuk had been overtaken, but was assumed to be little poorer in real terms.[12]

There were important differences between the groups, however. The Dnipropetrovsk 'clan' was in reality two separate financial-industrial groups. The first, Interpipe (which specialised in pipes, chemicals and oil processing), was run by Pinchuk, Leonid Derkach, head of the Security Services from 1998 to 2001, and his son, Andrii. The second, Privatbank (metals), was founded by another young Dnipropetrovsk tycoon, Serhii Tihipko, but taken over by Ihor Kolomoiskyi. Both groups were built up with *komsomol* money and used their political connections to gain control of productive, albeit investment-starved, businesses. In the late Kuchma era, the two therefore began to spend millions on PR, both at home and in the US, advertising their intention to go legit, although their links with new Russian capital – which came without any obligation to clean up corporate governance – remained close. For example, they helped Oleg Deripaska's Siberian Aluminium to win control of Mykolaïv's relatively modern Aluminium Works in 2000.

The Kiev group headed by Viktor Medvedchuk and Hryhorii Surkis, who still dressed like Gordon Gekko in the film, *Wall Street*, on the other hand, began life with protection rackets in Kiev's markets, before moving on to financial pyramid schemes. Although it then parleyed its initial fortunes and political muscle for substantial controlling packages in Ukraine's lucrative oblast energy supply companies, the clan was only rarely involved in actual production, and sought to entrench its precarious privilege through control of media markets and the security apparatus of the state – and through Medvedchuk's position as Kuchma's chief of staff after 2002. Medvedchuk claimed to be a lawyer, and bought up most of Ukraine's courts. The clan's most prestigious asset was the football club Dynamo Kiev, and their most dangerous activity was the systematic logging of every tree they could find in Transcarpathia, seriously contributing to flooding problems downstream in the Danube basin. Otherwise, the Kiev clan and the political party that fronted their activities, the SDPU(o), were little more than professional budget-leechers.

The Donetsk clan stood somewhat in between the other two, not in geographical terms – Donetsk is in Ukraine's far east – or politically, given the region's reputation for political muscle, but economically (see pages 10–11). The Donetsk clan earned large export revenues through steel and chemicals, but these were dependent on hidden state subsidies. The main clans also controlled the Ukrainian media. Medvedchuk ran the three biggest TV channels, the First National channel UT-1, Inter and 1+1. Viktor Pinchuk's Dnipropetrovsk group ran the next three, STV, New Channel and ICTV. The Donetsk media were mainly local, but Akhmetov also controlled the Kiev paper *Segodnia* ('Today').

## Kuchma Wins Virtual Re-election

As his friends and family grew rich, the increasingly unpopular Kuchma undoubtedly benefited from dumping public opprobrium on Lazarenko. Those who followed him were just as bad, however. Kuchma had a lot to hide. The 1999 election campaign was therefore a truly bizarre affair; in fact, it was not really an election at all, but more of a shadow conflict of proxies and fakes. In theory, Kuchma was standing against Communist Party leader Petro Symonenko and the Progressive Socialist leader Nataliia Vitrenko on the left, and former security chief Yevhen Marchuk on the right. In practice, however, all were cut-outs secretly sponsored by the presidential administration and the leading oligarchs.

Well aware of his image problems at home and abroad, Kuchma's advisers deliberately sidestepped the issues of corruption and a still stagnant economy by setting up a scenario (the Russian word is *dramaturgiia*) that would pit their man against a non-existent 'Red threat'. Kuchma's real enemies were Lazarenko and his business partner Yuliia Tymoshenko; Vadym Hetman's protégé Viktor Yushchenko; and, to a lesser extent, the veteran Rukh leader Viacheslav Chornovil. None ended up standing in the race.

Rukh was subject to yet another split in February 1999, after some hefty expenditure by the oligarchs to bribe both sides. Oleh Ishchenko, head of another energy company, Olhaz, provided an alleged $1 million,[13] the SDPU(o) financed more than twenty moles in the Rukh leadership and a third,[14] later, splinter group, laughably calling itself 'Rukh for Unity'.[15] Chornovil was killed in March in a collision with a Kamaz truck. Former SBU boss Marchuk was reported to have taken possession of a video on which Spetsnaz officers from the interior ministry admitted to organising the killing, but he claimed to have lost it. Marchuk decided to stand himself, to prevent any real right-wing challenge to Kuchma, allegedly using a supply of *kompromat* ('compromising materials') that he looked after with rather more care and attention, and which he gave to strong-arm nationalists, many of whom were former dissidents, to persuade them to support him. His 8.1 per cent share of the ballot drained away the right-wing vote. The two Rukh candidates squabbled over the remainder, with 2.2 and 1.2 per cent each.

Lazarenko's dramatic flight to the USA made it easier to deal with Kuchma's potentially most dangerous opponent, the Socialist Party leader Oleksandr Moroz, whom Lazarenko, and, possibly, Tymoshenko had planned to finance. Moroz was now harassed at every turn, both by the authorities and by their proxy, the fake 'Progressive Socialist' party leader Nataliia Vitrenko. On 2 October 1999, state media splashed a sensational story that grenades had been thrown at Vitrenko and her supporters at an election rally in the eastern town of Inhulets, near Dnipropetrovsk. Moroz's local election agent, Serhii Ivanchenko, and his brother were arrested and blamed (in that order). The two were sentenced to fifteen years in 2001, but by then the whole affair had been confirmed as a blatant set-up. Ivanchenko was pardoned in 2004.

That only left potential liberal opponents. Hetman's murder in 1998 was an apparent warning to Yushchenko not to stand. In 2002 it was alleged that Lazarenko had arranged the murder because Hetman, then boss of the Ukrainian Interbank Currency Exchange, had offered to finance Yushchenko's campaign. (The hit was allegedly cheaper than Shcherban, at only $850,000.) It was unclear, however, why Lazarenko would do Kuchma's dirty work, unless he was clearing the path for his own candidacy or that of Moroz. It was also possible that the murder was linked to the privatisation of the lucrative currency exchange.

Yushchenko, however, was badly hit by his mentor's death and did everything he could to avoid standing. Kuchma helped him to defeat a Communist-backed no-confidence motion in the wake of the 1998 currency crisis and revelations about NBU financing, as he didn't want an unemployed Yushchenko suddenly deciding he was tempted to run for office. But a deal was supposedly done. According to the journalist Kost Bondarenko:

In the Spring of 1999 Viktor Yushchenko . . . met with [the leading oligarch, then Kuchma's campaign manager] Oleksandr Volkov. Oleksandr Mikhailovich painted roughly the following picture in front of Yushchenko: 'Vitia, you can, certainly, stand for president, that's your right. But just think: what will you gain? You won't become president – this isn't your game and not your fated time. You could take votes off Kuchma and help either Moroz or [Communist leader] Symonenko to become president. You'd want this? And if Kuchma becomes president everything's the same: he won't forgive your intervention. And so – I propose to you a gentlemen's agreement: you decline to stand, support

Kuchma in the elections, and in exchange I'll guarantee you the post of prime minister after his victory.'[16]

With only Moroz left as a serious opponent, 'administrative resources' made sure that Kuchma won a (still not that impressive) 36.5 per cent in the first round. Secret tapes released a year later showed what these 'administrative resources' meant in practice:

EPISODE ONE, NOVEMBER 1999: Kuchma to Azarov, the head of the Tax Inspectorate:

KUCHMA: You should get together all your fucking tax inspectors . . . and warn them: those who lose the elections in the district will not work after the elections . . . You should sit down with every [collective-farm] head and fucking tell them: either you sit in fucking jail – as I have more [*kompromat*] on you than anybody else, or you produce votes. Right or wrong?[17]

Kuchma then switches to interior minister Yurii Kravchenko, with a message for his police:

KUCHMA: Tell them: guys, if you don't fucking give as much as necessary, then tomorrow you will be where you should be – yes . . . those fucking central oblasts [where Moroz's support was strongest] they should be clear, we are not gonna play fucking games with them anymore . . . we must win with a formidable margin . . . when they say 2 or 3 per cent, it is not a victory . . . not a fucking place can say that it's protesting [that is, voting against the authorities].[18]

While officials stuffed the ballot in Kuchma's favour, their discreet support helped Symonenko to second place with 22.2 per cent, and short-term sympathy for Vitrenko pulled her up to 11 per cent, making sure that Moroz, with only 11.3 per cent, would not make it into the second round. Faced with the alternative of the distinctly unpalatable Communist leader, Kuchma now had the 'lesser evil' scenario his technologists had promised, and won an easy victory in the second round, with 56.2 per cent against Symonenko's 37.8 per cent. Almost a million voters, however, (970,181 hardy individuals) went to the polls just to vote against *both* candidates.

Fittingly, however, Kuchma's virtual victory proved hollow, and his expected second honeymoon period non-existent. America pressurised him surprisingly hard to push his shadier associates into the background and appoint a real reform government, during his 'victory' visit to Washington on 8 December, under the auspices of the Binational ('Gore-Kuchma') Commission set up in 1996. The decisive factor was Ukraine's still truly dire economic situation. With a real risk of financial default looming, Kuchma decided Yushchenko was the only person who could front a fraught period of loan negotiations with the IMF – but he planned to give him only a year.

Kuchma had also made a similar promise to the sitting prime minister, Lazarenko's do-nothing successor, Valerii Pustovoitenko, but that had to be broken. On 14 December, Pustovoitenko lost his renomination vote by 206 votes to 44, largely because key Kuchma supporters sat on their hands – 131 deputies voted but abstained or were present but did not bother to vote. The vote was secret, because government factions voted for it to be such, including ten from the SDPU(o) and thirteen from the rival clan party Labour Ukraine, which was controlled by Kuchma's son-in-law, Viktor Pinchuk.[19] Yushchenko was now a shoe-in, and on 22 December he won the Rada's approval by 296 votes to 12.

Yushchenko's appointment may have been a typical tactical manoeuvre by Kuchma, but the consequences were enormous. Kuchma expected everything to return to normal when he pulled on the string, but Yushchenko had much bigger strategic plans, with he and his supporters hoping to use his time in office to build a broader base for a Ukrainian liberal movement and a proper market economy. He knew he would have to take on the oligarchs if he were to achieve anything, and that they would crush his plans if he did not undermine them first. Aware of his sudden strength, Yushchenko appointed Tymoshenko as deputy premier in charge of the energy sector. Tymoshenko later claimed that they were the 'only two' real reformers in the government,[20] but they would form an effective tandem and proved surprisingly adept at running with the ball.

## The Yushchenko Government

Independent Ukraine has virtually no oil or gas, though it has coal and nuclear energy. Its mines, however, are Dickensian, and nuclear expansion plans were mothballed after the Chernobyl disaster in 1986. Ukraine's pronounced energy dependence on Russia has been widely seen as both an economic and political problem, as has its apparently ever-expanding debt, although most of the debt was racked up by a particularly brazen scheme benefiting both Russian and Ukrainian oligarchs. Most of Ukraine's gas came from the Russian company Itera, which, as it was basically a front for the Russian gas giant Gazprom, in the late 1990s was getting its gas almost free, at a price of around $4 per thousand cubic metres. The Ukrainian state usually paid about $50 to $80, but at this point, Itera had chosen to receive only about a third of that. The rest, about $2 billion a year for each side, was divided between Ukrainian and Russian middlemen. The final possibility was to sell the gas on to central Europe, where customers typically paid $100 to $110 per thousand cubic metres. Even allowing for $10 in bribes to customs officials and others, this generated another estimated $360 million every year. Tymoshenko had often been accused of profiting from such schemes when she was in business with Lazarenko. She now moved quickly to shut them down.[21]

Well aware of the system's collective strength and the weakness of the domestic reform lobby, Yushchenko and Tymoshenko sensibly took on the oligarchs one by one. First to go was Ihor Bakai, head of Oil and Gas of Ukraine. Bakai had been running two scams. The first involved siphoning off Russian gas in transit to central Europe and selling it on to Slovak and Polish traders. The second involved Ukraine's energy debt to the Russian supplier Itera, repayments against which Bakai had sent instead to a dummy company, Itera International, in Cyprus, and thence to his own pocket, buying, amongst other things, a $5 million home in Naples, Florida. But, as Bakai had also helped to bankroll Kuchma's 1999 election campaign, he survived. His company generated an estimated $150 million every year in off-book profits, which was either used widely, to grease Ukraine's political machine, or narrowly, supposedly by Kuchma himself.[22]

Tymoshenko now exposed Bakai by admitting in Moscow that Ukraine's energy debt was $2.23 billion, rather than the $763 million claimed by Bakai, but helpfully pointed out that Oil and Gas of Ukraine had run up the debt and was responsible for repaying it. Bakai resigned in March 2000, reportedly also as a result of private American pressure, although in Kuchma's Ukraine old hoods didn't retire. Bakai soon bounced back. By October 2003 he was director of the presidential administration's mysterious 'Department of State Affairs', whose affairs included distributing lucrative property to the president's allies and running a vodka plant and holiday property in Crimea. Other 'affairs' included a $200,000 table and $2,000 teapots for Kuchma's office.

Another oligarch, Oleksandr Volkov, lost the tax exemptions that allowed him to sell imported oil at double the price. More generally, the new government claimed to have eliminated some 250 subsidies, tax breaks and licenses granted to the friends of the old regime. Most notorious of these was the 1992 joint venture law. In origin a sensible attempt to attract foreign investment, the definition of 'joint' had over time become extremely loose, and most such schemes were run by domestic oligarchs with 'sleeping' or more or less non-existent Western partners to save themselves an estimated UAH3 billion per annum (about $550 million), including UAH1.3 billion in unpaid excise and VAT.[23] Such ventures controlled nearly all of Ukraine's market for petrol and diesel, and a large amount of its alcohol imports.

The next challenge the government tackled was reform of the electricity system, the privatised parts of which were controlled through a network of shadow companies which were ultimately controlled by Hryhorii Surkis of the SDPU(o), who had won control of seven *oblenergos* in the late 1990s (each of Ukraine's regions or oblasts had its own energy company and were therefore known as *obl-energos*). Crucially, the *oblenergos* were only distributors. They could set a price high enough for their local monopolies to earn much public opprobrium (household energy supply having been basically free in Soviet times, so that in the mid-1990s it was common practice to leave gas ovens and hobs on all day, because of a shortage of matches), but Surkis only paid about 6 or 7 per cent of supply price and almost nothing in tax. By forcing him to cough up for both, a claimed $1.8 billion was added to the state budget.

The government had less success with its attempts to arrange a more transparent privatisation of three more *oblenergos* for a fairer price, $100 million. The three were sold to the American firm AES and to Slovakia's VEZ, but the latter later turned out to be a front for Aleksandr Babakov, a financier of the Russian nationalist party Rodina, who soon joined forces with Surkis and Medvedchuk. Moreover, the SDPU(o) duo would later win shares in nine more *oblenergos* from the Energy Standard Group, after organising the arrest of its head, the Russian businessman Konstantin Grigorishin, for 'cocaine and firearms possession' in October 2002. Grigorishin alleged that Medvedchuk and Surkis threatened to take him to a forest and 'bury him alive', and allegedly paid for a lurid full-page ad to make his claims in the *New York Times* on 19 December 2003.

The other side of the coin was the new government's attempts to make life easier for small- and medium-sized businesses, reforming first itself – slimming down government and bureaucracy – and beginning a tax reform that would ultimately lower the top rate of income tax from 40 per cent to 30 per cent (by January 2004, it would be down to a 13 per cent flat rate) and profit tax from 30 to 20 per cent. The reform, in other words, lowered taxes into a region where they were actually paid. Parts of the shadow economy started to move into the legal sphere.

In December 1999, a decree was issued to 'abolish' the collective farm system, though in mirror-image neo-Soviet style, this was supposed to be achieved almost instantaneously by April 2000. Nevertheless, this epochal change promised that all collective farm workers now had 'the right to freely leave [their collective farms] with land and property shares and may, on the basis of these shares, create private enterprises, private farms and agricultural cooperatives'.[24] There were many problems with bureaucratic delay and the land loans that were supposed to smooth the process, but the agricultural reforms, coming on the back on the 1998 devaluation, soon put more food in the shops. The grain harvest grew from 24.4 million tons in 1999 to 39.7 million in 2001 and 41.7 million in 2004, after a bad year in 2003. Ukraine returned to its famous status as a 'bread basket' net exporter, with nine million tons going abroad in 2001.

According to the Swedish economist Anders Åslund, the government's overall reform programme raised $4 billion in 2000 alone – some 13 per cent of official GDP.[25] The rounded nature of the maths probably reflects the fact that many scams were minimised, but not eliminated. The SDPU(o) still thought it was worthwhile to add to their *oblenergo* empire after Yushchenko was ousted. Undoubtedly, however, the general campaign against corruption and against barter and offset operations put huge sums back into the budget. The government was able to pay off the mountain of pension arrears and most of its wage arrears, providing an extra UAH18 billion ($3.3 billion) to the population at large – and deliver a balanced budget. A virtuous circle began, as the extra money kick-started economic growth. After a staggering cumulative economic decline of some 60 per cent from 1991 to 1999, with GDP still falling by 0.2 per cent in 1999, growth was 5.9 per cent in 2000 and 9.2 per cent in 2001. Yushchenko now had an ideal political slogan, based on the impression, and in large part the reality, of transferring money from the undeserving super-rich to the deserving poor. Both he and Tymoshenko began a steep rise in the opinion polls.

Not everything was rosy, however. Tymoshenko met much more resistance with her plans to reform the coal sector in November 2000. Although Ukraine avoided a payments crisis and actually voluntarily returned $94 million to the IMF in September 2000, there was no real resumption of the IMF lending which had been suspended because of pre-election abuses in September 1999, despite an initial indication that this might be possible by December 2000. Without the official IMF seal of approval, the oligarchs found it hard to borrow abroad – and improving relations with international financial institutions was what they thought Yushchenko was for. Yushchenko, on the other hand, was happy to make up the gap with Russian money. A majority shareholding in the Odesa oil refinery went to Lukoil (Vagit Alekperov), the Lysychanskyi refinery to Tiumen Oil (Viktor

Vekselberg), the Mykolaïv Aluminium Plant (a particular bargain; built in 1980 with French investment, all of its produce was of export quality) to Siberian Aluminium (Oleg Deripaska), and its less modern counterpart in Zaporizhzhia to Avtovaz (formerly Boris Berezovskii).

The Ukrainian oligarchs were seething and circling, however. In private, Kuchma made his intentions clear. As early as March 2000, he can be heard on secret recordings promising that, 'I'll destroy Yushchenko'.[26] Later he added: 'Yuliia must be destroyed.' Azarov replied: 'We are working on Yuliia. I have issued an order, she is not such a fool. She. . .' Kuchma concludes: 'We need a criminal case against her and to put her ass in prison.'[27] Tymoshenko was duly sacked in January 2001, and imprisoned in February. Yushchenko was brought down by more prosaic, but still corrupt, methods in parliament. On 26 April 2001, he lost a confidence vote by 263 votes to 69. The votes against him demonstrated who was who in Ukraine. First, they included the oligarchs' factions: Pinchuk's Labour Ukraine, the SDPU(o), the Donbas party Regions of Ukraine, Volkov's Democratic Union, and most of the National-Democratic Party now run by Pustovoitenko. The Communists also voted against Yushchenko, for a reported pay-off of UAH17 million (then $3 million).[28] The leading oligarchs Viktor Medvedchuk, Hryhorii Surkis, Viktor Pinchuk, Serhii Tihipko, Ihor Bakai and Oleksandr Volkov all voted against Yushchenko; but so did fake liberals such as Valerii Khoroshkovskyi (later economy minister), the fake 'Greens' and the Yabluko party (both were fronts for dodgy businessmen – see page 65); and such notable individuals as Oleksandr Zinchenko, who would end up as Yushchenko's campaign manager in 2004, and Volodymyr Satsiuk, who would play a controversial role in the final election show-down as deputy head of the Security Service. The fake left-wingers, for example, Nataliia Vitrenko, and the fake nationalists, such as Bohdan Boiko, all of whom were secretly funded by the oligarchs to split the opposition, also voted against.[29]

Instead of removing a president with apparent criminal tendencies, the Rada had voted to get rid of a prime minister who had begun to reverse a decade of corruption and economic decline. The disappointment was crushing. Kuchma tried to blunt criticism by appointing as Yushchenko's immediate successor Anatolii Kinakh, a colourless technocrat, albeit one then linked to the SDPU(o). But under the increasing pressure of cumulative scandal, he eventually turned to two tough men to survive. Viktor Medvedchuk was made his chief of staff in June 2002, and Viktor Yanukovych took over as prime minister in November that year. Rigged privatisations began again straight away, in May 2001. First under the hammer was Ukraine's (and one of Europe's) largest tyre factory, Rosava, which was sold for $400 million rather than the expected $2 billion (the scandal involved Ukrspetsiust, the justice ministry's agency for enforcing court orders on the storage and sale of confiscated property, famous for bank-rupting state enterprises by forcing the sale of seized assets at a fraction of their market value). Second were three thermal power stations belonging to Donbasenerho, which went for UAH160 million ($30 million) rather than the mooted UAH700 million, to an undisclosed buyer – the first of many sales to benefit the Donbas clan now that Yanukovych was at the helm. Dodgy schemes and scams again proliferated, such as removing the wheels from luxury cars at the border, so they could be imported as 'spare parts'.

----

The fact that so much was achieved by the Yushchenko government gives the lie to those who would later argue that the 2004 election simply pitted one bunch of crooks against another. The old regime had survived the onslaught of the reforms, but much had changed. The possible nemesis of the post-Soviet order was now discernible in Ukraine, unlike in Russia. Moreover, with both Yushchenko and Tymoshenko now out of office, a real opposition would be created. When Yushchenko was later asked when he decided to run for president, he replied, 'I would say that the final decision was made on 26 April 2001'.[30]

# 4

# Two Dress Rehearsals: Gongadze, Melnychenko, and the 2002 Elections

The Ukrainian revolution could, and should, have begun in 2000, although it wouldn't then have been 'orange' – a branding idea that came later. On 5 September 2000, Hryhorii Gongadze, the editor of Ukraine's first muck-raking internet website, www.pravda.com.ua, filed an exposé about one of President Kuchma's confidantes, entitled 'Everything About Oleksandr Volkov', which may not have been entirely comprehensive, but certainly added a lot of new facts to his published biography.[1] Gongadze had just complained to the interior ministry that he was being followed. He was right. But as he was being followed by a 'special team' from the interior ministry, as well as one from the Security Service of Ukraine (SBU), and probably had been since the summer, his complaint fell on deaf ears. On the night of 16 September, Gongadze walked out to dump rubbish at about 10:30 p.m., and vanished. The president added his concern to that of Gongadze's colleagues. Parliament began an investigation. Fifty days later, on 2 November, Gongadze's corpse was found in a shallow grave in woods south of Kiev. His head had been severed, probably with an axe.[2]

On the same day, Major Mykola Melnychenko, an officer in President Kuchma's Security Service who specialised in communications and counter-ing electronic surveillance (Melnychenko had also served Gorbachev in the last days of the USSR), received his passport. On 26 November he left with his family for Warsaw, and travelled on to the Czech Republic, where he was looked after by two businessmen acquainted with Oleksandr Moroz, the leader of the opposition Socialist Party of Ukraine and the aggrieved loser of the 1999 election, Volodymyr Tsvil and Volodymyr Boldaniuk. (Tsvil claims that Melnychenko and Moroz had been in contact since early 2000.) Two days later, with Melnychenko safely out of the way, Moroz made a sen-sational speech in parliament. Melnychenko had made hundreds of hours of secret tapes in Kuchma's office between October 1999 and October 2000, and had passed some recordings and summary transcripts to Moroz.

The first date was in the middle of Kuchma's re-election campaign, when Melnychenko, who had worked for the president since 1994, claims his patriotic vengeance had been provoked by overhearing the president's order to fake the grenade attack on the puppet candidate Nataliia Vitrenko and to blame Moroz. The second date came after Melnychenko's most sensational discovery led him to wrap up his work. The tapes were presumed to end on, or shortly before, Melnychenko's resignation on 23 October 2000, although he has never to date provided any tapes dated after Gongadze's disappearance on 16 September.

Melnychenko claimed to have acted alone, using a digital recorder placed under Kuchma's settee. This aspect of his story was never convincing, conjuring up an image either of furtive crawling under the sofa or of repeated visits after hours. It was later intimated that his recording device was actually hidden in the air-conditioning system, or in the TV remote control. Some have hinted that he was helped by Yevhen Marchuk, who by 2000 was head of the National Security and Defence Council.[3] Despite having headed the SBU in 1991–4 and, indeed, supported the 1991 Moscow coup, Marchuk was seen as relatively friendly to the West, or at least to NATO. He also had a long record of looking after his own interests, however. Others claimed the involvement of one or other domestic 'clan', painting a scenario of Lazarenko's revenge, Tymoshenko's skulduggery or the SDPU(o)'s naked ambition. It was alleged that the latter had arranged for Gongadze's body to be reburied where it could easily be found, to discredit Kuchma, replace him with Medvedchuk or Marchuk, and bring Yushchenko's reforms to a halt. There was no one conspiracy theory that commanded much common ground. Others were convinced of Russian involvement, both in the original taping operation and in Gongadze's death; that is, they believed that a Russian special team intervened to ensure that the kidnapping ended up as murder, to leave a weakened Kuchma more dependent on Russian help.[4] Neither was Melnychenko able to make the most of his treasure trove, a reported seven hundred hours of recordings on thirty-five CDs. He had a new computer in the Czech Republic and a crib sheet, but was only ever able to transcribe some sixty hours. When he left for America in April 2001, the rest was allegedly left in the company of Tsvil and Boldaniuk in Ostrava, who placed it on safe deposit in Liechtenstein. Their offer to supply copies to the SBU was politely declined.

But the scandal Melnychenko detonated was big enough without them. Moroz was able directly to accuse Kuchma of ordering Gongadze's disappearance. On the secret tapes Kuchma, or a particularly foul mouth remarkably similar to the president's, can be heard in various episodes, beginning in June 2000, when Gongadze had already been a thorn in the president's side for some time.

EPISODE ONE, 12 JUNE 2000.

KUCHMA: This Gongadze, yes?

LEONID DERKACH, long-time colleague of Kuchma from the Pivdemash factory in Dnipropetrovsk, and head of the Security Service from April 1998 to February 2001: Yes, yes.

KUCHMA: You can take care of him?

DERKACH: The time for him to mouth off will come to an end. I'll crush this fucker.

EPISODE TWO, 3 JULY 2000.

KUCHMA: . . . This goes to the prosecutor, right?

VOLODYMYR LYTVYN, Kuchma's then chief of staff: No, let loose [the notorious interior minister Yurii] Kravchenko. . .

KUCHMA: Simply shit – is there any limit, after all, son-of-a-bitch – he needs to be deported – the scum – to Georgia and thrown there on his ass!

LYTVYN: Take him to Georgia and dump him there.

KUCHMA: The Chechens should kidnap him and ask for a ransom!

EPISODE THREE, 10 JULY 2000.

KUCHMA: So that I don't forget, did you find this Georgian? [Gongadze was born in Georgia, hence his Georgian surname.]

KRAVCHENKO: I'm, we're working on him, that is. . .

KUCHMA: I'm telling you, drive him out, throw out, give him to the Chechens, let [undecipherable] and then a ransom.

KRAVCHENKO: We, we think it over. We'll do it in such a way that. . .

KUCHMA: Take him there, undress him, the fucker, leave him without his trousers, and let him sit there.

UNKNOWN VOICE: The shit (I would. . .)

KUCHMA: He's simply a fucker.

KRAVCHENKO: I – today I was informed. We're learning the situations, where he goes, where he walks.

UNKNOWN VOICE: Well, yes, he is somewhere on holiday ['Unknown' was well-informed: Gongadze had returned from Turkey just two days before].

KRAVCHENKO: We are doing a bit, a little bit more has to be learned, we'll do it. The team – such eagles – that will do whatever you want.[5]

Kravchenko's 'eagles', who were actually from the Sokil ('Hawk') unit, apparently did exactly as he promised. Three years later, it would be claimed – though the information was obtained with no thanks to the official investigation – that they contacted the notorious Kiev gangster Kysil, who supplied the actual killer.[6] Kravchenko agreed to resign in March 2001, but was soon back with a cosy job as head of the State tax administration in December 2002. The Prosecutor General Mykhailo Potebenko, on the other hand, not only survived, but organised the cover-up alongside Kravchenko's successor, Yurii Smirnov. Potebenko was allegedly bribed $100,000 to look the other way during another election finance scandal,[7] and was also rewarded with a seat in parliament, and therefore with immunity from prosecution, in 2002.

His successor, Sviatoslav Piskun, was appointed after international pressure to begin a proper investigation of the affair, and by 'the summer of 2003' therefore, a 'new, more vigorous, investigation under Piskun . . . was well under way'.[8] In private, Piskun's office had identified the likely killers: two men from the interior ministry acting under the alleged orders of Kravchenko and Mykola Astion, the head of Kiev's organised crime division, with Kysil's sub-contracted gangster, Yurii Nesterov, a notorious sadist from the 'Werewolves' gang, in tow. Nesterov allegedly tortured Gongadze before he died. Two whistle-blowers from the interior ministry, Liudmilla Levchenko and Anatolii Osypenko, named their boss Lieutenant-General Oleksii Pukach as the man who had overseen Gongadze's surveillance and stated that he had been present when Gongadze was bundled into his killers' car. It was even claimed that Pukach had strangled Gongadze with a belt. On 23 October 2003, Piskun's office had Pukach arrested on charges of destroying evidence. A week later, the president's inappropriately named commission on corruption met and came to a different conclusion, namely that Piskun was guilty of 'large-scale corruption'. He was then sacked.

Ihor Honcharov, the key witness against the interior ministry men, died in police custody on 1 August, after what an investigation by the British newspaper the *Independent* later revealed to be a lethal drug injection. He had also been savagely beaten in the stomach.[9] Honcharov had retired from the interior ministry in 1997, and had been arrested in May 2002, allegedly because of his own involvement arranging contract killings with the likes of the 'Werewolves'. Some called this black PR, others claimed that Honcharov was now working for Marchuk (who in June 2003 was moved to be minister of defence). Whatever the case, Honcharov left behind a sheath of letters detailing the trail of evidence and the many threats against his life. But with Honcharov dead and Piskun fired, Pukach, the key suspect, was released and allowed to flee Ukraine. Kravchenko, meanwhile, was temporarily in Russia. Piskun's successor was Hennadii Vasyliev, who resumed Potebenko's policy of inaction – or, more exactly, of prosecuting all those who made their own accusations in the affair. Not surprisingly, Vasyliev was forced out during the Orange Revolution, when the reappointment of Piskun drew some faint praise.

## The Tip of a Very Large Iceberg

The Gongadze affair was, unfortunately, entirely symptomatic of broader problems that had been developing for some time. As his prime minister Viktor Yushchenko set about cleaning up the Ukrainian economy in 2000, President Kuchma's authoritarian instincts were taking politics in an entirely different direction.

The Melnychenko tapes confirmed the extent of fraud during the 1999 election. They also record Kuchma's private vow to impose 'the toughest possible order' after it was over.[10] In January 2000, Kuchma announced he would hold an 'All-Ukrainian Referendum on Popular Initiative' in April. There was, of course, no such initiative. Or, rather, the real initiator was one of the president's shadier allies, once again Oleksandr Volkov, the subject of Gongadze's piece on 5 September, which had detailed Volkov's links from childhood with none other than the gangster Kysil (which didn't preclude Volkov working as a police agent), and his pursuit by the Belgian courts, who were interested in $15 million of unexplained transit through his accounts in Belgium between 1993 and 1997. Volkov's version of 'popular initiative' was a spontaneous nationwide craving to strengthen presidential power. Two of his questions were struck out by the normally docile Constitutional Court – one on the grounds of sheer incomprehensibility. The other four were approved by ludicrous margins of 82 to 90 per cent, on a turnout of 81 per cent, higher than in the recent presidential election. All told, this was basically an exercise in telling voters that they just didn't matter. (Amongst my own sociologically unrepresentative sample of friends, there was not one who could remember actually having voted.) Neither did the Constitution matter much to Kuchma's men, except in that it required them to win an additional two-thirds' majority in parliament (300 out of 450 votes), which they couldn't get. Only 251 votes were forthcoming in July, and a second attempt was scuppered by the Gongadze crisis, after which the whole expensive charade was quietly forgotten.

The opposition continued to be harassed. The Melnychenko tapes record Kuchma demanding in February 2000 that deputy Oleksandr Yeliashkevych, 'a fucking Yiddish sprout', should be dealt with. 'Fuck him up! Let's [do it]! Let the little Jew be handled by Yids!.'[11] Yeliashkevych was duly attacked and badly beaten. He was granted political asylum in the USA in October 2002. On 9 June, Oles Podolskyi, a former Rada deputy and associate of another opposition leader, Serhii Holovatyi (now part of Tymoshenko's bloc), was kidnapped.

EPISODE FOUR, 12 JUNE 2000.

INTERIOR MINISTER YURII KRAVCHENKO: Now about this gang, you remember, that distributed leaflets from Holovatyi?

KUCHMA: Yes.

KRAVCHENKO: I mean the day before yesterday he was located as far as Sumy oblast [north-east of Kiev], the one who was distributing them. They beat the hell out of him [laughter]. And he's yelling 'it's Holovatyi' [laughter]. When he gets home . . . the door burned out [unknown assailants tried to set fire to Podolskyi's friend's apartment moments after he had left, possibly getting the wrong one].

KUCHMA: Whose?

KRAVCHENKO: His [both laughing] . . . I have such a unit, their methods; they have no morals, no nothing . . . they have begun to silence things.[12]

Gongadze wasn't the only journalist Kuchma wanted silenced. Others to experience 'administrative' pressure after they were discussed on the tapes included Oleh Liashko of the paper *Freedom*, and Oleh Yeltsov, editor of another new website called 'Criminal Ukraine' (www.cripo.com.ua).

Virtually every conversation on the tapes indicates habitual abuse of the law. Kuchma at one point says chillingly: 'If we are the power, then the procuracy is an instrument of our power.'[13] In another conversation, Kuchma complains to no less than Viktor Yanukovych about his local patch in Donetsk, specifically stating that a local judge is not acting sufficiently harshly – Kuchma has a grudge against a certain Serhii Salov, who was Moroz's local election agent in 1999.

EPISODE FIVE, 30 MARCH 2000.

KUCHMA: . . . Your judges are the dregs. I am now obliged to come and testify! That's why you should take this fucking judge, hang him by the balls, let him hang for one night.

YANUKOVYCH: I understand. We will look into it.

KUCHMA: Judges, in general, are fuckers.

YANUKOVYCH: Well, they're the dregs. The boss of my [local] court there is hopeless. He's got to be changed.

KUCHMA: Well, I think now you'll look into it [in such a way] that he'll remember it his whole life.[14]

'My court' is, of course, a revealing expression. The tapes also reveal financial corruption to have been systematic and almost casual. Kuchma, who takes a cut on many things, is often referred to in private as 'Papa'.

EPISODE SIX, OCTOBER 1999: Kuchma is talking to Ihor Bakai, boss of Oil and Gas of Ukraine.

KUCHMA: . . .You said to me Ihor, I looked you in the eyes, and you said to me, that I'll guarantee you 250 million dollars for the election campaign. We need it now!

BAKAI (to Volkov): 48 million *hrivina* [then $11.6 million] and fourteen million dollars, that you confirm. . .

VOLKOV: I only confirm twelve.

BAKAI: It's not worth talking about – twelve or fourteen!

KUCHMA: Well, fine – twelve or fourteen, I don't give a fuck.

VOLKOV: We need a minimum of twenty-five million now – we needed it yesterday.

BAKAI (to Volkov): I'll give you twenty-five million on Tuesday. On Tuesday – twenty-five for starters.

KUCHMA: We need that much to win in the first round. Get ready twenty for the second round.

BAKAI: I'll give my own. But I want you all to know that all the money, which is just, it's all mine. . .[Bakai means it belongs to 'his' state-owned company, Oil and Gas of Ukraine.][15]

## 'Ukraine Without Kuchma': Kuchma Survives

The revelations contained on Melnychenko's tapes detonated a protest movement, but not one that turned out as either Moroz or Melnychenko intended. After an initially confused reaction, which was not helped by Rukh's compromised leaders condemning Moroz, or by inconclusive debates in parliament, a 'tent city' of protesters was set up in central Kiev on 15 December. The first demonstration was held two days later, by which time, fortunately for Kuchma, winter had already set in. The tent city was dominated by members of Moroz's Socialist Party and some Rukh rank-and-file, but few of the general public were present. The demonstrations pulled in a wider circle, but numbers were never large, and no more than 20,000 to 30,000 people attended, at most.[16] A second wave began with warmer weather and the reopening of parliament on 6 February 2001.

Kuchma's regime adopted a cynical survival strategy. First of all, its shadowy advisers, the self-styled 'political technologists' (see pages 86–7), pushed what they artfully dubbed a 'double object' campaign, that is, projecting the regime's own failings on to the opposition. By encouraging the general cynicism of 'they (politicians) are all the same', they hoped to demotivate the protesters.[17] The recent political cycle worked in their favour. After the fraudulent presidential election in 1999 and, even worse, the abortive referendum in 2000, popular willingness to protest was at a low ebb. (The 2004 election, on the other hand, would come after the opposition had won the 2002 Rada elections, only to see the fruits of victory stolen from them. The baseline of popular discontent would then be radically different.) Kuchma's advisers also benefited from a confused international reaction. As Yushchenko was still prime minister and still popular in the West, it was difficult to draw the line between criticising one set of authorities and backing another – which was a particular dilemma for the Ukrainian diaspora. Initially, most of the opprobrium came from the foreign press, foreign NGOs and individuals. Most foreign governments never made a formal break with Ukraine, but settled into a *de facto* (partial) boycott of the government's highest levels as time went on. The authorities and the oligarchs (especially Pinchuk) also paid for several technical analyses of the tapes to muddy the waters, deliberately multiplying versions of events so as to leave the average voter confused.

Secondly, the regime labelled the remaining protesters 'fascists'. This made absolutely no sense whatsoever – most of them were Socialists – until it became clear that the authorities were busy infiltrating fake nationalists from government-funded parties such as Trident and the Ukrainian

National Assembly (UNA), and equally fake 'anarchists' (most were students who had been paid a few dollars or skinheads keen for a fight) into the
opposition's ranks. Even when they were viewed with suspicion, they dominated coverage on state TV, and an escalating series of provocations, carefully staged violence and confrontations with the police was eventually used
to justify a crackdown. At the final showdown in Kiev on 9 March, the UNA
caused most of the trouble. The authorities responded by arresting members of the rival UNA–UNSO (Ukrainian Self-Defence Force), hoping
nobody would notice the difference.

Thirdly, the authorities sought to keep the protesters leaderless. The political system that Ukraine had developed in the 1990s had decapitated, evis-
cerated and recycled most of what were once the opposition parties. Most
major politicians now worked within the system. The one exception to this
was Yuliia Tymoshenko, who, after her expulsion from government on 19
January, had organised a National Salvation Forum on 9 February, which
was intended to force Kuchma out of office. The government responded just
as quickly, however. Tymoshenko was arrested on 13 February, allowing her
barely a week to lead the protests. Yushchenko was still prime minister, but
his protests on her behalf were muted. In any case, her leadership was con-
tested by the Ukraine Without Kuchma movement (mainly a youth organisation), set up earlier in December 2000, and, more controversially, by the
For Truth group formed on 13 February. For Truth was led by several of the
leaders of Rukh who had allowed themselves to be enmeshed in Kuchma's
schemes back in 1999. It was therefore exploited by the authorities to divide
the protests, although its rank and file members were genuine enough.
Rather disingenuously, For Truth claimed they couldn't work with the tent
city protest this time, because it was controlled by the left (sic) – as if there
was no question of greater good. The notorious 'letter of the three', ordered
by Kuchma, but also signed by Rada chair Ivan Pliushch and by Yushchenko,
was released the same day, accusing the demonstrators of 'instigating an
atmosphere of hysteria and psychosis' and representing 'a Ukrainian brand
of National Socialism'.[18]

Signing this letter was undoubtedly Yushchenko's biggest mistake,
although his then chief of staff, Oleh Rybachuk, would claim three years
later that: 'You ought to know what was signed, and what appeared in print.
I was the chief of the prime minister's staff and I saw the text that
Yushchenko had signed. I can state with all responsibility: the text had been
changed by the time it got published. We know who, at which computer.
This is the country we live in. . .'.[19] A generous interpretation of
Yushchenko's behaviour was that, thinking like a post-Communist banker,

he wanted more time in office to allow his reforms to take effect. He did not get much, however; in April, only two months after the letter was published, he was ousted, though he at least recovered a lot of ground with one of his best ever speeches: 'As a citizen, I am convinced that democracy in Ukraine has suffered a serious loss . . . I am not going to leave politics. I am leaving, in order to return!' There was still plenty to play for. The next parliamentary elections were due in March 2002.

Despite much misguided talk of the West inspiring and even financing the Orange Revolution three years later in 2004, the key lessons were all local. As Dmytro Potekhin, head of one of the NGOs set up to promote a clean election, later put it, quoting his Serbian contact, Aleksandar Maric, '"Every success is preceded by a failure". So I attribute what we achieved [in 2004] to lessons learned from the flawed protests organised by the Ukraine Without Kuchma movement [almost] five years ago.'[20] On the other hand, Kuchma was certainly *persona non grata* in the West after 2001. When it was made clear that he would not be welcome at the Prague NATO summit in November 2002, he turned up anyway. So a decision was taken to list the countries in French, so that l'Ukraine would not be next to les États Unis or la Grande-Bretagne. (Normally, Blair of the UK and Bush of the USA would have sat right by Ukraine.)

The opposition would also learn from its attempts to revive the protests on successive anniversaries of Gongadze's disappearance. Tymoshenko spent two months in the squalid Lukianivskyi prison before being freed by one of Ukraine's few remaining independent judges, Mykola Zamkovenko, in March 2001 (Zamkovenko was dismissed in July 2001). The protest in September 2001 was therefore fairly muted, but in September 2002 Tymoshenko led a protest campaign dubbed 'Stand Up, Ukraine!', which, although unsuccessful, debuted many of the 'theatre of opposition' methods that would be used in 2004, including mock trials of the authorities, an attempted revival of the tent city (though this was cleared away after one day), and the uninvited arrival of protestors to demand air time on official TV. Moroz joined in, as did even the Communists, albeit briefly. Yushchenko, meanwhile, attended the first demonstration, but generally kept his distance. The protests continued through October, but then petered out.

### The 2002 Elections

Kuchma may have survived the Ukraine Without Kuchma campaign, but he still had to face the elections for parliament that were due in March 2002.

Yushchenko, who had committed himself to politics in his resignation speech, would now be his main opponent. Yushchenko sensibly sought to build as broad a coalition as possible. As a natural centrist, his first great achievement was to get most of the traditional right to support him as well. His sometime friend, sometime rival, Yuliia Tymoshenko, was left to run on a more radical ticket, and pick up some of the more nationalist elements, but almost everyone else went with Yushchenko, mainly because they were fed up with losing. Both main parts of the now divided Rukh were included, as was its liberal offshoot Reforms and Order. If anything, Yushchenko was a little bit too inclusive, adding some far-right elements such as Oleh Tiahnybok of the paramilitary Social-National Party, who would provide ammunition for his opponents, and the émigré-based Congress of Ukrainian Nationalists, the direct descendant of the OUN (known by its Ukrainian acronym, KUN, 'K' for 'Kongres'). After their role in undermining the Ukraine Without Kuchma campaign, however, the fake right, including Bohdan Boiko's Rukh, the UNA and Trident, was sensibly kept at a distance.

On the other hand, Yushchenko campaigned with a radically different message to the traditional right. Cultural nationalism, and the language issue in particular, was downplayed and replaced by a pragmatic emphasis on his economic achievements in office, and a value-based emphasis on regeneration, respect for the citizenry and clean government. Yushchenko also pushed his own image, including his faith and family values, to the fore (see plate 6). In one small but telling example, he reworked the traditional nationalist rallying cry of 'Glory to Ukraine!', which in OUN circles was followed by 'To [its] Heroes Glory!' Yushchenko now finished most of his speeches with 'Glory to God!' first. The new bloc was called 'Our Ukraine', and its skilfully constructed propaganda contrasted the real, 'our' Ukraine with 'their' Ukraine, the foreign country of the Kuchma government and the oligarchs. Its adverts reprised Ronald Reagan's campaigns of the 1980s, with a sunny, optimistic 'morning in Ukraine' feel. This was the first step towards the highly successful rebranding of the opposition as 'orange' in 2004 (see pages 72–3). In 2002, at least, the opposition had already left behind the one-trick national movement of old. The Our Ukraine 'brand' was now an eclectic mix of patriotism, pragmatism, folklore and folksy, and traditional religious rhetoric, but it was no less effective for that.

Although several of his advisers were opposed to the idea, Yushchenko wanted to reach out as far as possible to the centre. He even toyed with the idea of running both a right and a centre bloc. He negotiated long and hard with various elements of the regime, including many offshoots of Donbas politics, such as the Liberal Party and the New Generation youth movement, and even talked with controversial figures such as Rinat Akhmetov and Mykola Azarov. But only the Liberals joined in the end, and they didn't do so for long. Yushchenko's one big catch was Petro Poroshenko's Solidarity Party, even though Poroshenko had been in the SDPU(o) from 1998 to 2000, and then the Party of Regions until December 2001 and had even at one time been a serious candidate to lead the latter party. Solidarity was much more important for its social base in rural Ukraine, particularly in Poroshenko's home region of Vinnytsia, and for Poroshenko's financial resources.

Yushchenko also included almost two dozen businessmen on the list; including some serious potential financiers. Initially, this was, of course, good news, a sign that the governing elite was losing unity, and a means of challenging their massive advantage in 'administrative resources'. It was also a sign that the Kuchma regime had less than total control. Yushchenko's key business supporters would later set up the faction Razom ('Together') within Our Ukraine, but there were initially three main groups of separate interests: namely the business empires of Petro Poroshenko and Yevhen Chervonenko, and a looser group consisting of Davyd Zhvaniia, Mykola Martynenko and Oleksandr Morozov. Interestingly, given later events, at least six of the Our Ukraine businessmen made up a so-called 'Russian bloc', which was linked to companies such as Lukoil (Dmytro Sandler) and Russian Aluminium (Oleksii Yaroslavskyi and Ernest Haliev).

Poroshenko, who in the past had enjoyed close business ties to Our Ukraine's enemies such as Volodymyr Lytvyn, then head of Kuchma's presidential administration, was Ukraine's Willy Wonka, the 'chocolate king' who ran the foodstuffs company Ukrprominvest, five confectionary factories and the Etalon brewery, which produces a rather fine Ukrainian version of Weissbier. He also controlled the Lutsk car plant, part of the magnificently named Leninska Kuznia ('Leninist Blacksmith') shipyard, which makes gunboats, and was on the board of Mriia ('Dream') Bank. Crucially, he also owned the one opposition TV station, Channel 5, which had been set up in 2003. As Russia was his number one export market, Poroshenko was a pragmatist who supported good relations with the north. His diverse holdings, some acquired from the Kuchma 'privatisation' programme, made Poroshenko the one Yushchenko supporter who looked almost like an oligarch.

Yevhen Chervonenko founded the drinks company Orlan (although allegedly he started by smuggling red caviar and then by selling Ukrainian beer in more desirable Polish bottles) and was one of Ukraine's leading freight operators. Davyd Zhvaniia owned the energy company Brinkford, a machine-tool construction plant in Luhansk, and, in Crimea, the Kerch-based shipbuilders Zalyv and the Bakhchisarai factory Bundindustriia. Zhvaniia was also vice-president of the bank Glomain Holding Ltd, registered in Cyprus – which raised a few eyebrows. Martynenko had interests in the power sector and Morozov headed the European Insurance Alliance, one of Ukraine's biggest new insurance companies. Yaroslavskyi ran Techproject Ltd., and, like Haliev, was part of the 'Kharkiv clan' based around Ukrsibbank.

Yushchenko's businessmen were mostly younger than the oligarchs of old. Poroshenko was born in 1965 and Zhvaniia in 1967. Some could call themselves self-made men; while others had been made only with external help. The most crucial difference between them and those who supported the established regime was, however, perhaps not age or business culture, but the fact that none represented the type of cash cows (monster steel plants, *oblenergos*) won by the likes of Akhmetov and the SDPU(o). Nearly all ran active businesses, which would benefit from a less active state.

Even more controversially, Yushchenko gave key roles to several former members of Kuchma's innermost coterie, whose conversion to the opposition cause occured at the very last minute. Roman Bezsmertnyi, mocked behind his back as 'Little Medvedchuk' (after Kuchma's notorious new Chief of Staff), had been a member of the nationalist Republican Party in the early 1990s (he wrote a dissertation on the neo-fascist OUN ideologue Dmytro Dontsov), but had defected to Kuchma via the National-Democratic Party, where he met Yushchenko, occupying the strange constitutional position of Kuchma's 'representative' in parliament and helping plan Kuchma's 1999 election campaign. Even more controversially, he had been ever-present on TV during the early days of the Gongadze scandal, competing to be Kuchma's most ardent public defender. Bezsmertnyi, whose name means 'immortal' in Ukrainian, was now parachuted in as campaign manager, where he spent much of his time excluding 'radicals'. Yushchenko also took on board Yurii Yekhanurov, despite his closeness to the head of the presidential administration, and Volodymyr Lytvyn, as he had worked well with the former as a deputy prime minister in 1999–2001. The businessmen and the arrivistes, moreover, had more places on the Our Ukraine list: Rukh had twelve seats in the top forty, the liberal party Reforms and Order four, Solidarity five, and the business bloc ten. Yushchenko's men were lower down than the former 'Kuchmisty': Bezsmertnyi was at number thirteen but his chief of staff, Oleh Rybachuk, was at twenty-nine.

Yushchenko's association with some of these people may seem surprising, but he needed the money. He wanted to demonstrate his moderation, and his willingness to cooperate with politicians of any origin. Ultimately, he also hoped to split the governing coalition (although in the short term the boot was mainly on the other foot) and gain some share of 'administrative resources' and some shelter from negative campaigning. Creating a moderate image was also crucial to his plans for selling Our Ukraine. To Yushchenko's more radical critics, however, he was simply inviting too many obvious cuckoos into the nest.

Tymoshenko also set up her own bloc in December 2001. It was again a mixed bunch, held together by the force of her personality. In addition, she had changed her image. In the 1990s she was post-Soviet superwoman, but since 1999 she had busied herself learning Ukrainian and patronising more right-wing causes, while remaining politically a social-democratic populist. She still dressed in Dolce and Gabbana, but now did so with a more Ukrainian touch. The election bloc named after her therefore contained some strange bedfellows. There was her old party, Fatherland, and some other remnants from Hromada, including the historian Petro Tolochko, an advocate of close and friendly ties with Russia, but also some right-wing parties like the above-mentioned Republicans (Ukraine's oldest political group, set up in 1990) and right-wing mavericks such as Stepan Khmara. The bloc also provided a home for some independent-minded deputies, for example, the former justice minister Serhii Holovatyi and the 'Anti-Mafia' crusader Hryhorii Omelchenko. As mentioned in Chapter 2, Tymoshenko was happy to sell the coalition as the 'Bloc of Yuliia Tymoshenko', therefore BYuTy, and even happier to campaign as a one-woman band. On the other hand, the Tymoshenko bloc had a striking campaign symbol – a box with a small opening and an arrow as an exit sign, with the simple slogan 'There is a way out'.

Yanukovych, meanwhile, was preparing for the election in a rather different way. One of the Melnychenko tapes records him describing to Kuchma how he is setting up the Party of the Regions in the Rada. 'We're raising payments [bribes] to the ceiling!', he states, in the manner of a technical report, and boasts that deputies of every party are queuing up to take the bribes, including various Communists. [21]

EPISODE SEVEN, 31 AUGUST 2000.

KUCHMA: Well, at the same time you must pull Fatherland to pieces, the fuckers, and the Communists of course.
YANUKOVYCH: And the Communists.

KUCHMA: Well, the fuckers, and take about three from Moroz, and he'll fall to pieces.

. . .

YANUKOVYCH: There are also those, who are [already] today in the factions, in the majority [the pro-Kuchma forces] as it were, who will behave themselves just right [i.e. will toe the line once they join].

KUCHMA: Yeah, fucking right!

. . .

YANUKOVYCH: They feed on you, the vipers, fasten on to everything!

Bribes and threats came naturally to the authorities. This was how they had first set up a temporary 'majority' in parliament in January 2000, how they had forced Yushchenko out of office in 2001, and how they would install Yanukovych as his successor in 2002. The regime now tried to stitch together the various clans for the election in the same way. The Dnipropetrovsk, Kharkiv, Donbas and rural clans had all created virtual parties with nice-sounding labels. Viktor Pinchuk's party, Labour Ukraine (Trudova Ukraïna), from Dnipropetrovsk, went by the initials TU. The National-Democratic Party (ND), having once been a broad party of government, was now just a vehicle for the Kharkiv clan. The Party of the Regions (R) represented the business elite of one region, the Donbas, and the Agrarian Party (A) represented collective farm bosses in the countryside. For a time, the authorities seriously thought of running them together under the truly awful name 'TUNDRA' (the same in English and Ukrainian); but quickly thought better of it and decided to bury their differences under the name 'For A United Ukraine', which was a bit better. The Kiev clan ran their own party, the SDPU(o) independently.

The authorities also set up a range of fake 'clone' parties to steal the opposition's votes. None was constructed with particular subtlety. Two fake Communist parties were set up to keep the official Communists in line. Because Yushchenko was supposed to be a liberal reformer, a favourite among the young, the authorities set up a fake liberal party, Yabluko (a copy of the Russian 'Yabloko'),[22] and a fake liberal youth party, the bizarrely-named KOP (even in Ukrainian, *Komanda ozymoho pokolinnia*, or 'Winter Crop Generation Team', it wasn't clear what this meant).[23] Because Tymoshenko was a woman, a fake women's party was set up, and covert support was given to another female firebrand, Nataliia Vitrenko. Vitrenko, leader of the 'Progressive Socialists', was also expected to take votes off the Socialists. All these parties were privately funded by the authorities and the oligarchs, and were given extensive coverage on official TV.

The result was a triumph for both Yushchenko, whose 'Our Ukraine' bloc came first on 23.6 per cent, and Tymoshenko, with 7.3 per cent, while Moroz's Socialist Party made a good comeback performance on 6.9 per cent. By comparison, the old opposition, Rukh, had won only 9.8 per cent of the vote at the previous parliamentary elections in 1998. The reinvented Tymoshenko scored best in more radical regions in the West. Yushchenko won most of his extra votes in central Ukraine, vindicating his rebranding strategy. The Communists dropped from 25 per cent of the vote in 1998 to 20 per cent. Despite very expensive campaigns, the two governing parties were not a success. For A United Ukraine won only 11.8 per cent, and the SDPU(o) only 6.3 per cent.

The three-headed opposition still won 112 seats out of 225, only one short of a majority. The authorities had been caught out by the degree of international supervision, and by the innovative use of an exit poll largely

*The results of the 2002 elections – the proportional vote*

|  | Vote (per cent) | Seats |
|---|---|---|
| *Opposition* | | |
| Our Ukraine (Yushchenko) | 23.6 | 70 |
| Tymoshenko bloc | 7.3 | 22 |
| Socialists (Moroz) | 6.9 | 20 |
| *Communists* | 20.0 | 59 |
| *Authorities* | | |
| For A United Ukraine | 11.8 | 35 |
| SDPU(o) | 6.3 | 19 |
| *Fakes* | | |
| Vitrenko bloc | 3.2 | |
| Women For The Future | 2.1 | |
| KOP | 2.0 | |
| Communists | 1.8 | |
| Greens | 1.3 | |
| Yabluko ('Apple') | 1.2 | |
| Others* | 1.9 | |

* New Generation, Workers', Christians, Rukh for Unity, Against All, New Force, Justice, Ukrainian National Assembly

Source: www.cvk.gov.ua

funded by Western embassies on voting day. The point of the exit poll was not to predict the outcome with speed to bolster TV ratings, as it is in the West, but to create a background of expectations that would make fraud more difficult. Moreover, in Ukraine it normally took at least several days to produce official results, so an early exit poll on election night itself would provide a marker which would make it harder to corrupt the counting process. The exit poll had Our Ukraine on 25 per cent (1.4 per cent higher than the eventual official result), the Communists on 20.5 (+ 0.5 per cent), For A United Ukraine on 10.6 (− 1.2), the Tymoshenko bloc on 7.9 (+ 0.6), the SDPU(o) on 7.1 (+ 0.8) and the Socialists on 6.1 (− 0.8).[24] The parallel count organised by the 'For Fair Elections' NGO estimated that For A United Ukraine won only 9.4 per cent (− 2.4 per cent), with the SDPU(o) unchanged at 6.3 per cent and the opposition parties consistently up, with Our Ukraine again on 25 per cent (up 1.4 per cent); the Communists on 21.2 (+ 1.2); the Tymoshenko bloc on 8.6 per cent (+ 1.3) and the Socialist Party on 7.9 per cent (+ 1).[25]

By local standards, this was fairly limited fraud. The mere threat of the exit poll had forced the authorities to limit themselves to small-scale, but still significant, abuses, such as the crude manipulation of local voting protocols ('1' vote altered to '19' and so on); the resurrection of 'dead souls' (28,000–30,000 of the undead were brought back to life in Luhansk alone), often inhabiting whole invented buildings. In the Donbas, local voting 'technology' was no more sophisticated than thugs patrolling polling stations,[26] or the 'directed voting' of entire workforces. Volodymyr Boiko, director of the giant Mariupil Illich steelworks in southern Donetsk, for example, was reputed to control 100,000 to 200,000 votes in return for his fourth place on the party list.[27] Overall, 'administrative resources' delivered between 5 and 10 per cent of the official count.[28] Moreover, the opposition would have won outright without the fake parties. None of these won the necessary 4 per cent to win seats in the Rada, but they did their job as 'clones'; collectively, they won 13.5 per cent, the majority of which would otherwise have gone to the real opposition.

## The Steal

The opposition celebrated on election night. Their victory in the general popular vote was only one half of the story, however. The other half of the Rada's 450 seats were elected in local territorial constituencies, on a first-past-the-post basis. Here, 'administrative resources' could be much more effectively deployed; various unsavoury oligarchs found a refuge, and the regional clans could clean up in their own back yards. The opposition only won 54 of these 225 extra seats, and the Communists another seven. The authorities, on the other hand, both by electing their own under various labels and by pressurising independents to join their ranks, won 161. In Donetsk, the new 'Regions of Ukraine' machine swept up nineteen out of twenty-three seats. The other four were easily persuaded of their affront to the local monopoly and soon joined 'The Party' as well.

This was still not enough for a 'majority' when parliament assembled, however, so the establishment began to put all sorts of pressure on opposition members to defect. First, several 'cuckoos' were persuaded to leave Yushchenko's nest. These were mostly leading business 'sponsors' that the nationalist right had always distrusted, including Dmytro Sandler, Oleksii Yaroslavskyi, Ernest Haliev and the governor of Sumy, Volodymyr Shcherban. Second, loyal Our Ukraine businessmen came under intense 'administrative' pressure: Yevhen Chervonenko (trucking, soft drinks) and Volodymyr Shandra (roofing) claimed political measures cost their businesses millions.[29] In March, the offices of Petro Poroshenko's Ukrprominvest were raided 'by mistake'. In May, it was the turn of Shandra's rubber factory in the western town of Khmelnytskyi. Nine different companies in five different cities associated with Brinkford, Davyd Zhvaniia's joint stock company, were also paralysed as a result of two raids on 13 and 16 August, which had been ordered by the prosecutor's office. By August, Oleh Rybachuk claimed twenty businessmen in or linked to Our Ukraine had suffered from the authorities' attentions. In December 2002, Oleksandr Stoian, leader of the official trade unions, changed sides to save his job from an opponent backed by the SDPU(o). In October, the authorities in Kiev arrested and roughed up Konstantin Grigorishin, head of the Russo-Ukrainian joint venture Energy Standard Group, which then controlled eleven oblast energy companies coveted by the SDPU(o) (at the time he had $370 million invested in Ukraine). Grigorishin immediately blamed Medvedchuk, who was angry that Grigorishin had refused to finance the SDPU(o) instead of Our Ukraine.

Carrots were also used alongside the sticks; bribes were commonplace. Yurii Orobets claimed he was offered $500,000 to defect.[30] In all the 'operation' to create a majority cost an alleged $15 million.[31] Once it was over, For A United Ukraine split back into its constituent parts, but persistent pressure meant they continued to grow. By January 2003, the authorities had another twenty-five members in their swollen ranks, the opposition had lost another twenty-two and the Communists another six. Only in this way did the authorities 'win' control of parliament – a crucial resource in the key battle to come. And, of course, the dress rehearsal would profoundly affect the way the much more important presidential election was fought in 2004. On the other hand, the Gongadze and Melnychenko scandals had weakened the authorities before the re-match in 2004, which was therefore notable for a big extension in both domestic NGO monitoring and international involvement. Ukraine had a real opposition again for the first time in ten years. The earlier 2002 elections were also a huge psychological break-through. Having cowed the population with the 2000 referendum and the suppression of the Ukraine Without Kuchma movement in 2001, the authorities had suddenly shown their vulnerability. Their largely Russian advisers, however, claimed they had not been allowed to play dirty enough, and would demand *carte blanche* in 2004.

# 5

# The Campaign

After the dress rehearsal at the 2002 parliamentary elections, it seemed likely that the crucial presidential contest in 2004 would be a two-horse race between Yushchenko and whomever the authorities decided to put up. So it proved, though this chapter will also look at some of the other players and some of the possible scenarios that were missed. Paradoxically, Yanukovych was a bad choice who almost won.

## Yushchenko Flat-lining

Every revolution has its moderate and its radical wing. In spring 2004, no one called Viktor Yushchenko a revolutionary. Since 2001, had kept his distance from Tymoshenko's constant campaigning to force Kuchma out of office. Personally, Yushchenko was often disorganised and lazy; politically, he was cautious. He believed that the constant demonising of the old order was what kept the old opposition in opposition, and that the authorities would allow him to come to power by constitutional methods. And this included Kuchma, whom critics accused Yushchenko of toadying to in private, focusing especially on a notorious reference to him as his political 'father'.[1] This was, of course, unfair. Yushchenko knew that Kuchma's favourite political tactic was to balance all the main groups around him, and that if he could stay in that particular magical circle, he would be part of that balance. Ukraine needed to avoid the fate of Belarus, or even Russia, where the opposition had been cast into outer darkness, and the only apparent political choices were autocracy or implosion.

Yushchenko had led the opinion polls for two years, consistently scoring around 23 to 26 per cent – in other words, keeping the support Our Ukraine had won in 2002, but not advancing on it. Rumours of factional struggle and dissatisfaction in his staff were rife, especially with so many formerly separate parties making up the coalition. Paradoxically, problems were also caused by Yushchenko's success in winning (mainly small and medium) business support. Not all of the money was wisely spent, although the Yushchenko campaign was spared the financial bacchanalia that was apparent on the other side (see pages 120–1 and 156–7). In July 2004, Roman Bezsmertnyi was suddenly demoted from being Yushchenko's campaign chief and made 'head of campaign staff'. Bezsmertnyi was increasingly disliked by the Our Ukraine businessmen, who stood to lose everything if Yushchenko went down, although Zhvaniia, his number one backer, stayed loyal, keeping him in a degree of favour. The agreement with Tymoshenko (see below) also led to pressure to up Our Ukraine's game, with Tymoshenko at one point even proposing herself as chief of campaign staff.

However, Yushchenko's natural caution led him to replace one regime turncoat with another: Oleksandr Zinchenko. Zinchenko's father, appropriately or not, had worked in KGB counter-intelligence. Young Oleksandr had himself worked as a censor for *Komsomolskaia pravda*, before becoming a typical *komsomol* businessman. He returned to Ukraine from Moscow in the early 1990s and moved in SDPU(o) circles, helping to set up their Inter TV channel in 1995, which became a notorious source of black PR against Yushchenko in 2002. The Melnychenko tapes illuminate Zinchenko's paradoxical position as head of the Committee on Freedom of Information, as he agrees with Kuchma in private that there is far too much freedom of information in Ukraine. Zinchenko complains specifically, 'there's one thing I didn't like: how quickly they [the opposition] succeeded in forcing public opinion to divide the country, relatively speaking, that Surkis and Medvedchuk are oligarchs and Yushchenko and Tymoshenko are not oligarchs'.[2] After the 2002 elections, when Zinchenko was elected deputy chair of the Rada, however, he quarrelled increasingly frequently with Medvedchuk, especially over the politicisation of Inter, and began to feel the heat on his business interests. In September 2003 he was expelled from the SDPU(o) and was ready to jump ship – though clearly he changed sides very late indeed.

Zinchenko made little organisational difference to Yushchenko's campaign, but he provided a certain spark. One faction in the Yushchenko camp, particularly Mykola Tomenko and Borys Tarasiuk, wanted to keep Yushchenko 'pure'. They worried that cooperating too closely with Tymoshenko would encourage the authorities to paint her as black as possible and damn Yushchenko by association. They also worried that Oleksandr Moroz, as another possible ally, was still too close to the Communists and that his Socialist Party had still to reform its party ideology. Zinchenko persuaded Yushchenko otherwise. He was less concerned than Bezsmertnyi about links with radicals, and by the summer of 2004 the Yushchenko campaign was reaching out to both Tymoshenko and new student groups such as Pora (see page 74). A potential broader coalition was shuffling into shape. Organisationally, however, there were still problems. On the ground in eastern and southern Ukraine, the Yushchenko campaign existed only on paper. Its representatives on the local election commissions would be easy prey for the authorities' 'administrative pressure'.[3] They would be able to give detailed reports of the eventual election fraud, but would be able to do nothing to stop it.

## Why Orange?

Like the British Labour Party after eighteen years out of power between 1979 and 1997, the Ukrainian opposition knew it had to reinvent itself. More exactly, its pragmatic wing was prepared to pay the price of reinvention, but its other wing preferred to remain pure in opposition. First of all, the slogan of the Orange Revolution seeded the idea that Ukraine could have its own version of 'velvet revolution' (as in Czechoslovakia in 1989), 'singing revolution' (the Baltic states, 1991) or 'rose revolution' (Georgia in 2003). (Kuchma's coterie labelled their takeover of parliament in January 2000 the 'velvet revolution', but the phrase never really stuck because it wasn't exactly revolutionary and it was mainly achieved with bribes.) Orange was chosen as the opposition's colour partly because the decisive phase of the election was expected to be the build-up to the first round of voting in October, when Kiev's main street, Khreshchatyk (the name means 'crossroads', and the street is the site of an ancient spring ravine) is lined with horse chestnuts and autumnal leaves. By the time the world's cameras focused on the actual revolution, however, it was mid-winter, and all the natural orange had gone.

Second, Ukraine's national colours are blue and yellow (symbolising sky over corn). These are now the official colours of the state and the state flag, but at demonstrations they tend to be monopolised by the 'national-democratic' opposition, which in the 1990s kept losing elections. In the Donbas, the Soviet propaganda stereotype, which narrowly associates the colours with the wartime OUN, rather than with the Ukrainian People's Republic of 1918 or the west Ukrainians' participation in the 'Springtime of Nations' in 1848 (when the flag was also flown), still holds sway. When Rukh concentrated mainly on a cultural agenda – broadening the use of the Ukrainian language in particular – no more than 20 to 25 per cent of the electorate voted for it. Some initial attempts were made at the 1998 Rada elections to broaden Rukh's appeal and lead it out of the culturological ghetto, with some very personal ads for Viacheslav Chornovil and a strong anti-corruption emphasis in Rukh's main slogan 'Power to the People, Bandits to Prison!', but it was only the economic achievements of the Yushchenko government in 1999–2001 that really laid the basis for reinvention. The national colours of blue and yellow were therefore kept in the background in 2004 (as even more so were the red and black also once favoured by the OUN), and orange came to the fore. The idea was to emphasise an all-national, value-based campaign, which was overwhelmingly peaceful and a little bit jolly.

Orange was also the colour of Ukraine's second football team, Shakhtar Donetsk, the pride of east Ukraine, which was an irony, but also a minor factor in neutralising some opposition. Dynamo Kiev, on the other hand, usually play in blue and white (and sometimes yellow), which were Yanukovych's campaign colours. Ultimately, however, the choice of orange would have unforeseen consequence of overriding importance, landing Ukraine one of the modern world's most precious commodities – brand recognition.

### The Radicals: Pora

Every revolution has its vanguard. A prominent role in the Ukrainian events would be played by the youth activist organisation Pora, which was actually made up of two organisations, one of which was deliberately not organised. Pora would provide the opposition with extra strength, compared to 2002, and was also symptomatic of its changing tactics. Pora was modelled on rough regional equivalents such as Serbia's Otpor ('Resistance') that helped bring down Slobodan Milošević in 2000, Georgia's Kmara! ('Enough!'), which was prominent in the 'Rose Revolution' of 2003, and the rather less successful Zubr ('Bison') in Belarus, which had conspicuously failed to oust local desperado Aliaksandr Lukashenka in 2001. All three were youth movements of non-violent protest. Equally important, though less of an obvious parallel, were the lessons learnt from the Slovak equivalent OK'98, which had helped to bring down another semi-authoritarian strongman, Vladimír Mečiar, in 1998, by building an NGO coalition dedicated to combating election fraud and improving voter turnout. Pora was, however, also specifically Ukrainian. In Ukrainian, its name meant 'It's Time', i.e. it's time for the old guard to go; and also inverted the title of the patriotic hymn 'Ne Pora' ('Now is Not The Time', 1880) by the west Ukrainian writer Ivan Franko (1856–1916). It was much punchier than the name 'Wave of Freedom', which had been suggested at one time.

The first version of Pora, nicknamed 'Black Pora' after its black and white logo and headband, was a continuation of the radical wing of the unsuccessful 'Ukraine Without Kuchma' and 'For Truth' movements of 2001. Many of its activists were irreconcilables, permanent oppositionists, many from west Ukraine, several of whom had been on Muskie scholarships to the USA, who sat down and thought about how to avoid repeating the mistakes they had made in 2001.[4] Black Pora's leading light was Mykhailo Svystovych, later editor of www.maidan.org.ua, but it remained deliberately leaderless and amorphous, mainly for ideological reasons, but also because a cell structure was its best defence against repressive measures by the authorities. The conspiratorial method was popular amongst the young. It also *worked*. Unlike its equivalents in 2001, Pora was not infiltrated by *provocateurs*, and the Orange Revolution passed off without a single broken window or baton charge.

Discussions about the group's strategy began in November 2003 and Black Pora made its first public appearance on 29 March 2004, the day the clocks changed in Ukraine, with a ticking clock, which was intended to mark out Kuchma's remaining time in office, as its symbol and a mysterious 'What is Kuchmizm?' sticker, inviting people to visit its irreverent website, www.kuchmizm.info. Two weeks later, their answers appeared on other stickers: 'Kuchmizm is poverty', 'Kuchmizm is banditry', 'Kuchmizm is corruption'. 'Yellow Pora', whose *de facto* head was Vladislav Kaskiv, came up with many of the same ideas at the same time, appearing only slightly later with a yellow logo in which the letter 'o' appeared as a clock at fifteen minutes to midnight, and with the website www.pora.org.ua. 'Yellow Pora' were rather more entrepreneurial, both politically and economically, and more Kiev based. They were also more prepared to talk to the press – indeed that was part of their raison d'être. Black Pora had a strong negative message, but avoided being openly pro-Yushchenko, while Yellow Pora, on the other hand, were happier to work unofficially with the Yushchenko campaign. Yellow Pora flags began to appear at Yushchenko rallies. Roman Bezsmertnyi helped coordinate, if not control, their actions, and a useful division of labour would be established during the protests on the Maidan, with two informal 'agreements' on 15 October and 15 November on a division of labour. There were even suspicions that Yushchenko's headquarters had helped set up the 'copycat' Yellow Pora to steal the brand and steer it more in his own direction. Some of its web material did seem to be copied from the Black Pora group.

The two Poras held a unification congress of sorts on 19 August 2004.[5] Their joint membership was necessarily imprecise, but estimates of about

20,000 seemed about right. Both versions of Pora provided three novel strands in their approach. The first was gleaned from the book by the Amercan Gene Sharp, *From Dictatorship to Democracy: A Conceptual Framework for Liberation* (1993), which had also been popular in Serbia in 2000. Sharp, dubbed the 'Clausewitz of non-violent warfare', has since the 1960s advocated 'strategic non-violence', which is neither passive nor a means of avoiding conflict, but a means of identifying and engaging with the weak points that any regime will have. It is not money, he argues, but a change in mindset that is crucial to bringing about change. Moral confidence is an opposition's most important asset, especially in encouraging the thousands of foot soldiers, who support any establishment, to defect.

The second element was the use of 'Situationist' tactics designed to mock the authorities and dispel the fear of repression. These included the ticking clock, posters of a jackboot crushing a beetle, the slogan 'Kill the TV Within Yourself' and carnival-like street parades, intended to block the buses used to ferry 'professional voters' to the ballot box on polling day. Pora also put out a satirical paper, *Pro Ya. i tse*, 'About Ya[nukovych] and Stuff'. *Yaitse* means 'egg', a reference to the comic egg attack on Yanukovych in September 2004 (see page 99). The third element, copied from Slovakia in 1998 but now transferred to the internet, was the development of an NGO network to combat the regime's 'administrative resources'. Pora certainly did not lead the development of the network, but was symptomatic of its growth and a key link in the organisational and internet chain. Back in 1999, Kaskiv had helped to found the 'Freedom of Choice' coalition of NGOs, which helped monitor and analyse the election, with a website at www.campaign.org.ua. It developed its role in 2002, and in 2004 benefited from astute financial support from the West (so there may have been some slippage of funds over to Pora). In this way, at least, Yellow Pora acted as a kind of 'semi-official partner for the OSCE mission'.[6] But it was very semi-official. With one or two minor exceptions, the OSCE maintained the very independence that Russia and the Yanukovych camp so disliked.

Another NGO was Znaiu ('I know', i.e. I know my rights), a more studiously neutral organisation set up to encourage people, especially the young, to vote (www.znayu.org.ua). According to Znaiu's leader, the twenty-eight year old Dmytro Potekhin, his group won a $650,000 grant from the US-Ukraine Foundation, with an extra $350,000 for the third round, topped up by $50,000 from Freedom House.[7] The money went on ten million leaflets, a toll-free helpline and ads in various papers explaining voters' rights. It also paid for visits by incoming US congressmen. Twelve thousand copies of the Sharp book were published with money from his Albert Einstein Institute and distributed through www.maidan.org.ua. Znaiu avoided anything that smacked of political campaigning, but was happy for Black Pora, at least, to deliver its 'negative message' on the dangers of fraud.

Some have cast doubt on the effectiveness of Pora before the protest campaign proper.[8] It activated students, but not the wider numbers who were to be outraged by the electoral fraud that provided the revolution's key spark. It overlapped with other smaller groups seeking to perform similar tasks, so that the youth movement actually became somewhat fragmented. These included Chysta Ukraïna (Clean Ukraine, www.chysto.com, with a paper, *Za chystu Ukraïnu!*), Student Wave, Sprotyv (Resistance) and Student Choose Freely. Nevertheless, the regime considered Pora a big enough threat to plan active measures against it.

The procurator Hennadii Vasyliev led a secret group plotting against Pora and related NGOs. The group included his deputy, Viktor Kudriavtsev, the Kiev police chief, Oleksandr Milenin, Mykhailo Manin (deputy minister) from the interior ministry, and Ihor Smeshko from the SBU. On 15 October, the police raided the Kiev office of Pora, supposedly finding a homemade explosive device, 2.4 kilograms of TNT, electric detonators, and a grenade, even though Pora members videotaped them and their sniffer dogs leaving empty-handed, forcing them to come back later when no one was around. Pora claims 150 people were detained nationally, and fifteen charged, including one 'leader', Yaroslav Hodunok of the Ukrainian People's Party. On 22 October, agents raided the apartment of Mykhailo Svystovych, in connection with the alleged discovery of explosives. Kudriavtsev also convened a secret meeting of the SBU and interior ministry in October, where plans were made to arrest up to 350 Pora and other student activists three days before the first round, and plant them with drugs and forged money – but the plan met with 'silent protest and open sabotage'.[9]

## Yushchenko's Allies: Attempts at Divide-and-Rule

The 2002 elections had caught the authorities in a pincer movement. In total contrast to 1999, when nearly all the regime's real opponents had been substituted by fakes, the authorities had faced three real opposition parties, and its efforts against them had proved divided and weak. In 2004, it was the opposition parties who were determined to be the ones playing divide-and-rule.

Given her ambiguous role when first entering politics in 1997–9, a number of the regime's advisers initially thought Tymoshenko could be scared or bought off, while others suggested that she could be manipulated into standing on her own, to take votes off Yushchenko. Both factions assumed that the constant black PR and legal pressure they placed her under throughout 2002–4 would destroy her campaign. They even created two whole websites devoted to besmirching Tymoshenko's name: www.aznews.narod.ru and http://timoshenkogate.narod.ru. However, a series of planned killer blows had little effect. In May 2004, Volodymyr Borovko, an alleged SBU agent in her party, provided the authorities with a video tape on which Tymoshenko apparently discussed the possibility of bribing a judge with $125,000 to secure the release of her four arrested colleagues from United Energy Systems (see pages 22–3). In September, Russia weighed in with charges against her – a measure supposedly agreed in private between Medvedchuk and his Kremlin counterparts, first Aleksandr Voloshin then Dmitrii Medvedev. Tymoshenko's more radical statements were constantly replayed in the official media, the most notorious of these being the comment that, 'Donetsk should be fenced off with barbed wire' – which she, of course, claimed never to have said.

This all seemed to have the opposite effect to the one intended, largely because Tymoshenko decided that she would be destroyed unless the regime could be brought down. The more the authorities campaigned against her, therefore, the more she campaigned against them. Tymoshenko knew how to fight dirty, and was often a better Bolshevik than them all. She also knew when it was time to play it clean (at least in public). On 2 July 2004, she formally declared she would not run in the election and signed a deal with Yushchenko under the heading 'Force of the People' – not a formal coalition as such, as Tymoshenko agreed to back Yushchenko, but a declaration of unity and a division of campaigning responsibilities. Tymoshenko had won 7.3 per cent of the vote in 2002. Now that she was on board, Yushchenko's rating (23.6 per cent in 2002) moved consistently over 30 per cent. On the other hand, the agreement missed an opportunity to combine the efforts of the various campaign teams in the most effective way. Tymoshenko was supposed to campaign in the eastern oblasts, where her efforts were largely wasted. Not only did Tymoshenko remain steadfast, however, but in private she was playing the same game of divide-and-rule as the authorities, making a series of secret contacts with the Donetsk clan, including Rinat Akhmetov, with old enemies such as Viktor Pinchuk and with the SBU – in short with anyone who had their doubts about Yanukovych.[10]

The authorities began to have greater hopes that they could manipulate Oleksandr Moroz's Socialist Party. The Socialists are one of the few parties in Ukraine with a real grass-roots structure. Our Ukraine therefore hoped to cooperate with the Socialists in central Ukraine, where they were weaker and the Socialists correspondingly stronger. From the opposite perspective, the powers-that-be sought to use the Socialists to block off Yushchenko's growing popularity in central Ukraine. It also made perfect sense for them to negotiate with the Socialists, as the moderate opposition, to try and preserve certain interests. Crucially, the Socialist leader, Oleksandr Moroz, had long been personally committed to the idea of constitutional reform.

In February 2004, a secret plan to exploit the Socialists, drawn up by the Russian 'political technologists' advising the regime, found its way on to the web.[11] Unfortunately, this time there was more of a bite at the bait. According to the main authority on the Ukrainian left, the Socialists in 2004 were 'not interested enough in ideology and were too often engaged in intrigue'.[12] It was certainly true that the party had shadowy business interests to protect. Its major sponsor, Mykola Rudkovskyi, had interests in an oil well in Poltava, and had also helped the fugitive Melnychenko. The party had at one time had many more sponsors, including the eventual deputy head of the Security Services, Volodymyr Satsiuk (see page 98), but most were scared off in 1999. The party also had its share of ambitious individuals, such as its campaign chief Iosyp Vinskyi, who maintained private contacts with Medvedchuk and consistently opposed cooperating too closely with Yushchenko or Tymoshenko. Both Vinskyi and Rudkovskyi argued that, as the party gradually evolved towards European-style social-democracy, this would move it closer to the fake social-democracy of the SDPU(o). However, more sensible voices, such as Yurii Lutsenko, one of the key organisers of the Ukraine Without Kuchma campaign in 2001, knew that such development should take the party closer to the real opposition instead. The party had one eye on the next parliamentary elections in 2006, for which it hoped to receive friendlier coverage on SDPU(o)-controlled TV. The Socialists were also interested in money, and took plenty from the SDPU(o) before the first round.[13] The leaked plan actually intimated that Moroz could be levered into the presidency, gratefully to serve his masters' interests thereafter – which was never likely.[14] On the other hand, in December the party would return to the game of constitutional reform favoured by Medvedchuk, though it is unclear how much of a victory for him this ultimately was (i.e. fixing the constitution in case Yushchenko came to power – see pages 80–1). After the elections, the Socialists were happy to see Medvedchuk's party collapse. In other words, they took the money and ran.

The one party the regime could rely on was the Communists. They had never really been an opposition party, in any case, and Tymoshenko, and even Moroz, on occasion, quite rightly didn't trust them. Their leadership was also corrupt, particularly the older generation 'inner party' that stood behind the formal party leader, Petro Symonenko. Stanislav Hurenko, for instance, who had last been leader of the old party back in 1990–1, was still around and had good private relations with his former aide-de-camp, the chair of parliament, Volodymyr Lytvyn. The Communists were also privately close to the Donetsk clan, to whom they had lent their parliamentary lobbying skills to develop their various business scams in the 1990s. So complicit were they in fact that, although Symonenko formally ran in 2004, the Communist leadership was prepared to acquiesce in a highly risky opt-out from actually campaigning. Without the Communist 'gift' of 15 per cent (the party's 20 per cent vote in 2002 collapsed to 5 per cent this time), Yanukovych's campaign would never have got off the ground.

## The Authorities' Options

### Option One: Changing the Rules, Constitutional Reform

One of the great ironies of the Orange Revolution is that the authorities might possibly have won the election if they had used different methods. However, there were too many players on their side, too many cooks with too many plans, and they ultimately ended up working against one another.

The first plan, which was much discussed after a fatuous ruling by the Constitutional Court in December 2003 that cleared the way for a Kuchma third term, was to repeat the election steal of 1999. (The Ukrainian Constitution says 'one and the same person shall not be the president of Ukraine for more than two consecutive terms'. As it was passed in 1996, however, the court's Kuchma appointees argued that his original election in 1994 was governed by the 1991 Law on the Presidency instead, despite the fact that its wording is not much different: 'one and the same person shall not be the president of the [then] Ukrainian SSR for more than two consecutive terms'. Some lawyers thought the ruling opened the interesting question of just who had been president between 1994 and 1999.) Kuchma, however, had a health scare at this time, and besides, with his ratings at rock bottom, at less than 5 per cent, it was difficult to see how he could claim another win except by the crudest of frauds.

Some members of the established regime argued that the whole controversy was a feint on Kuchma's part, a characteristic 'lesser evil' ploy, designed to frighten moderate deputies into backing constitutional reform (see below), and moderate voters into backing some possible 'third force', which, bizarrely, Kuchma thought again could be himself, in a different guise. One secret plan, leaked in June 2004 but supposedly drawn up in November 2003, was labelled 'Kuchma's Third Term: How it Should Be'.[15] It envisaged creating 'directed chaos', setting Yanukovych against Yushchenko, and east Ukraine against west, so that the elections could be cancelled to restore 'order', and Kuchma's term promulgated as a 'lesser evil'. Clearly, this was intended to be a serious option, as the election did indeed end up polarised in this way, and Kuchma began to pose as a conciliator in December. It is also true that Kuchma himself seems never to have quite liked or trusted Yanukovych. His characteristic ploy of divide-and-rule would be under threat if the Donetsk clan came to unrestricted power. Yet another document, leaked later in 2004, explicitly stated that political reform would ease the fear of 'Donetsk authoritarianism' and muscular business expansion after the election.[16]

Kuchma was simply deluding himself. He may have given up on the rest of the world in the years of semi-isolation since the Gongadze scandal broke in 2000, but the people around him had not. Stealing the election too blatantly would damage their hopes of rehabilitation in the West. The preferred option of Viktor Medvedchuk, Kuchma's chief of staff, was therefore to change the rules so radically as to deprive any incoming president of real power. It was perhaps natural for him to think in such terms, as no one ever thought of Medvedchuk himself as having any electoral appeal. Medvedchuk had business interests to protect from the Donetsk clan, and was therefore not particularly enamoured of Yanukovych. The two men's forceful personalities also led to many a private clash.

The Rada spent much of the first half of 2004 locked in struggle over the project of constitutional 'reform' which was sponsored by Medvedchuk and, with sufficient prompting, the Communists. There were many overlapping proposals, but they all included different ways of reducing the power of the next president. One plan was to delay the presidential election until the following parliamentary elections due in March 2006. Another was for the Rada, not the people, to select the next president in Autumn 2004 (300 out of 450 votes would be necessary) and extend its own four-year term an extra year, until 2007. The third plan envisaged the 2004 presidential and 2006 parliamentary elections going ahead as planned, but under new terms, whereby the 2006 parliament would be elected for five years rather than for four, and would have the right to select a new president, who would serve for five years until 2011. Whoever was (popularly) elected in November 2004 would therefore have a very short term before parliament voted for a successor within three months of its election in March 2006 – although in theory the '2004 president' could take part in that vote.

Whatever the detail – and there was a lot of it – and the sophistry of arguments deployed in support of the plan, this was just plain cheating. Yushchenko was the favourite to win, and Medvedchuk was simply trying to deny him the fruits of victory. When the plan was discussed in parliament, it was particularly galling to listen to the old guard lecturing the opposition on the dangers of authoritarian rule. The final package failed in a dramatic vote on 8 April, only six votes short of the necessary two-thirds' majority (294 instead of 300 deputies out of 450 voted in favour of it). Despite massive pressure from Medvedchuk and, according to Volodymyr Lytvyn, the chair of parliament, at least five falsified votes, the proposal failed because several reluctant 'oligarchs' refused to support it,[17] including Oleksandr Volkov, Derkach father and son, the former mayor of Uzhhorod, Serhii Ratushniak[18] and Volodymyr Syvkovych, an associate of the Russian businessman Konstantin Grigorishin. Some of these men clearly disliked Medvedchuk and had other plans in mind.

The opposition had something to celebrate at last. Nevertheless, even after his setback in April, Medvedchuk hoped to re-animate the issue on the eve of the vote, even, possibly, between the first and second rounds. He was stymied because the authorities' artificial 'majority' in the Rada fell apart in September. Three factions suspended their allegiance: the so-called Centre; the People's Agrarians; and Democratic Initiatives – the latter not because of any point of principle, but because its fancy name was a mask for the Kharkiv 'clan', who objected to the pooling of the state's shares in two oil companies, Halychnya and Tatnafta, to a third company, Ukranafta, a deal that basically benefited the rival Privat group from Dnipropetrovsk. The deal unravelled, and the majority reravelled. A deal on the Constitution was eventually done, in December. But its apparent failure at this time was one reason why some of Yushchenko's opponents decided to poison him.

### Option Two: A Strategy of Tension

The authorities also toyed with the idea of creating a 'strategy of tension', or 'organised chaos', either as a means of intimidating some voters and scaring others into supporting them, or as an excuse to delay or neuter the election, but they were too divided, or insufficiently ruthless, to push such a strategy to any extreme conclusion. On 20 August 2004, a bomb went off in the Troieshchyna market on the edge of Kiev, killing one person and injuring eleven. It was followed by a smaller bomb two weeks later.[19] The attacks were immediately blamed on extremist supporters of Yushchenko – though what motive they would have had for such an unprovoked attack was far from clear. Troieshchyna was actually the stomping ground of the gangster Kysel and of various shadowy rackets linked to Medvedchuk, and three of those arrested were later found to work for the fake nationalist parties secretly funded by the authorities (see below).[20] In December, many of the charges against those arrested would be withdrawn.[21] Bombs were also planted on the premises of the student movement Pora. Alarms started ringing when Yevhen Marchuk, the relatively neutral minister of defence, was dismissed in October.

On 23 October, an estimated 100,000 rallied peacefully in Kiev outside the headquarters of the CEC, to demand it conduct a fair election. Ignoring such disappointing restraint, the authorities staged a double provocation: first a violent 'assault' by Yushchenko 'supporters' on the building itself, then, later that evening, an 'attack on the militia' that seems mainly to have been carried out by other militia in plain clothes.

This was on the whole lower-grade provocation, which mainly served as black PR, and to keep the opposition disoriented. But there was always the temptation to do more. Towards the end of the campaign, Andrii Kliuiev wanted to organise fake terrorist attacks in the Donbas, with dozens of deaths that could be blamed on Yushchenko, but the SBU refused to cooperate with this plan, and likewise the interior ministry's special forces. Even established organised crime structures refused to have anything to do with it.[22] The younger Kliuiev was the acknowledged paymaster for 'incidents' such as the trouble outside the CEC on 23 October.[23] These types of measures were always in the background, part of the attempt to intimidate the opposition and keep its options narrow; they were essentially part of the game of bluff. It is in this light that later measures, including the miners' demonstrations, the movement of Crimean troops, and the threat of 'separatism', should really be seen (see pages 133–4 and 145–6). Overall, however, the opposition was not intimidated by the measures the regime took, and anything more extreme carried too high a cost for most elements in the establishment, all with one eye on their survival strategies, to consider seriously.

A different type of provocation was organised during the mayoral elections held in the west Ukrainian town of Mukachevo, Transcarpathia, in April 2004. Thugs were deployed and ballot boxes stolen to reverse the result. The Our Ukraine candidate, Viktor Baloha, claimed 19,385 votes (57 per cent) against the 13,848 won by the SDPU(o)'s Ernest Nuser. An exit poll gave Baloha 62 per cent.[24] Baloha was therefore distinctly surprised to lose by 12,297 votes to 17,416 in the official count. No less than 6,307 local voters were also surprised to find that their votes were now invalid. These

1 An optimistic – and very Soviet – view of what Ukraine would look like under Viktor Yanukovych.

2 Another type of endorsement: support from the Archangel Michael, 'With love, Viktor Yanukovych'.

3 Viktor Yanukovych – official campaign poster.

4 Yanukovych satirised by Pora. *Kuchmizm – tse Ya* ('Kuchmism – is Me'). In Ukrainian and Russian *Ya* (Я), 'Me', also stands for Yanukovych. His campaign colours adorn the jailbird's cap.

5  Viktor Yushchenko: 'I Believe in Ukraine'.

6  Yushchenko, his family, and family values.

УКРАЇНА

УРЯД

Хто везе - того й поганяють!

ДОБРИЙ ГОСПОДАР КОНЯ НА БАТІГ НЕ МІНЯЄ!

7 'Don't Spare the Lash!' The message being that Yanukovych provides strong leadership, and Ukraine should not change mid-course.

8 The Yanukovych 'attack'. The prime minister is hit either by 'several large objects' or by a single egg.

9  Yuliia Tymoshenko, in a studiously glamorous pose.

10  'Mona Yuliia'.

11 Yes! (*Tak!*). Yushchenko shown as an American puppet, with his slogan 'Our President!' changed to 'Your President!'

12  'Yes! For Bushchenko'. Yushchenko is at the top and bottom, in between are Bush's eyes.

14 And more. On the left, Ukraine of three sorts: West Ukraine is depicted as the first class and Central Ukraine the second, relegating South-East Ukraine to third class. On the right, a scare story about energy prices.

13 More black PR. On the left, Yushchenko's campaign logo (see plate 5) is inverted to give him donkey's ears. On the right, Bush shouts his support, 'We are for "Our Ukraine!"'

15 *Yanuchary*, East Ukrainian Janissaries.

16  A less than flattering view of Yanukovych (Я) supporters.

17  Storming the barricades. Yuliia as Marianne, after Delacroix's *Liberty Leading the People* (1830), flanked by Yushchenko on the right and the Socialist Yurii Lutsenko on the left.

18 The militia face a Yushchenko flag.

19 Tymoshenko presents them with a flower.

20  Viktor Yushchenko, before and after the poisoning.

21  The crowd on the Maidan at the height of the protest.

**УГОДА**

про організаційно-кадрове забезпечення
діяльності Коаліції "Народна Сила"

Ця угода укладена з метою забезпечення перемоги кандидата в Президенти України від Коаліції , блоків "Наша Україна" та БЮТ (далі Коаліція), формування нової парламентської більшості, Кабінету Міністрів, оновлення на демократичних засадах центральної та регіональної виконавчої влади, силових структур, органів правосуддя. Угода є конфіденційною та регламентує організаційно-кадрові питання Коаліції. Угода укладена між Блоком "Наша Україна" та Блоком Юлії Тимошенко, далі засновники Коаліції, про наступне:

1. З метою забезпечення безальтернативності перемоги Коаліції, зміцнення її єдності та консолідації зусиль для реалізації Програмних завдань і подолання соціально-економічної кризи Коаліція висуває кандидатами на посаду Президента України – В. Ющенка, на посаду Прем'єр-Міністра України – Ю. Тимошенко. Після перемоги на президентських виборах В. Ющенко вносить кандидатуру Ю.Тимошенко на посаду прем'єр-міністра для затвердження Верховною Радою. В. Ющенко силою власного морального авторитету, переконливістю головних програмних засад і збалансованістю кадрової політики сприяє результативному голосуванню Парламенту з цього питання. Фракції Блоку "Наша Україна" та Блоку Юлії Тимошенко голосують за цю пропозицію в повному складі.

2. Засновники Коаліції визначають, що добір 55% кадрового складу органів державної влади доручається Блоку "Наша Україна", а 23% кадрового складу – Блоку Юлії Тимошенко. Проект рейтингової оцінки та номенклатура посад додається (Додаток №1).

3. 22% посад з номенклатури, що вказано в Додатку №1 резервується засновниками Коаліції для забезпечення формування нової парламентської більшості.

4. Розподіл посадової номенклатури, що відповідає квоті засновників Коаліції та залучених до формування нової парламентської більшості політичних сил, затверджується Президією Коаліції.

   З метою зняття конфліктів під час вирішення кадрових питань, сторони погоджуються розподілити всю кадрову номенклатуру на 4 групи в залежності від суспільної вагомості зазначених посад, та окремо по кожній групі вносити пропозиції, щодо кадрових призначень за наступною чергою: дві пропозиції вносить Блок "Наша Україна", одну пропозицію вносить Блок Юлії Тимошенко, одну пропозицію вносить третя сторона, яка може репрезентувати одну або декілька політичних сил. Далі такий алгоритм повторюється поки кожна з сторін не використає свою номенклатурну квоту. Посади за чергою вільно обираються сторонами з усього загального реєстру (додаток №1) та вносяться іменні кандидатури для призначення.

5. Кадрова політика стосовно посад, що не увійшли у рейтинговий список (в т.ч. керівні посади міністерств, відомств, регіональних адміністрацій), проводиться за узгодженням засновників Коаліції, з урахуванням принципів, зазначених в п. 2.

6. Для забезпечення патріотизму, професіоналізму та порядності нового кадрового складу органів державної влади України, недопущення до влади корумпованих та заангажованих кланами чиновників, засновники Коаліції до виборів узгоджують у межах, визначених вище квот, прізвища кандидатів на посади, що визначені Додатком №2.

7. З метою відновлення незалежності і об'єктивності діяльності загальнонаціональних телевізійних компаній і каналів, засновники Коаліції спільно визначають засади нормалізації ситуації на електронному мас-медійному ринку.

8. Для забезпечення персональної відповідальності за результат виборчої кампанії засновники Коаліції затверджують закріплення регіонів за керівниками політичних та штабних структур Коаліції (Додаток №3).

9. Виходячи з затвердженого кошторису на проведення виборчої кампанії на регіональному рівні засновники Коаліції забезпечують фінансування регіонів пропорційно чисельності виборців. Фінансування здійснюється через голів партій (та блоків) та інших кураторів регіону – членів Координаційного комітету.

10. Зміни до цієї угоди вносяться за погодженням засновників Коаліції та засвідчуються їх підписами.

Від Блоку "Наша Україна"                              В. Ющенко

Від Блоку Юлії Тимошенко                           Ю. Тимошенко

22  The secret agreement between Yushchenko and Tymoshenko.

events were designed to test the limits of achievable fraud, and to demotivate voters by showing them that their voices would not be heard. Fortunately, the level of international protest was for once relatively strong.

### Option Three: Yanukovych the Populist

The third option for the established regime was to concentrate on the actual election. To do this, the authorities needed an agreed candidate, but it is not clear why they chose Yanukovych. A more centrist candidate could have been sold to the electorate much more easily, as could a candidate without a criminal past, or someone who had occupied a post more prestigious than, as Yanykovych, a driver in the Soviet era. (Kuchma, for instance, it will be recalled, had headed the giant missile factory Pivdenmash.) Someone less renowned for his or her ability to speak both Russian and Ukrainian equally badly would have also been a better choice – Yanukovych would famously misspell his own job title and qualifications in his official application to stand in the election.[25]

It seems, however, that in November 2002, the up-and-coming Donetsk clan simply informed a president much weakened by the Gongadze affair that it was their turn to nominate the prime minister. Many of the other 'clans' were clearly less than keen on this idea. Yanukovych scraped together only 234 votes (he needed 225 out of 450 to be approved), some of which cost up to $200,000 to obtain.[26] This may also have been a financial proposition as far as the president was concerned, but, more importantly, it suited Kuchma's main priority of providing a counterbalance to the power of the SDPU(o), that is, the Kiev clan, whose leader, Viktor Medvedchuk, now headed the presidential administration, and was able to count the outgoing prime minister, Anatolii Kinakh, as his informal ally. The SDPU(o) was happy to cede the premiership to forestall what they thought was the greater danger (though in the light of later events, this now seems deeply ironic) of the Donetsk group forging some kind of alliance of convenience with Yushchenko. (The Donetsk group, which actually produces things and depends on foreign trade for its profits, temporarily considered that Yushchenko might front their operations. The SDPU(o), however, prefers empire-building within the state and mass media; a semi-isolted Ukraine therefore suited these purposes.) Yanukovych's transfer to Kiev also left Rinat Akhmetov more clearly in local control of Donetsk. He was therefore happy to stop making overtures to Yushchenko and cough up the cash for the cut-price privatisation of Ukraine's biggest steel company, Kryvorizhstal, in 2004.[27]

There was some discussion of replacing Yanukovych as prime minister and therefore most-likely candidate in December 2003, but the Donetsk clan held firm. Thereafter, the regime had too little time to launch any alternative. The Donetsk clan was thinking narrowly about expanding its own business and political interests, and not strategically about the type of candidate best placed to win the election. They also vastly underestimated the difficulties that their thuggish political culture would have in translating to the rest of Ukraine, and even to the rest of east Ukraine. The latter factor may explain why the possible 'centrist' candidates, particularly Serhii Tihipko, the new head of the National Bank, took fright. Tihipko had grown into his own PR image as an urbane international capitalist equally at home in international playgrounds such as Davos in Switzerland, as in his home city of Dnipropetrovsk, and was put off running if he had to use Donetsk-type 'technology' to do so. Conversely, Tihipko's white collar image did not sell him to voters in the Donbas. He ended up as Yanukovych's campaign manager instead.

Other possible centrists also had their weaknesses. The economy minister, Valerii Khoroshkovskyi, was too young; the Odesa governor, Serhii Hrynevetskyi, too obscure. The most interesting candidate might have been the Rada chair, Volodymyr Lytvyn, but as he figured in damning portions of the Melnychenko tapes, his survival strategy depended on his continued control of parliament. Certainly, a campaign fronted by someone such as Tihipko or Lytvyn would have been very different, but so many other factors would have changed as a result – a stronger Communist vote would have been likely without Yanukovych, for instance – that it would be rash to say more. But the authorities' advisers certainly missed a trick. They did not do what this seasoned cynical observer expected them to do in 2002–4, which was to box Yushchenko in by running strong flanking candidates on both his right and centre-left. The choice of Yanukovych, the centripetal candidate, failed to cut off the opposition's advance towards newer, softer voters in central Ukraine.

Another possible reason for the regime's backing of Yanukovych is that the constitutional reform package was designed partly with him in mind, and that he was a pliable candidate behind whom Kuchma could continue to exercise power after 2004. (Yanukovych certainly wasn't the sharpest tool in the box, so this may have worked.) Another theory is that the choice of an east Ukrainian was dictated by the campaign strategy prepared by the Russian 'political technologists' (see below). In the years of diplomatic semi-isolation since the breaking of the Gongadze scandal in 2000, Kuchma's regime had fallen under stronger Russian influence than would

Opinion poll ratings of Yushchenko and Yanukovych in 2004, in an assumed second round.

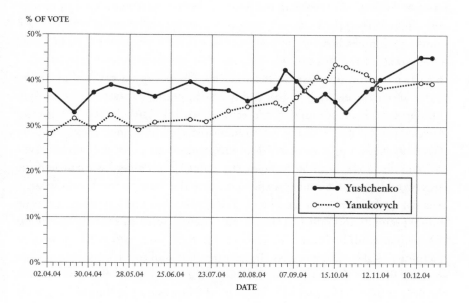

Source: supplied by Valerii Khmelko, KIIS

otherwise have been the case; and for the Russian 'geopolitical project', it made sense to choose the candidate who was as antithetical to west Ukrainian 'nationalism' as possible. Some Russians even hoped to provoke a simmering undercurrent of Galician (west Ukrainian) separatism, in order to build a stronger Russo-Ukrainian condominium without them. Rather more Russians had appreciated the advantages of a semi-isolated Ukraine and hoped that that trend would continue under Yanukovych. Attending to Russia's needs, however, was not the right way to appeal to the median Ukrainian voter.

It is also possible that the authorities just got it wrong. They were over-confident in their ability to sell anybody, and over-reliant on the 'administrative resources' they presumed would guarantee victory in any case. It is also likely that there is an element of truth in all these theories, and the cumulative effect was that the Yanukovych campaign lacked the clear direction it needed.

Although he himself was 'white collar', Serhii Tihipko, as Yanukovych's campaign manager, sought to craft a positive, populist campaign. For this strategy to work, however, Yanukovych should have adopted a more 'oppositional' image. His belated rhetoric about 'old power' (Kuchma) and 'new power' (himself) in December came far too late to make any real difference. After an initial rise in the polls in the spring, Yanukovych's progress was therefore stalled in the summer, with Yushchenko still ahead. Yanukovych himself grew dissatisfied. With three months to go, this created an opening for the Russian advisers, most of whom arrived in town around this time, to promote their chosen strategy. There was a great deal of uncertainty about the election at this point which, because it occurred so late in the day may have stimulated the attempt to kill Yushchenko. To bolster Yanukovych's popularity, the government planned huge increases in welfare payments, including a dramatic doubling of the state pension from UAH137 to UAH284 ($54), but had to delay these until September, as even then the rises would prove ruinously expensive. But the tactic proved temporarily effective. Yanukovych surged ahead in the polls, rising by ten points between mid-September and mid-October (from 34 per cent to 44 per cent in a putative second round). Factor analysis by the Kiev International Institute for Sociology (KIIS) suggests that three-fifths of Yanukovych's rise came from the over-fifties – those who were already on a pension, or who would be, in the near future.[28] The pensions hike and the moves on the Russian language to appeal to relatively elderly Russophones (see below) reinforced one another, but the former came first, and Yanukovych's rise in the ratings immediately followed.[29] On the other hand, the move revived popular fears of inflation from the 1990s.

### Option Four: The Russian Card

Most of the Russians who arrived in Kiev in 2004 described themselves as 'political technologists'. (I have explained this strange term elsewhere.[30]) The 'political technologist' is much more than a 'spin doctor' such as Peter Mandelson in the UK. The latter spins a story between its origin and its interpretation by the media. The political technologists who proliferate throughout the former USSR, however, like to think of themselves as political metaprogrammers, masters of the local political universe. First, the scope of their work is extremely broad. Countries such as Russia and Ukraine are often called 'directed democracies' (the Russian term is *upravliaemaia demokratiia*) and the job of the technologist is one of direction, shaping and even creating governing parties and politicians, and trying to do the same to the opposition, as well. Second, they dress up manipulation and fraud as 'technology', but their work is often corrosive and crude. They usually work for the authorities, and usually stop at nothing to win.

Ukrainians have two contradictory images of so-called political technologists. Often, they are feared as omnipotent; their schemes are seen as too clever to detect and too effective to oppose, and their cunning plans as always able to deliver another victory for the undeserving and dim-witted powers-that-be. On the other hand, fictional Russian political technologists make a brief appearance in Andrei Kurkov's novel *Penguin Lost*, and are depicted as feckless misanthropes, 'bastards to a man', with 'such a taste for luxury.' 'There's hardly [a pre-prepared manifesto] we can't use three times over', they declare. 'The main thing is to clear off before the successful candidate starts implementing it.' The 'golden rule of the image maker is "Never be there for the result." The client gives you hell if he loses, his rivals give you hell if he wins.'[31] (Kurkov is Ukraine's most popular writer in translation, particularly big in Germany, thanks to his bleakly comic evocation of the seedier side of Kuchma's Ukraine.)

In reality, of course, some 'technologists' were good at their job, and some were not; but there was undoubtedly an over-supply of Russians working in Ukraine in 2004. The money was good, many were seconded by the Kremlin, and Russia had just finished its own election cycle, so a few had time on their hands. According to Andrei Riabov of the Moscow Carnegie Foundation, 'Ukraine is a Klondike, an El Dorado . . . business is drying up at home'.[32] (Putin's constitutional changes after the Beslan tragedy in September 2004, which abolished Duma constituencies and elected governors, meant there would be fewer elections to manipulate.) The most famous 'technologist' of all, Geleb Pavlovskii, of the Foundation for Effective Politics (FEP) in Moscow, was often in town, albeit claiming he was only working on a 'Russian contract' (i.e. for a client based in Russia). In one interview, he reeled off a long list of his colleagues: 'Marat Gelman, Stanislav Belkovskii, Igor Mintusov, Sergei Dorenko . . . all became Kievites' for the duration.[33] Some, like Gelman, who had worked in Ukraine on and off since 2002, became over-familiar faces. Working in the dark was part of the secret of their success. Other frequent flyers to Kiev were Sergei Markov, Viacheslav Nikonov and Igor Shuvalov, who had worked for Kuchma in 1999 and, despite an expenses scandal, for the SDPU(o) and 'liberal' projects in 2002. Shuvalov had stayed on to oversee the so-called *temnyky* (weekly instructions to the media on how to cover – or not cover – events).

Kuchma's chief speechwriter and the deputy head of the presidential administration, Vasyl Baziv, complained that Gelman and Russian businessman Maksim Kurochkin, aka 'Mad Max', the director of Pavlovskii's Russia Club, which was based in the Premier Palace Hotel, Kiev's number one house of fun for the nouveaux riches, 'made themselves at home' at the presidential administration on Bankivska Street.[34] The Russia Club was notorious for its dodgy finances,[35] and the Premier Palace wasn't much better; it was widely assumed to be funded by circles close to the mayor of Moscow, Yurii Luzhkov, Russian businessman-politician Aleksandr Babakov (a friend of Gelman) and their Ukrainian associates, Hryhorii Surkis and Viktor Medvedchuk. In fact, the whole Yanukovych campaign was awash with money, and some were more interested in creaming it off. An apparent attempt on Kurochkin's life was made on 6 November, when a nearby Volkswagen exploded as he approached his car after midnight with two bodyguards. After the Orange Revolution he fled to Russia, just before the new authorities in Kiev accused him of fraudulent last-minute property deals involving the Dnipro Hotel in Kiev and three sanatoria in Crimea.

The Russians were almost all working for the Yanukovych side, although Gleb Pavlovskii was approached in September 2004 by the Our Ukraine financier, Petro 'Poroshenko [who] made an open commercial proposition to cooperate with the Yushchenko team'.[36] (Pavlovskii politely declined the intellectually challenging idea of working for both sides.) One interesting exception was Aleksei Sitnikov of the Moscow firm Image-Kontakt,[37] who had also worked for Mikhail Saakashvili during Georgia's 'Rose Revolution' in 2003, allegedly advising him on the art of demonstration and virtual revolution (i.e. using the media to make it seem all 'the people' are on your side). Sitnikov didn't stay long, however.[38] Sergei Markov also claimed that another leading Russian agency, the magnificently-named Nikkolo-M (the Russian spelling of Niccolo Machiavelli), was working for the Yushchenko side,[39] but contacts again seem to have been only superficial. Minor roles were also played by Andrei Piontkovskii from Russia and Mirosław Czech from Poland.

The Russian political technologists had also been in Kiev, pushing up hotel prices, for the 2002 elections, when their work had mainly involved selling the establishment parties For A United Ukraine and the SDPU(o), and setting up the fake or 'clone' parties. Their earlier work was therefore only a partial success; their standard excuse the claim that, 'the election's dynamic became who was for Kuchma and who was against – and we were squeezed in the middle'.[40] If their analysis was correct, they faced a choice of tactics for 2004 – within their own limited repertoire, that is. One approach, more loosely associated with the faux-celebral Marat Gelman, in his other life a 'post-modernist' gallery owner, involved deconstructing the binary scenario that had tripped them up in 2002, by introducing a variety of 'virtual objects' to create the impression of a more complicated picture. These could be either stage-managed events designed to change the political atmosphere, or actual but virtual participants in the election, like the fake candidates and parties who had been more prominent in 1999 and 2002. The second approach, broadly more typical of Gleb Pavlovskii, who tended towards Russian great power nationalism, was to keep the polarisation scenario, but to change its *dramaturgiia*.

This is how they talked. What they meant was that they needed to reinvent the election's central theme. Instead of 'good opposition' versus 'bad authorities', it would have to be 'east versus west' within Ukraine. Pavlovskii and Markov therefore advocated playing the Russian card. It is not difficult to see why they thought this strategy would be a winner. First, they were Russian. Second, Putin enjoyed a very high approval rating in Ukraine – 60 per cent or more – and they thought they could craft the campaign in his shadow. Third, their sociological research (and they did do some solid work to justify their exorbitant fees) showed them that just over half the population used the Russian language as a first language, and their leading questions produced very negative images of 'Ukrainian nationalists' in eastern and southern Ukraine. An early try-out to test this theory in April 2004 had briefly pushed Yanukovych ahead in the polls. That month, the Ukrainian parliament had ratified the agreement on a Single Economic Space with Russia, Belarus and Kazakhstan, and, in a blatant provocation, the National Council on TV and Radio had announced that all channels would have to start broadcasting in Ukrainian. The nationalist wing in Our Ukraine fell into the trap, enthusiastically cheering the measure, which funnily enough was never implemented. Subsequent publicity about Yanukovych's criminal past and the events in Mukachevo meant the gain was only temporary (see figure on page 85).

Half the strategy was public. On 27 September, only a month before the vote, Yanukovych made a dramatic late commitment to make Russian an official language, to allow for dual citizenship of Ukraine and Russia, and to abandon all moves towards NATO (the first two would require specific changes to the 1996 Constitution, and none had been in his original manifesto). Russia waded in with help. During the Russian–Ukrainian summit in Sochi in August, Putin agreed to remove VAT on oil exports to Ukraine. Ukrainian petrol would therefore be 16 per cent cheaper, at a cost to the Russian budget of $800 million. Moreover, as crude price soared over $50 a barrel, Russian suppliers held prices constant in Ukraine till the election. There were also rumours that Kuchma had secretly promised to remove the Ukrainian fleet from the bases it shared with the Russian Black Sea Fleet (in Crimea, on Ukrainian territory since 1997) in return for Putin's support.[41] Russia also announced, as of 1 November, that Ukrainians would be allowed to stay in Russia for up to ninety days without registering, and, from January 2005, would be granted freedom of entry into Russia with only their own domestic documentation.

The covert parts of the strategy can be seen in the plan leaked in June 2004, which was reportedly drawn up by Marat Gelman (see above). In private the technologists argued they could overcome the problems of 2002 if they were given freeer reign. The 'main scenario for the campaign', declared the report, must be 'directed conflict'. 'Our task is to destabilise the situation in the regions (maybe involving political games, but not the everyday economy)', which might hurt the oligarchs' business interests, 'and drag Yushchenko into this process.' The report could not mention a potential conflict without suggesting it be exploited. It recommended stirring up animosity between Ukrainians from east and west; between Poles and Ukrainians; between Ukraine's various Churches; and between Slavs and Crimean Tatars. Overall, though, its preference was clear. 'The task of the media [in other places, 'our media'] is to interpret this as an ontological "East-West" conflict, a political conflict between Our Ukraine and the Party of the Regions, and a personal conflict between Yushchenko and Yanukovych.'[42] The tone grew more impatient later in the campaign, when another leaked document urged 'the escalation of confrontation on all possible lines: Galicia–East, South, West (USA–Europe) – Russia, Russian language, the threat of the growth of extremism, etc'. It also mentioned the need to 'organise a social movement in the south-eastern regions of the country against Yushchenko and his circle coming to power, as a reactionary, Pro-American, radical candidate' – and the need to depict the opposition as the 'aggressive' party.[43]

Unlike some other plans, which stayed on the drawing board, much of this came to pass. Trouble was only narrowly averted in Crimea in March, after nine Crimean Tatars were stabbed by skinheads. The Tatars were the ones who were then jailed for the offence. A blatantly political provocation followed in July 2004, when Serhii Kunitsyn, head of the local administration in Crimea, changed the local criminal code to create an offence of 'squatting', punishable by up to two years in prison. The Crimean Tatars had been deported *en masse* by Stalin in 1944 and not allowed to return until the late Gorbachev era. Most of the 260,000 or so who came back therefore lived in shanty-towns or self-builds, as their property was long gone. Kunitsyn now ordered several militia raids on Tatar areas, some allegedly using chemicals. The Crimean Tatars' traditional non-violent methods held with difficulty. A big majority voted for Yushchenko, but not in the disciplined unanimity of recent years, as some stayed at home in frustration with both their leadership and the general situation. Almost every Slav voter in the Crimea, however – that is, both Russians and Ukrainians – apparently backed Yanukovych. In the final round in December, 178,755 supported Yushchenko (15.4 per cent) and 942,210 (81.3 per cent) Yanukovych. As of 2002, the Crimean Tatar electorate was 186,000 (12 per cent of the total).[44] The provocations also had a wider purpose, as the opposition, now led by Yushchenko, traditionally supported the Crimean Tatars: 'Yushchenko must be represented as an enemy of Russians in Crimea', the report argued, and of Slav culture in general. 'If Ukraine can't defend the interests of Slavs in Crimea, then' Yanukovych or 'nearby Russia is always prepared to offer support'.[45]

One big problem with this overall strategy was that Yushchenko really wasn't a nationalist. Moreover, to his great credit, he refused the invitation to fight the election on such terms. The powers-that-be therefore covertly supported four virtual nationalists in his stead. All were previously obscure, but they were soon all over state TV acting out the role of the 'nationalist threat'. All were secretly financed by the SDPU(o) and Yanukovych's party, which in public constantly used the wartime imagery of the OUN–UPA to demonise what it dubbed the *nashisty* (from the equation of 'Our Ukraine', *Nasha Ukraïna*, with *fashisty*).[46] The fake four were a sorry bunch, however. Roman Kozak of the little-known OUN in Ukraine, was not the brightest of men. Dmytro Korchynskyi, an 'intellectual provocateur' on SDPU(o) TV,[47] was over-exposed. The powers-that-be hoped that Andrii Chornovil, son of the veteran dissident they allegedly had murdered in 1999, would have inherited some of his father's charisma, but he hadn't. Bohdan Boiko, of the fake party 'Rukh for Unity', had a long record of political treachery and financial corruption in his native Ternopil, where he distinguished himself by speculating in the local sugar crop when head of the local council in the mid-1990s. Kozak, Korchynskyi and Kovalenko at the UNA were soon dubbed the Ukrainian 'KKK'.

Still, they strove to damn Yushchenko by mock-association, demonstrating uninvited in his support and receiving plenty of coverage on official TV. Kozak's TV ads were even placed right before Yushchenko's, so that viewers could hear his call to 'Vote for Yushchenko. Together . . . we will kick the Russians and Jews out of Ukraine!' Kozak ended up spending the third highest sum on TV advertising. The four won only 0.35 per cent of the vote; but their constant over-exposure on east Ukrainian TV (Inter and 1+1), and their hysterically unrealistic calls to close Russian schools, ban the Russian language, and introduce a visa regime with Russia had a definite, if unquantifiable effect on building up anti-Yushchenko stereotypes in the east.

Nor were there many real nationalists for the authorities' PR machine to exploit, though there were some important exceptions. Clean Ukraine rather unwisely depicted Yanukovych as leading a gang of *Yanuchary*, a traditional nationalist insult for east Ukrainians. The 'Yanuchary' (in English, 'Janissaries') were soldiers in the service of the Ottoman Empire in Cossack times, traitors to their own faith and nation, who were press-ganged into service when young, made to forget their origin, converted to militant Islam and were often sent to raze their own villages to the ground (see plate 15).[48] Ukrainian intellectuals published two open letters that did Yushchenko no favours by reverting to an older, more intemperate nationalist tone, attacking '"prime minister" Yanukovych [for] promising to grant the language of pop music and Russian criminal slang the absurd status of "second state language"',[49] and prejudging voters' rights by claiming that 'today we have no right to give away a single Ukrainian vote to Yanukovych'.[50]

Three other 'technical candidates' were designed to 'activate' radical leftist and Russophile voters in east Ukraine, this time from their own side of the fence. Opinion polls showed that this segment of the electorate was disillusioned with the powers-that-be, but also susceptible to the black PR against both the West and west Ukraine. The technologists therefore argued it was better to use proxies to stimulate them into action. The technique was known as a 'relay race', with 'technical' (fake) candidates being paid to stir up anti-Yushchenko sentiment on the basis of crude anti-Western propaganda and then 'pass it on' to Yanukovych in round two, despite the risk that they would take votes from him in round one.[51] Not only was the seemingly implausible Nataliia Vitrenko wheeled out to play this role (the fact that she could play it at all was testament to the degree of media control in the east, where part of the electorate had not been exposed to her exposure as a fake), she was joined by Oleksandr Yakovenko, leader of the faux-radical fake party, the Communist Party of Workers and Peasants (secretly funded by the Donetsk clan), and Oleksandr Bazyliuk of the justifiably obscure Slavic Party. The three dutifully hammered away at all the black PR themes prepared for Yanukovych, claiming that Yushchenko was an 'ultra-nationalist' and an 'American puppet', and that his wife was an 'American spy'. The technologists seemed right: Vitrenko eventually won a useful 1.5 per cent and Yakovenko 0.78 per cent, though Bazyliuk flopped with 0.03 per cent.

The Orthodox Church of the Moscow Patriarchate played a similar proxy propaganda role – or, at least, one faction or 'group of influence' in its fairly pluralistic leadership did so. Despite wild talk that 'the Donestkies must work on the Orthodox messianic idea if they want to strengthen their

influence in Ukraine', as the Donbas had originally been settled by fron-
tiersmen-priests,[52] most of east Ukraine was now dominated by post-Soviet
agnosticism. Yanukovych's main backer, Rinat Akhmetov, was, in theory at
least, a Muslim. (Most of the Russian political technologists were not
exactly religious men.)[53] On the other hand, as the Moscow Patriarchate
was still technically part of the Russian Church, it was the most easily available institutional channel for Russian influence in Ukraine. Yushchenko was
backed more informally by most of the two smaller Orthodox Churches,
and by the Greek Catholics.

Both the Russian Patriarch Aleksei and Volodymyr (Sabodan), leader
of the Moscow Patriarchate in Ukraine, blessed Yanukovych, the latter
at Kiev's prestigious Caves Monastery. Volodymyr publically endorsed
Yanukovych on UT1 TV on 10 November, stating that, 'I view him as a true
Orthodox believer, who would deserve to be the head of our state'.[54] In
November a typical stash of unsigned leaflets was found in a church near the
Moldovan border attacking Yushchenko as 'a partisan of the schismatics
[that is, the rival Orthodox Churches] and an enemy of Orthodoxy' and
calling his wife a 'CIA agent'.[55] Priests politicised their sermons, and the
Church's opaque finances helped channel several covert operations for
Yanukovych (see page 109). The Church also helped the Yanukovych team
send out flyers from no less than the Archangel Michael, the patron saint of
Kiev, 'with love' from Yanukovych to his flock, but obviously implying
divine endorsement for the prime minister (see plate 2). In return, the government handed the Patriarchate the St Volodymyr Cathedral in Crimea on
the eve of the election.

Fortunately, as the Church was attacking one of its own, Patriarch Aleksei
was prepared to make peace after the election, meeting Yushchenko on his
visit to Moscow, and stressing that 'we [now] respect the will of the people
of Ukraine'.[56]

### Russia

As one of Yanukovych's campaign slogans had it: 'Ukraine – Russia;
Stronger Together'. Putin obviously agreed, but there was still a real debate
in both the Kremlin and the Russian press until September 2004, not about
whom to support, but about whether to back Yanukovych exclusively or to
take a more balanced approach. Putin's gamble on Yanukovych alone seems
to have been a personal decision, albeit one prompted by Pavlovskii,
Kuchma and above all by Viktor Medvedchuk, who loudly and repeatedly
claimed he could deliver the necessary result. Putin's chief political fixer,

Vladislav Surkov, deputy head of the Kremlin administration, convinced him that the same methods that had entrenched 'directed democracy' in Russia would work in Ukraine. Or rather, he didn't have to. Both men worked within the same set of assumptions, within a world view that saw their methods as omnipotent and any opposition as marginal.

One further problem for the Yushchenko camp was that its natural allies in Moscow, the Russian liberals, had tumbled out of the Duma in December 2003. Ironically or not, the Ukrainian opposition's message now came through two other channels. First were those Russian businessmen who had done well in Ukraine when Yushchenko was prime minister in 1999–2001. Not the controversial exiles such as Boris Berezovskii, but men like Oleg Deripaska, who had bought the Mykolaïv aluminium plant, Mikhail Fridman of the Alfa Group, who had bought the giant Lysychanskyi oil refinery, and Vagit Alekperov of Lukoil, who had bought the Odesa refinery and the Oriana caustic soda plant and set up a lucrative chain of petrol stations. In fact, some of them had done less well thereafter. Once Yanukovych was prime minister, the expansion of the Donetsk group had often been at the expense of opportunities for Russian investors. Overall, Russian investment was down an estimated 20 per cent. A second channel was through the Security Services. Oleh Rybachuk maintained this channel and claims it was open right to the very top, all the way through the campaign.[57]

Putin chose not to listen. He does not seem to have been thinking about economics, but about geopolitics. Once Ukraine was more firmly within Russia's orbit, then so many other things (the proposed 'Single Economic Space', Moldova, the South Caucasus, a more secure southern flank, an end to EU and NATO expansion, and even easier management of Belarus) would fall into place. Significantly, the end to debate in Russia coincided exactly with Yanukovych's declarations on the Russian language, dual citizenship, etc, on 27 September. Clearly, Putin, the former KGB apparatchik, had no time personally for Yanukovych, the former convict. The Ukrainian opposition, particularly its satirical wing, derived much succour and amusement from the scenes shown on Ukrainian TV during the Kiev military parade on 28 October, the eve of the first round, when Yanukovych, disrespectfully munching sweets, offered one to a clearly astonished and frankly disgusted Putin.

This was only the last of frequent-flyer Putin's many high-profile visits to Ukraine, because he was convinced his own popularity was an asset. He received extensive coverage on official Ukrainian TV, including a ninety-minute phone-in broadcast, live on three national channels on 26 October, when 80,000 questions were received, which was unprecedented in Ukraine

(Kuchma hadn't faced a real voter for years). Putin wasn't necessarily wrong to assume that he was helping the campaign. One theory has it, however, that his support showed up Yanukovych's weaknesses, and made it too obvious even to those who felt culturally close to Russia that Yanukovych was politically dependent on the Kremlin (as did the bizarre idea of putting up Yanukovych billboards in Moscow). Despite this, others still insist he bolstered a flailing candidate. Whether or not this was true, Putin clearly erred massively in supporting Russian political technologists' methods. The most telling aspect of his message of congratulations to Yanukovych on Monday 22 November, the day after the second round vote, was that it could only have been based on their fraudulent exit polls, as the official result was not then out. Putin also misjudged the ability of the political technologists to guarantee victory, but then he was not alone in that.

## Bushchenko

In October, when the outcome of the election still hung in the balance, the authorities' black PR against Yushchenko went into overdrive. Given the simultaneous presidential election in the USA, a new figure appeared in the campaign – 'Viktor Bushchenko' (Bush + Yushchenko = Bushchenko).[58] 'Yushchenko,' it was claimed, 'is a project of America, which doesn't need a strong, independent Ukraine' (see plates 11–13). Posters and adverts appeared, which showed George Bush appearing from behind a Yushchenko mask and saying 'Yes! Yushchenko is Our President!', except that the 'P' was crossed out to read *rezydent*, a KGB term for an agent in a foreign country ('President' in Ukrainian is spelt 'Prezydent'). 'Bushchenko' also appeared as Uncle Sam, asking 'Are you Prepared for Civil War?', and saying 'Bosnia–Herzegovina, Serbia, Kosovo, Iraq. . . You're next!', and as a cowboy riding (a map of) Ukraine.

Much of this Cold War imagery was actually distinctly old-fashioned. Another poster showed a mosquito in the colours of the stars and stripes, sucking Ukraine's blood. The national hero, nineteenth-century poet Taras Shevchenko, was enlisted to say 'Yankee go home'. A petrol price scare combined two messages: the dangers of invading Iraq and the benefits of links with Russia. It should be pointed out that it was the Yanukovych government, very willing to re-enter the international arena via the 'coalition of the willing', which had sent Ukrainian troops to Iraq, where they made up the fourth largest contingent, to curry favour with Washington, whereas Yushchenko at the time promised to bring them home. Yushchenko's wife was constantly subject to the crudest of attacks, and Yushchenko himself was lambasted for leaving his first, 'proper Ukrainian' wife, Svitlana Kolesnyk. Finally, a notorious poster showed a Ukraine divided into three different 'sorts': with the first class west Ukrainians and the second class central Ukrainians discriminating against the third class in the east and south. Much of this propaganda was distributed indirectly, through the 'technical candidates'. When an entire warehouse of posters was found by Our Ukraine in October, Roman Kozak and Oleksandr Yakovenko were sent along to claim it was all theirs.[59] Kozak, supposedly a Ukrainian nationalist but none too bright, ended up distributing Pavlovskii's Russia Club leaflets on 'Why Russia Supports Viktor Yanukovych'.[60]

Much of the black PR depicting Yushchenko or his supporters as ardent nationalists was relayed to the USA, via Yanukovych's adviser Eduard Prutnik and the Odesa-born American citizen Aleksei Kiselev, who helped employ half a dozen American companies on Yanukovych's PR.[61] The accusation of anti-Semitism was particularly damaging in America, particularly after an anti-Semitic diatribe, including the claim that there were 400,000 Jews in the SS, was planted in the paper *Village News* earlier in the campaign,[62] which some on the Ukrainian right were stupid enough to defend. The Ukrainian authorities couldn't have it both ways, however, and the global attention given to the domestic 'Bushchenko' campaign in October 2004 helped pave the way for their abandonment by Washington during the Orange Revolution.

It should also be stressed that, although the traffic wasn't just one-way, the Yushchenko camp did nothing as bad as this. They focused on Yanukovych's criminal record like a dog with a bone, and exploited it to symbolise the general corruption of the regime as a whole, but both points were fair comment. One advert made in Yanukovych's style, saying, 'If you are for Yanukovych, go and fight in Chechnia' could be considered black PR, but the opposition didn't churn out blatant lies on an industrial scale. Instead, Yushchenko constantly talked of dignity, moral values in government and respect for the citizen in a way that Yanukovych could not.

### The Poisoning

Neither did the opposition try to kill their opponents. Yushchenko's former chief of staff, Oleh Rybachuk, claims his sources, former agents in both the Russian and Ukrainian secret services, had told him as early as late July 2004 that a plot to kill his boss existed, and that they had warned that poisoning would be the most likely method, although at first it seemed that Yushchenko's minders were more worried that he would succumb to a fatal car crash – another favourite Ukrainian tactic. An early scare came on the evening of 12 August, when Yushchenko was out campaigning in southern Ukraine. As his Audi attempted to pass a KamAZ truck on a road near Kherson, it swerved three times, almost forcing him off the road. His entourage stopped the truck and got the local traffic police to detain the driver, but he was released without charge.[63] Even the type of truck was a favourite. The very same model had been involved in the crashes of Viacheslav Chornovil, Valerii Malev, head of the export company embroiled in the 'Kolchuha scandal' (the alleged sale of a radar system to Saddam Hussein during the build-up to the invasion of Iraq in 2003), and of Anatolii Yermak in February 2003, a crusading Rada deputy from the 'Anti-Mafia' group.

Yushchenko could hardly not travel, however. Back in Kiev, late on 5 September after a normal evening with his aides, Yushchenko set out for what was then supposed to be a secret meeting with the heads of the SBU, Ihor Smeshko and his deputy Volodymyr Satsiuk.[64] The meeting, postponed from the previous evening, was arranged by one of Our Ukraine's businessmen, Davyd Zhvaniia, who was the only other person to attend the rendezvous at Satsiuk's *dacha* in the forests outside Kiev (which was not a cabbage patch, but a villa set in five hectares). Oleh Rybachuk was not present, despite being the normal contact man with the SBU. Neither was Yevhen Chervonenko, who was in charge of Yushchenko's personal security. Chervonenko claimed that he abandoned normal precautions, which included tasting all Yushchenko's food, at the SBU's request, and that Yushchenko initially kept his other colleagues in the dark about the meeting.[65] Rumours have circulated about the presence at the meeting of an unnamed 'fifth man', supposedly a Georgian, a presumed friend of Zhvaniia (possibly Badri Patarkatsishvili – see page 176).

According to Zhvaniia, although it later became notorious, the September *dacha* dinner was just one of a series of meetings and other contacts designed 'to prevent possible "disorder" and forcible methods', and to persuade the SBU and other organs 'not to go over the limits, written for them in the Constitution'. The last meeting was in November, after the second round, again at Satsiuk's dacha.[66]

Yushchenko left his bodyguards at home. According to Satsiuk, the meeting lasted from 10 p.m. until 2:45 a.m. The four men dined on boiled crayfish with beer, a salad of tomatoes, cucumber and sweetcorn, vodka with meats and a final round of cognac – all prepared by Satsiuk's personal chef.[67] When Yushchenko got home, his wife says she smelt 'something metallic' on his breath. One version of events has it that he vomited on the way home, which may have saved his life, although this remains obscure as the vomiting could be attributed to the drink, which would be difficult to admit to in Ukraine's macho culture.

As he immediately fell very ill, Yushchenko has continued to state that he believes he was poisoned at this time. On the other hand, Yushchenko got what he wanted from the meeting, which, judging by the amount of alcohol consumed, seems to have been cordial enough. During the campaign, one faction in the SBU remained broadly neutral, while another actively helped the Yushchenko team, remaining in secret contact with Rybachuk to pass on the recordings they made of the Zoriany fraudsters. Contrary to later reports that it defected to the opposition *en masse*, the SBU was obviously split at this time between professionals and recent political appointments by Kuchma and Medvedchuk. Smeshko embodied the split, as he was both. Just to make things more complicated, he had close links to the Russian GRU (the military's 'Main Intelligence Directorate'), *and* had served as Ukraine's first military attaché in Washington from 1992 to 1996. Satsiuk was a late political appointment in April 2004, and was widely seen as Kuchma's, or more exactly, Medvedchuk's, man in the SBU. He had previously served as a Rada deputy in Medvedchuk's party, the SDPU(o) and, before that, for the socialists.

The next day, Yushchenko went to see some local Ukrainian doctors, who thought he had food poisoning. On 9 September, after four days of rapidly worsening health, with severe stomach pain and swollen organs, and lesions appearing all over Yushchenko's face and body, Chervonenko spirited him off to a luxury clinic in Austria – just in time to save his life, but, it was thought initially, too late to identify the toxins in his body. Half of his face was paralysed, and a catheter had to be inserted for pain-killing injections. Yushchenko discharged himself after a week, but was forced to return for ten days' more treatment in early October, by which time his advisers began to worry that his whole campaign was unwinding.

A fake statement from the Austrian clinic, the Rudolfinerhaus in Vienna, claiming they had found no evidence of poison, was faxed to Reuters, who assumed it to be genuine and gave it wide publicity, which was, of course, then parroted back in Ukraine. According to one report, the fax was traced to the PR company Euro RSCG, which was linked to Viktor Pinchuk and his favourite foreign spin-doctor, the Machievellian Frenchman, Jacques Séguéla.[68] Pinchuk's TV channels, such as ICTV, also exaggerated Yushchenko's past health problems, after the records he had given to the parliamentary commission investigating the affair were leaked, and the claims by the Rudolfinerhaus's Dr Lothar Wicke that he was sacked, and physically threatened, for refusing to support the poisoning diagnosis. More callously, the official media poured scorn on Yushchenko's claims, claiming that his terrible appearance was the result of a bad hangover, a botched botox injection, or even herpes. A later slur claimed a rejuvenation operation using foetus cells had gone badly wrong. Oleksandr Moroz disgraced himself by saying that Yushchenko shouldn't eat so much sushi (*sic*), but should stick to simple peasant fare, like *borshch* (a beetroot-based soup, which is much nicer than it sounds), potatoes and lard.[69]

The government camp also replied with an 'attack' on Yanukovych, when 'several large objects' were thrown at the prime minister when he was campaigning in west Ukraine on 24 September. Yanukovych was rushed to hospital, but found time to blame the incident on extremist supporters of Yushchenko. However, Poroshenko's Channel 5 captured the event on video, and the 'several large objects' were revealed to be one solitary egg. On tape, Yanukovych seemed surprised and initially failed to react, but went on to over-react with a dramatic collapse (see plate 8).[70] As often, the attempted replay was a poor copy of the original – on 10 December, Yushchenko's poisoning would be confirmed to have been both frighteningly real and nearly fatal.

The poisoning seemed to be a direct attempt on Yushchenko's life, although Rybachuk claims that his contacts had warned him 'that the goal would not be to kill Yushchenko but to make him an "invalid", in order to knock him out of the campaign'.[71] It seems unlikely the poisoners could have been so precise. In December, TCDD dioxin poisoning was confirmed after further tests at the Rudolfinerhaus and three other laboratories in Germany and the Netherlands, although Rybachuk instead referred to the mycotoxin T-2, used in 'Yellow Rain', the Soviet version of Agent Orange, that was allegedly used for chemical warfare in both South-East Asia and Afghanistan. If it was fat-soluble dioxin, it could have been administered via fatty foods such as lard, fish (sushi), beer or another Ukrainian favourite, *smetana* (a yoghurt-like addition to soup), some, but not all, of which were on Satsiuk's reported version of the menu. As little as five milligrams would have been lethal. Dioxin collects in the fatty tissues of the sweat glands, which would explain Yushchenko's terrible acne-like appearance. It acts late, however. If Yushchenko had died in September, the later symptoms might never have appeared, and dioxin poisoning would never been diagnosed. It was also alleged that Yushchenko may have been poisoned twice, with the September dose coming second as a trigger for an earlier, more subtle dose administered on an unknown occasion; or that he was given two poisons on 5 September, with Alpha-Fetoprotein used to speed up (and disguise) the effects of the dioxin.

A strange sequel occurred on the eve of the second round of the election, when police reportedly found a car outside Yushchenko's headquarters, loaded with two kilograms of plastic explosive and a remote-control detonator. Two men who were later arrested (Russians travelling on false passports, says Rybachuk) supposedly told police that unnamed officials in Moscow promised them $200,000 to assassinate Yushchenko. Despite the publicity given to this saga on Channel 5, there were obvious holes in this particular story The plotters supposedly had to ask where Yushchenko's headquarters were located, which seems unprofessional to say the least. They are located near the American embassy, which is always crawling with security. It was entirely possible that the SBU had played up the story, hoping to blur its role in the September poisoning.

On 24 December 2004, the Channel 5 programme 'Secret Zone' broadcast a secret conversation, which had supposedly taken place between two agents of the Russian Federal Security Service (FSB), the main successor to the KGB, one in Kiev and the other in Moscow, which had allegedly been leaked by the patriotic part of the SBU. Initially, the conversation also seemed implausible, particularly because the two agents constantly feigned surprise. The extract that follows is translated without comment,[72] but was linked to the alternative version of the poisoning, which was circulating in Kiev. This claimed that the attack had been ordered by Kuchma's chief of staff, Medvedchuk, and one of Yanukovych's key allies, deputy prime minister Andrii Kliuiev, who enlisted help from their Russian contacts, one of whom was supposedly the political technologist Gleb Pavlovskii. According to this theory, Satsiuk was not informed about the poisoning, and may even have been set up.[73] The poison was supplied via Satsiuk's cook or by a waiter, both of whom had fled abroad.

The Yushchenko team continued to blame the (old) regime for initiating the plot. In January, the new interior minister Yurii Lutsenko claimed: 'We know who brought the poison through the border, which parliamentary deputy transported it, which official brought it to the place of the crime, and who mixed it with the food.'[74] It was also intimated that the dioxin could be 'fingerprinted' so as to establish the precise laboratory it came from, out of an extremely narrow list homing in on Russia, and that the complicated poisons used bore the hallmarks of the KGB's infamous 'Laboratory No. 12'. Hinting so openly at Russian involvement, however, may well have been a reflection of the practical difficulties involved in taking such an investigation to a conclusion. By the spring they were backtracking.

The following conversation is not dated, but is clearly supposed to have taken place after the poisoning.

MOSCOW: All the specialists say this is totally delirious.

KIEV: I predicted this earlier. . .

MOSCOW: That they will use. . .

KIEV: They will. And they will turn [the blame] on Russia.

MOSCOW: In general, totally delirious.

KIEV: Not only that, the Americans will also turn [the blame] on Russia.

MOSCOW: I'll say. Although, as far as I understand, they too are sick of Yushchenko.

KIEV: Possibly. . .

MOSCOW: And more likely than not, if they did it, it was them.

KIEV: Aleksandr Ivanovich. There are several options. The moment Russia says that it had nothing to do with it, there are people with significant evidence. And that Pavlovskii will have to run pretty far.

MOSCOW: What are Pavlovskii's people associated with. . .

KIEV: In this matter?

MOSCOW: . . .with Yushchenko, could they have poisoned him?

KIEV: No, [he's the] author of the idea. The author of the idea and the organiser. The ideological inspiration, do you understand?

MOSCOW: What's with you? That wanker proposed such an idea?

KIEV: Absolutely.

MOSCOW: And there are people who can confirm this?

KIEV: Yes, who can confirm this. Not in the press, but at the prosecutor's, well, with depositions.

MOSCOW: Really?

KIEV: Absolutely, what did you think?

MOSCOW: Are you saying this seriously?

KIEV: Absolutely. Not only that, the people are abroad. Spirited away, as required. When I say there was a large-scale operation under way, I'm not making journalistic jokes.

MOSCOW: So right now you are saying serious things about that plan, because up till now all that was a joke. Nobody knows about this.

KIEV: Well, how would that be funny?

MOSCOW: But absolutely no one knows about these tricks of Pavlovskii.

KIEV: The point was to make his [Yushchenko's] face ugly, to disfigure the Messiah, and to brand him with the mark of the beast.

MOSCOW: Lord! My God! So he gave this assignment to someone?

KIEV: Yes.

MOSCOW: Mama Mia!

KIEV: As for details, I don't know whether he hired retired or active special operations operatives to prepare this.

MOSCOW: Probably retired.

KIEV: That I cannot say.

MOSCOW: It's just totally delirious!

KIEV: And so, doesn't it resemble . . . cynically-speaking.

MOSCOW: No, but that rascal, he is capable of anything, I have no doubt. But to come up with such a thing.

KIEV: But, excuse me, to split up the country into two parts, having provoked a civil war – is that worse, better, or what?

MOSCOW: That is even worse.

KIEV: Cynically-speaking, that's right.

MOSCOW: Well, it still fits into the framework of some sorts of political things . . . but in general this is already some sort of criminal act.

KIEV: Yes.

MOSCOW: Well, well.

KIEV: And violence in polling stations, that's also a criminal act.

MOSCOW: Well, yes.

KIEV: The organisation of violence – that's [his] position. To squeeze, to create fear, so that people are afraid to take a step. To breeze into town and intimidate [people] publicly and ostentatiously – that's his style.

MOSCOW: And the premier [Yanukovych] knows about this, no?

KIEV: In 99 per cent of cases, the premier didn't even guess. He just sincerely feels deceived.

MOSCOW: Simply, because I watch how he speaks [in public] and I see that he sincerely feels himself deceived.

KIEV: 99 per cent of the time he knew nothing.

MOSCOW: Then who in his headquarters coordinated these things with Pavlovskii?

KIEV: Kliuiev, Prutnik.

MOSCOW: Those two wankers?

KIEV: Yes. Well, there are also a few other people of lesser calibre.

MOSCOW: Well, understood, but they were like the executors. But they had to have coordinated with someone? With those two?

KIEV: He didn't coordinate, he came up with ideas. Glebushka [Pavlovskii] came up with ideas, and they picked up on them.

MOSCOW: And implemented them?

KIEV: Well, to the extent of their abilities. The idea of the mark of the beast, he took part directly in carrying it out, found specialists.

MOSCOW: They'd gone out of their minds! He, none other than Pavlovskii?

KIEV: Yes.

MOSCOW: Himself?

KIEV: Well, I don't know, through someone.

MOSCOW: Well, he found specialists, by himself, to complete the assignment. O My! There's a fine present for you!

KIEV: I tell you honestly, this [blame] will be turned on the Russian Special Services. And then we will have to wash ourselves here – no one will look at Pavlovskii even through a microscope. The [blame] will be turned on state politics.

MOSCOW: Lord, My God!

KIEV: That trump is still up the sleeve.

MOSCOW: And what – does Yushchenko know about all this?

KIEV: Naturally.

MOSCOW: And with evidence?

KIEV: Now that I cannot say. Informed – yes.

MOSCOW: But information can also be false. And what evidence?

KIEV: He is informed and intends at some opportunity to release this information.

MOSCOW: And who are these people that [they] say were spirited out of the country, they're who – the executors?

KIEV: People, who took part. . .

MOSCOW: In the discussion?

KIEV: In the process. At the executive level. It's the devil's work.

MOSCOW: Oh my! That's how it is. . .

KIEV: When we were spraying spit in relation to Pavlovskii, we should have foreseen, understanding what was going on, predicted the scale. . .

MOSCOW: Well, honestly speaking, with all my experience, I could never imagine that someone would go for this.

KIEV: It's not surprising at all. Unfortunately, this is typical of those guys. For sure, Gelman could have thought of it. This is absolutely normal for them. Such approaches. Both Gelman and Shuvalov. Markov is simply stupid, so he could never even imagine that sort of thing, but they are definitely cut from the same cloth. But, you understand, they are not poisoning people. They are poisoning natives, cannibals.

MOSCOW: Lord, My God! Fine. . .

KIEV: I hope, of course, that this card will not be put into play, and held up as an object of inadequate reaction by Russia.

----

By 2004, the Ukrainian authorities were used to fixing elections, having had some good practice in 1999 and 2002. This time, however, the stakes were much higher. The existence of a strong opposition and the prospect of real change produced a much dirtier fight. A decision had been taken that Yanukovych would win, whatever it took, but it was not necessarily a decision that could be implemented. There were too many rival plans at work, although the dangerous decision to play east against west, both within Ukraine and more generally, had put Yanukovych within sight of a possible victory. But this was still not certain. Too many of the authorities' other methods were too obviously cynical. As Sergei Markov later said of the pensions hike: 'Yanukovych needed to have a social idea behind this initiative to make it work, but there wasn't any.'[75] The authorities would rely on so-called 'administrative technology', that is, crude fraud, albeit inventively marshalled, to close the gap.

# 6

# The Fraud

The authorities were badly prepared for the first round on 31 October. They thought they were going to win, and that only the minimum amount of fraud would be necessary to achieve that result. Yanukovych had been ahead in the polls for almost a month, after the doubling of the state pension.[1] If the poll could have been held sooner, Yanukovych might have come out ahead, but the blatant largesse soon pushed inflation up and the exchange rate down (and would ultimately leave a gap in the budget of UAH8 billion, some 5 per cent of GDP), which scared off other, equally pragmatic voters in east Ukraine, who well remembered the hyper-inflation of the early 1990s.[2] The Yanukovych camp had other reasons for confidence, however. The economy in general, at least in terms of headline figures, was doing well. Their man was prime minister. The opposition had little media or money. To their way of thinking, the job had been done.

The Zoriany tapes record the Yanukovych special team's actions and reactions on the day of the first round vote. Panic sets in as it becomes obvious that Yushchenko is clearly in the lead.[3]

EPISODE ONE, 31 OCTOBER, 00:59: Serhii Larin, a Rada deputy and the leader of Yanukovych and Kliuiev's Party of the Regions, is talking with an unidentified speaker.

UNKNOWN: The turnout's low. It's terrible! Odesa, Mykolaïv, Dnipro [Dnipropetrovsk] and Kharkiv.
LARIN: All right. That will do. Don't say anything on air.

EPISODE TWO, 31 OCTOBER, 16:15.

UNKNOWN: (speaking on Larin's phone) Get everyone ready for action [turnout in Odesa is 48 per cent].
UNKNOWN 2: That's what I'm doing. I understand everything.
UNKNOWN: In Odesa, the turnout must be 80–85 [per cent]. You understand?
UNKNOWN 2: Yes.
UNKNOWN: Do whatever you like.
UNKNOWN 2: I understand.

EPISODE THREE, 31 OCTOBER, 17:07.

UNKNOWN: [Kliuiev?] Why is the turnout so low in Donetsk and Dnipropetrovsk oblasts?
LARIN: We'll take care of that.
UNKNOWN: Do it quick.
LARIN: We're raising the turnout.
UNKNOWN: Do it.

How did they do it? The secret 'Zoriany' team were linked by fibre optic cables to the CEC, so that they could intercept and manipulate the results in Yanukovych's favour. Suspicions were aroused by the long time it took for protocols sent by e-mail from local election commissions to arrive at the CEC – and by the fact that they would then all arrive in a rush. What was initially thought to be a 'transit server' was in fact simple trespass. Assisted by CEC personnel, the 'moles' had access to the CEC's own transit database, where the electronic versions of every local protocol were stored. This intranet remained intact – it wasn't hacked into by some outside server. But as the Zoriany team had access, they could simply alter the results electronically. The data then went to the CEC central server, where it was checked, summarised and placed online at www.cvk.gov.ua. The hackers then destroyed the CEC transit database completely, to prevent identification of their remote access point.[4] However, other evidence was discovered on 1 December, when a lorry laden with snow was stopped by chance as it tried to pass unnoticed through the cordon of demonstrators outside the presidential administration. Underneath the snow were piles of documents, some listing election committee members against receipts for payments of $100 a time.[5]

EPISODE FOUR, 2 NOVEMBER, 10:19: the conspirators express their thanks
to Serhii Katkov, their key mole in the CEC (see page 3), as the gap has
just changed 'to our advantage'. Kliuiev is talking with yet another
Rada deputy from the Party of Regions, Oleh Tsariov.

SERHII KLIUIEV: I'll tell you what, Oleh, we need to give that bloke
[Katkov] some dosh, because if he hadn't reacted in good time and
hadn't phoned us. . .
TSARIOV: I haven't got anything on me.
KLIUIEV: Come and see me at my office, give him a *trioshka** and say
thank you. If he hadn't given us a bell, we'd be really in the shit.

EPISODE FIVE, 3 NOVEMBER, 22:35: the two bosses of Ukrainian Telecom
refer to how the deed was done, and how their tracks must be covered.

LIVOCHKIN: I've just sent you a message. The thing that worries me is that
we should 'sweep up' there and call it a day.
DZEKON: We've 'swept up' everything there . . . Everything there's closed
up. We disconnected everything for the night. Everything's all right.

The Zoriany team, however, were just the last link in the chain. The election fraud had been planned since the spring and most of the other 'technologies' also depended on the complicity of the CEC and its equivalent
local election commissions. This could be achieved with bribes or intimidation, but the proliferation of covertly financed 'technical candidates' was
thought by the technologists to be a more reliable method. These might
serve other purposes, perhaps as *agents provocateurs* or as 'flies' to nibble at
opponents' support, but most were designed solely to exploit the provision
in the electoral law for each candidate to nominate 'trusted persons' to local
election committees. There were twenty-three candidates in the election. As
discussed in Chapter 5, four were 'nationalist projects' and three were hired
guns on the far left. There were also six technical candidates with no other
apparent role: Mykola Hrabar, Ihor Dushyn, Vladislav Kryvobokov,
Volodymyr Nechyporuk, Mykola Rohozhynskyi and Hryhorii Chernysh.
All were so obscure there will be no need to mention them again. All were

* *trioshka*: literally 'a three'. Slang for some kind of threefold payment,
which could refer to $3,000 or similar larger amount, a BMW three
series, or even a three-bedroom flat.

polling less than 1 per cent, but were able to nominate the same number of 'their' supporters (i.e. Yanukovych's supporters) to the committees as the main candidates – that is, between 400 and 450 each. Yanukovych could therefore count on thirteen out of twenty-three 'trust' groups, an estimated 60–65 per cent of all members of election committees at all levels, to do his bidding.[6] This percentage was increased where necessary by arbitrarily disqualifying opposition representatives at the last minute, or by physically preventing them from doing their work. The election process was therefore corrupted at an early stage.

Come voting day, blatant intimidation was therefore possible at polling stations 'controlled' by this method, as were other so-called 'technologies', such as padding the turnout with 'dead souls' (the impersonation of former voters, voters who were actually alive during previous elections) and 'cookies' (extra ballot papers). One 'technology' that had been used before was known as the 'carousel'. The fact that blatant cheating is dubbed 'technology' and its various sub-genres given specific names is, of course, highly indicative. Individuals were organised in teams and handed pre-marked (fake) ballots. At every voting station they visited they would ask for a new (genuine) ballot, deposit the fake, and move on. According to one estimate, if each member of the carousel made ten votes each, this would have added half a million votes to Yanukovych's total.[7]

Another abuse involved voting away from polling stations. The fraudsters were now keen to use any ruse to get ballot boxes where they could be more easily stuffed, or where votes would be cast as 'advised', and this was most easily done by the abuse of absentee voting provisions for the old and infirm. Levels of absentee voting in the east and south were massive – and far exceeded any plausible number of real invalids, even given the dire public health crisis throughout Ukraine. In polling station number 76, constituency number 59, in Donetsk, for example, 748 out of 2,248 voters (a whopping 33.2 per cent) supposedly cast their ballots at home, and only five of these were for Yushchenko.[8] In four out of six constituencies in Mykolaïv (numbers 129–132, the towns of Mykolaïv and Bashtanka) absentee voting was 30 per cent.[9] A total of 1.5 million absentee ballots were cast in all.

Another 'innovation' for 2004 was the so-called 'electoral tourism' referred to Chapter 1 (see page 6), the mass transport of activists by bus and special trains from one polling station to another for repeat voting. Normally, everyone in Ukraine votes where they are registered. Traditionally, those away from home, on temporary visits, etc., should have a paper to this effect inserted by the interior ministry in their internal passport to show officials when they vote at another polling station. However, in May 2004, the hardline interior minister, Mykola Bilokon, issued a secret directive that this practice would not be necessary at the 2004 elections, opening the door to a variety of frauds that allowed between 1.5 and 2 million fraudulent votes into the system.[10] The most notorious involved the special trains provided by the railways minister, Hryhorii Kirpa. When Our Ukraine deputy Mykola Tomenko raised the issue of the trains in the Rada on 19 November, the deputy prosecutor, Volodymyr Dereza, wrote back that: 'the total number of additional trains put in use inside Ukraine by the Southern, Odesa, Southwestern, Prydniprovska, and Donetsk railways [all sub-regions of southern and eastern Ukraine] over the period of October–November 2004 was 125'. The prosecutor's office also determined that UAH10.6 million (about $2 million) was paid for the use of the trains, which 'were ordered and paid for by the regional branches of the Party of the Regions and of the SDPU(o), [Russian] Orthodox associations, various enterprises, and some others'. The trains also carried huge amounts of anti-Yushchenko propaganda.[11]

Some of the voters used in this way were paid, but some were willing to provide their services free of charge, indicating a definite anti-Yushchenko sentiment in the east, but also the peculiarities of local political culture. As the Yanukovych vote was already high in the east, electoral tourism was most important in central Ukraine. Buses and trains from the east went mainly to regions such as Poltava, where two-thirds of the local election commission was under the control of Yanukovych and local authorities could be relied on to cooperate. Significantly, central Ukraine was the region where the Yushchenko vote rose most clearly between rounds two and three – not just because the mood had changed, but because the special trains were no longer running.[12] In the three oblasts adjacent to the east, Yushchenko's vote went up from 69 per cent to 79.4 per cent in Sumy, from 47.1 per cent to 63.4 in Kirovohrad, and from 60.9 per cent to 66 per cent in Poltava. His vote also rose sharply in Transcarpathia, from 55 per cent to 67.5 per cent, as the traditional local 'bosses' from the SDPU(o) were unable to boss the voters quite so forcefully in the third round.[13]

Conversely, in areas of strong Yushchenko support, where the local electoral commissions were still 'controlled' by the authorities, inaccuracies were deliberately added to voting lists. These might include a wrong address, patronymic or surname. Profuse apologies would be made to the affected voters when they came to the polling station on election day, but they wouldn't be allowed to vote. Within a given constituency this process was carried out randomly, but it was only done in pro-Yushchenko regions, where the assumption was that not too many of the excluded were likely to want to vote for Yanukovych.

In non-controlled stations, the *khustynka* ('kerchief') method was used. Yanukovych people would wear some distinguishing mark, a kerchief or suchlike, to guide their supporters (both their natural supporters and those under various forms of duress) to cast their votes, usually on behalf of the dead souls recorded on a list kept by the man or woman in the kerchief, in their part of the polling booth.

The authorities had much less success with their campaign to drum up votes for Yanukovych amongst Ukrainians in Russia. The Kremlin organised a blatantly pro-Yanukovych congress of Ukrainians in Moscow on 8 October 2004 and talked excitedly of gaining 200,000 extra votes. However, once the Ukrainian courts had tightened up on registration requirements, it was actually easier for Ukrainians living in the West to vote, as they tended to have the right documentation. (2.9 million ethnic Ukrainians live in Russia, having moved in Tsarist or Soviet times. Only Ukrainian citizens could vote, however, and too many of these worked in Russia's black economy.) Only four polling stations were eventually opened in Russia, and a total of 13,000 ballot papers were issued.[14] In the second round, 93,496 Ukrainians voted abroad, with Yushchenko having a slight edge (54.7 per cent to 43.4 per cent).

### Polling 'Technology'

According to Volodymyr Paniotto of KIIS, 'all these operations enabled [the Yanukovych camp] to forge the results of the election [by] up to 10–15 per cent . . . [across] the whole of Ukraine'.[15] Simple fraud needed a cover story, however, which was supplied in this instance by so-called *reitingovyi pressing*. In October 2004, Yanukovych was temporarily ahead in the polls, supposedly because of sympathy for his unfortunate egg-related accident and, rather more plausibly, because of his belated promises to east Ukrainian voters and the dramatic doubling of the state pension. An innovation that year, however, involved 'exit poll technology'. As the authorities' scope for possible fraud had been sharply reduced by the independent exit poll released on election night in 2002, this time they conducted rival exit polls of their own.[16] It showed just how bad the situation in Ukraine was that no one was prepared to believe the official results; the real struggle was to establish which version of the parallel exit polls people would be more likely to believe. Obviously, however, the fake exit polls were primed to predict Yanukovych's fake victory.

The (real) 'National Exit Poll' was a giant NGO initiative, which was collaboratively conducted by the Centre for Social and Political Research (SOCIS), KIIS, Social Monitoring, the Razumkov Centre and Democratic Initiatives, although all conducted their polls separately. KIIS and Razumkov ran 'anonymous' polls in which they thought respondents were far more likely to give their true opinion. By this method, KIIS had Yushchenko with a lead over Yanukovych in the first round of 44.8 per cent to 38.1 per cent (later corrected slightly, to 44.6 per cent versus 37.8 per cent), and Razumkov had Yushchenko ahead by 45.1 per cent to 37 per cent. SOCIS had Yushchenko ahead by 42 per cent to 41.1 per cent in an 'open' poll, where voters were more likely to feel as intimidated as they did when they were actually voting. Only Social Monitoring had him trailing by 40.1 per cent to 41.2 per cent.

SOCIS president Mykola Churylov caused a sensation by announcing completely different results on TV at 10:30 pm, now claiming that his figures had Yanukovych ahead by 42.7 per cent to 38.3 per cent.[17] He never produced any physical evidence for this turnaround, and never explained by what methodology he had arrived at such figures, which gave Yanukovych an even bigger fake lead than anything the CEC would manage to concoct. Churylov had clearly been manipulated by the Yanukovych campaign, and his colleagues would later leave the Sociological Association of Ukraine in disgust. A second 'Ukrainian Exit Poll', conducted by the Ukrainian Institute for Social Foundation for Research (a government think tank), the Centre of Political Management, the Institute of Sociology and others, initially had Yushchenko ahead by 42 per cent to 40 per cent, but also reversed it later on, to claim he was behind by 39.3 per cent to Yanukovych's 43 per cent.[18] Finally, the agency Public Opinion Foundation (FOM), behind which stood Russian money and Pavlovskii's FEP, failed to release its results. It claimed to have abandoned its poll because of an excessive number (over 40 per cent) of interviewees refusing to state a preference; although it leaked a false report that it had Yushchenko on 39.2 per cent and Yanukovych on 43.5 per cent. It was later suggested by the Ukrainian Marketing Group which had helped carry out the poll that, on the contrary, their research had provisionally placed Yushchenko on 43.5 per cent and Yanukovych on 38 per cent.[19] Pavlovskii, in other words, had used very similar figures to those actually obtained, but had switched the candidates' names.[20] The parallel count organised by the Yushchenko camp had their man on 40.2 per cent and Yanukovych on 38.9 per cent.[21]

## The First Result

The count also went badly for the authorities. Administrative resources failed to deliver a fake vote in line with their fake polls. The more votes that were counted, the closer Yushchenko came to first place, even in the official results. According to the chief presidential consultant, Liudmila Hrebeniuk, Yushchenko was ahead all the time.[22] Counting was suspended twice as Yushchenko threatened to surge ahead; first on 1 November, with 94.24 per cent of the votes counted, and nearly all the late-reporting areas, mainly in busy Kiev and the rural west, likely to favour Yushchenko.[23] During the night, an alleged 50,000 to 150,000 votes from Kiev and Kirovohrad were lost.[24] Counting was invalidated (subject to appeal) in three constituencies: 200 and 203 in Cherkasy, and 100 in Kirovohrad, where Yushchenko had led by 25,000. Other, 'reserve' ballots were allegedly substituted.

As a result, when counting resumed the next day, 2 November, the gap widened for the first and only time – then began to close again. A second, much longer, suspension was therefore ordered, with Yushchenko about to take the lead. The Zoriany tapes record the background work during the suspension. 'Valerii's' surname is unknown, Serhii Kliuiev was a Yanukovych fixer, and Serhii Kivalov was head of the Central Election Commission or CEC – see Chapter 1. The authorities had three types of *kompromat* on Kivalov, relating to fake degrees handed out when he was head of the Odesa Law Academy, the business dealings of his daughter Tetiana and her company Vivat-Femida!, and some sweetheart land deals.

*Progress of the first round count*

| | | | | | | | | |
|---|---|---|---|---|---|---|---|---|
| Percentage of bulletins counted, 1/11 | 50.27 | 63.36 | 73.48 | 81.42 | 84.32 | 91.76 | 93.85 | 94.24 |
| Yanukovych | 45.48 | 43.28 | 42.78 | 41.82 | 41.43 | 40.39 | 40.14 | 40.12 |
| Yushchenko | 34.25 | 36.26 | 36.64 | 37.53 | 37.92 | 38.90 | 39.14 | 39.15 |
| Percentage of bulletins counted, 2/11 | 94.89 | 95.38 | 96.60 | 97.67 | | | | |
| Yanukovych | 40.22 | 40.34 | 40.03 | 39.88 | | | | |
| Yushchenko | 39.01 | 38.88 | 39.16 | 39.22 | | | | |
| Percentage of bulletins counted, 10/11 | 100 | | | | | | | |
| Yanukovych | 39.26 | | | | | | | |
| Yushchenko | 39.87 | | | | | | | |

Source: www.cvk.gov.ua and the running score kept at www2.pravda.com.ua/archive/2004/October/31/cvk.shtml

EPISODE SIX, 9 NOVEMBER 2004, 17:34.

VALERII: I called and wanted to consult; today is the day of final resolution. Are all actions agreed? Is this true?

KLIUIEV: Yes, what results do you have?

VALERII: Let me see. Yushchenko has a 0.55 per cent advantage right now. But if we can wait a bit longer, tomorrow the courts' decisions will come into force and we will be leading. I tried to reach you, but your assistant took the phone. Later Serhii Vasylovych [Kivalov] has invited us round. I asked Misha to call [Stepan] Havrish [then Yanukovych's representative on the CEC]; Havrish said 'don't get involved, it's already agreed'. Kivalov also told us that 'everything is agreed; the councils have been called.' I know that you also participated in the council, but I also know that I need to receive an order from you directly.

KLIUIEV: That's correct.

VALERII: So here is the plan: we start the conference in a slow manner at six, receive some appeals, speak about methodology and simply stretch time to go into the next day. We need to wait until tomorrow, because tomorrow the Cherkasy court's decisions will come into force.

KLIUIEV: Districts number 200 and number 203.

UNKNOWN: Exactly; this is the exact number of votes we need to lead.

KLIUIEV: Great! Everything is correct. Start the conference today and slowly proceed into tomorrow. Well done. It's good that you called me, thank you.

When the official result was finally announced on 10 November, it was finally admitted that Yushchenko was in front, but it was claimed that he was only leading by 39.9 per cent to 39.3 per cent. The CEC failed to cover some tracks, even on its official website, where in seven regions (Crimea, Donetsk, Dnipropetrovsk, Odesa, Rivne, Cherkasy and Chernihiv) it recorded more votes cast than ballot papers handed out – 129,596 in total.[25] The long time taken to fix the result also had a paradoxical side-effect: Yushchenko was now psychologically in front just before the second round.

Oleksandr Moroz was declared third, with 5.8 per cent, and Petro Symonenko fourth, on 5 per cent. The Communist leader Symonenko scored an implausible 3.3 per cent in the traditional red stronghold of Donetsk (less than his national average) and only 5.8 per cent in the neighbouring mining region of Luhansk, compared to a massive 86.7 per cent for Yanukovych (80 per cent in Luhansk) and a miniscule 2.9 per cent for Yushchenko (4.5 per cent in Luhansk). This was highly suspicious. One source claims that: 'Almost 670,000 [votes] in Donetsk and Luhansk were added to Yanukovych with their [the Communist leaders'] approval.'[26] Nationally, Vitrenko won 1.5 per cent, Kinakh 0.9 per cent, and Yakovenko 0.8 per cent. Again, however, the fake candidates that the Yanukovych team wanted to do well nationally, were not allowed to do well in the Donbas. Despite being supposedly the most anti-Yushchenko candidates in the most anti-Yushchenko region, Vitrenko was only recorded at 0.8 per cent in Donetsk and Yakovenko at only 0.6 per cent.

Nationally, all the other candidates scored less than 0.5 per cent and 2 per cent voted against all. The turnout was 74.9 per cent. The minor candidates had helped shift the *dramaturgiia* in Yanukovych's favour, but they were squeezed by the 'polarisation scenario'. Their overall vote was too low to provide the cover story that their endorsement of Yanukovych could account for his victory in the second round. Moreover, Yushchenko was able to secure an agreement with Moroz for his support in round two, despite the flirtation of part of his party with the SDPU(o), albeit at the price of agreeing to a package of constitutional reforms (see pages 148–53). Kinakh also backed Yushchenko. Yanukovych was, of course, supported by the faux-leftists Symonenko, Vitrenko and Yakovenko.

### The Second Round

The authorities therefore upped the ante for the second round on 21 November. The honest exit pollsters from KIIS were offered first double, then quadruple their previous payment, that is, $100,000, to defect with SOCIS, but declined (this at least showed that Ukraine was not as ruthlessly authoritarian as some post-Soviet states).[27] This time, the KIIS–Razumkov poll, with a massive 15,000 interviews, had Yushchenko as the clear winner, with 53.7 per cent to 43.3 (this was later re-weighted to 53 to 44), with 3 per cent against both. Even the tainted 'People's Choice' poll undertaken by SOCIS and Social Monitoring had Yushchenko ahead by 49.7 per cent to 46.7 per cent. The authorities were therefore much more reliant than they had been in the first round on the efforts of the Zoriany team, which this time interfered much more blatantly in the counting process. They also fast-forwarded the count, so as to catch potential protesters on the nap. A lead was established early for Yanukovych, which Yushchenko was apparently unable to close. This time there would be no dramatic closing of the gap. With 65.6 per cent of the votes counted, Yanukovych led by 49.5 per cent to 46.9 per cent, and the gap then barely changed. Whereas the count for round

Change in voter turnout compared to 31 October

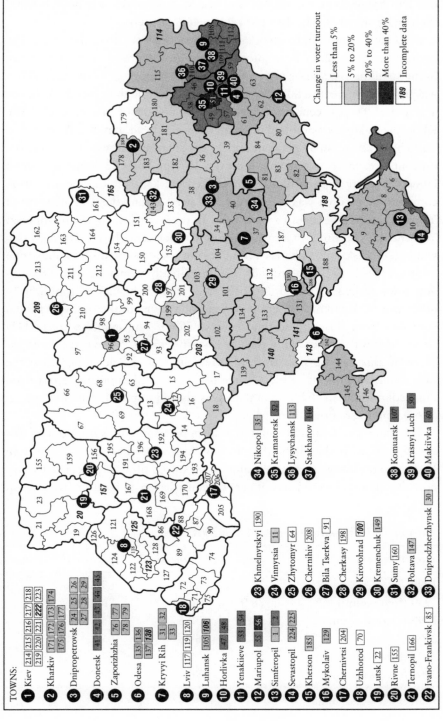

Source: adapted from www.ourukraine.org./newsletter/issue58/24November 2004

one had dragged out for almost two weeks, Yanukovych was now declared the winner overnight, by 49.5 per cent to 46.6 per cent.

It seemed immediately obvious how the deed was done, however. The opposition had already been informed that the key fraud would take place in the small hours, and be concentrated in east Ukraine.[28] National turnout was up by 5 per cent to 80.7 per cent. In east Ukraine the official result was a massive 92 per cent to 6 per cent in favour of Yanukovych. The KIIS–Razumkov exit poll had Yanukovych well ahead, but Yanukovych and Yushchenko were on 84 per cent and 13 per cent, respectively. Falsifying the turnout was more important, however. In Yanukovych's home region of Donetsk, where Yushchenko's supporters were kept off the local election commission, turnout was supposedly 96.7 per cent and the vote in favour of Yanukovych 96.2 per cent to 2 per cent. In three constituencies in Donetsk, Yushchenko's recorded vote was a mere 0.6 per cent. In the Donbas as a whole (Donetsk and Luhansk), Yanukovych's vote went up by almost one million votes between the rounds. He had already won a massive 2.88 million votes in the first round. Now the CEC claimed he had 3.71 million. In other words, Yanukovych's entire margin of victory in the overall national vote was from this implausible increase alone. The map (see page 115) shows how turnout soared in the key eastern regions.[29] The utter implausibility of this can be seen from all previous voting behaviour, when the turnout in Donetsk was always *below* that in west Ukraine and, apart from the second round in 1999, when there was also widespread fraud in the east, also *below* the national average.

The Yanukovych faction countered the opposition's objections to the official figures with the claim that two million votes had been falsified in Yushchenko's favour in west Ukraine. It produced no hard evidence to support this claim, however, except general statistics on emigration, to back up

*Turnout in Ukrainian elections, 1998–2004*

| Turnout (per cent) | Lviv | Donetsk | National Average |
| --- | --- | --- | --- |
| 1998 | 77 | 63.1 | 69.6 |
| 1999 (first round) | 78.9 | 66.1 | 70.2 |
| 1999 (second round) | 85.7 | 77.5 | 73.8 |
| 2002 | 67.8 | 64.6 | 65.2 |
| 2004 (first round) | 80.8 | 78.1 | 74.9 |
| 2004 (second round) | 83.5 | 96.7 | 80.9 |

Source: www.cvk.gov.ua

the claim that many west Ukrainians were out of the country at the time of the vote, working in Polish sweat shops, on construction sites in Portugal and as nannies in Italy.[30] The accusation also ignores the basic point that Yushchenko's supporters simply did not control the levers of administration in the west and centre of Ukraine. The key powers at election time were the local governors, who since 1994 had been directly appointed by the president (Kuchma), and the Territorial Election Committees (TECs), nearly all of which were controlled by the authorities via the 'technical candidate' method. West Ukraine, with little local industry of its own, was also notorious for oligarchs 'parachuting' in from further east. Lviv, for example, was largely controlled by the 'Agrarian Party' and the SDPU(o), and Viktor Medvedchuk's brother, Serhii, was head of the local tax administration. Many local politicians had joined the Kuchma gravy train. Bohdan Boiko, for instance, was once head of Ternopil council, but ended up as a fake nationalist in the pay of the SDPU(o). Lviv was where the notorious railways boss Hryhorii Kirpa polished his skills, taking over local sanatoria with a series of offers owners were unable to refuse. He moved to Kiev as a reward for helping to fix the local vote for Leonid Kuchma in 1999.

Just to emphasise the point, four governors who failed to deliver the local vote – even in the west the order was at least 10 per cent for Yanukovych[31] – were dismissed by the supposedly neutral Kuchma after the first round.

On the Zoriany tapes, the following conversations can be heard.

EPISODE SEVEN, 31 NOVEMBER, 20:07.

SERHII LARIN (another deputy from the Party of Regions and a Yanukovych campaign stalwart): Have a word with Inter [the TV company controlled by the SDPU(o)]. They must announce that there are a lot of violations in western Ukraine. Do you have them under control or what?

UNKNOWN: Yes, all right.

31 NOVEMBER, 20:31.

LARIN: The request is this: [TV must say that] lawlessness is rampant in western Ukraine.

UNKNOWN: We've just said that.

LARIN: It has to be put more strongly in the commentaries – like 'it's just unprecedented'.

## Money

Money was, of course, crucial to the campaign. One much-quoted, if well-rounded, figure stemmed from the comment that: 'According to opposition sources, Russia ... supplied half of the $600 million that Yanukovych is spending on his campaign – including a $200 million payment from the Kremlin-controlled energy giant Gazprom.'[32] Gazprom channelled its money through Oil and Gas of Ukraine and the shadow structures coordinated by Prutnik and Kliuiev (see below). The Russian magazine *Profil* put the figure at $900 million, and claimed Vladislav Surkov, the Kremlin deputy chief of staff, personally approved $50 million.[33] Another source claimed $95 million for just the second round.[34] Most estimates for the Yushchenko campaign, on the other hand, were closer to $50 million. Significantly, at least two Russian oligarchs who had been impressed by the Yushchenko government in 1999 to 2001, the oil tycoon Mikhail Fridman, head of the Alfa Group (estimated wealth $5.6 billion, actually born in Lviv in 1964) and the Russian Aluminium boss Oleg Deripaska ($3.3 billion), were contemplating an investment on his side, but both were warned off once the Kremlin made up its mind on one-sided intervention in September 2004. Viktor Vekselberg of TNK–BP (estimated wealth $2.5 billion, born in Drohobych, west Ukraine in 1957) was another Russian 'oligarch' rumoured to be close to Yushchenko.

Even the Yushchenko camp had to be coy about its expenditure, because official spending limits were so low. According to their final disclosures, the Yushchenko campaign spent only UAH16.8 million ($3.2 million), and the Yanukovych team only UAH14.4 million ($2.7 million) on the 2004 election.[35] The unofficial estimates, on the other hand, were simply enormous, even in comparison with American elections, which are costly enough, and get costlier every year. In 2000 George W. Bush spent an official $193 million against Al Gore's $133 million. In 2004, Bush and Kerry between them topped $600 million. It seems astonishing that a Ukrainian campaign could cost anywhere near the same, especially given that the US GDP is 150 times as large as Ukraine's.

The answer is in the disparity of tactics used. The vast majority of campaign spending in America goes on media advertising, especially on TV. Yushchenko's possible $50 million also went mainly on advertising and on maintaining the organisational sinews of a normal campaign. The massive outspend by the Yanukovych side, on the other hand, was typical for the ruling authorities in the former USSR because, not to put too fine a point on it, the money was spent on different things. An entire vote farming industry had to be financed. An army of state officials had to be paid off, from corrupt election officials to hospital managers in Donetsk who closed their half-empty wards and then claimed every bed was occupied by an infirm Yanukovych voter.[36] According to an analysis by the Committee of Voters of Ukraine, no fewer than 85,000 officials were involved in election fraud; that is, one third of the entire 'civil service'.[37] In one city alone, Zaporizhzhia in east Ukraine, documents left on the computer of former local administration boss Volodymyr Berezovskyi (no relation to the Russian tycoon Boris Berezovskii) indicated payments of $8.6 million to officials working for Yanukovych. In addition, special teams and political technologists had to be paid for. Technical candidates and their campaigns had to be financed. (Their anti-Yushchenko propaganda was normally ordered by weight.) The state media machine had to be kept working; the reluctant journalists who eventually rebelled had to be paid off. Trains and buses to transport repeat voters did not come cheap. Finally, the complex cross-subsidies that enmeshed 'official' businesses in 'official' campaigns meant that money could be taken out of campaign funds, as well as put in. Smaller business basically paid tribute, normally by being asked for an advance payment on taxes not due until March 2005 (another reason why the new authorities would face budget problems after the Orange Revolution was over). Bigger businesses would take money out – a certain amount of rake-off was an accepted norm, and the more squeamish needed extra payment in return for their dirty work. And finally, the pensions hike ordered by Yanukovych was so ruinously expensive that some money had to be taken out to pay for that as well.

Most of the spending was channelled through a shadowy company called Donechchyna, although it began to leak funds abroad after the second round. Eduard Prutnik was most often mentioned as the 'coordinator of financial sources'.[38] The most detailed analysis of campaign spending was carried out by the 'Freedom of Choice' coalition of domestic NGOs and was posted on their website, www.coalition.org.ua.[39] Much of its information was based on inside sources, and its calculations are generally accepted as broadly accurate, and not too out of line with the guesstimates cited above.[40]

'Signatures' refers to the collection of the 500,000 voters' signatures necessary to stand in the election the first place. Unscrupulous or plain lazy candidates would farm this tiresome task out to professional collectors. 'Mass actions' are demonstrations, rallies, etc. 'HQs/Staff' are the normal human labour needed in any campaign. 'Regional Press' involves a high percentage of so-called *zakazukha*, that is, paid propaganda dressed up as

*Campaign spending in the 2004 election, millions of US dollars*

|  | Yushchenko | Yanukovych | Moroz | Symonenko | Parliamentary* | Technical# |
|---|---|---|---|---|---|---|
| Signatures | 0.1 | 2 | 0.1 | 0.1 | 1.2 | 3.5 |
| Mass Actions | 4 | 25 | 0 | 0 | 0 | 0 |
| HQs/Staff | 21 | 106 | 14 | 14 | 2 | 3 |
| Regional Press | 3.2 | 13.6 | 1.2 | 1.2 | 0.6 | 0.5 |
| Bigboards | 0.1 | 8.4 | 0 | 0 | 1.5 | 0 |
| Internet | 0.8 | 4.5 | 0.2 | 0.1 | 0.2 | 0.2 |
| Election Control | 3 | 53 | 2 | 1 | ** | ** |
| TV Ads | 4 | 42 | 2 | 2 | 0 | 4 |
| Radio Ads | 4 | 9 | 3 | 2 | 0 | 0 |
| Posters, Leaflets | 5 | 35 | 4 | 4 | 13 | 6 |
| Purchase of Election Commissions (ECs) | 0 | 32 | 0 | 0 | 0 | 0 |
| Provocations | 0 | 30 | 0 | 0 | 0 | 0 |
| Bribing Electors | 0 | 32 | 0 | 0 | 0 | 0 |
| Total | 46.2 | 392.5 | 26.5 | 24.4 | 18.5 | 17.2 |

* After the first four main candidates, the rest are divided into two groups. The first are those considered 'parliamentary' candidates, with some real support: namely, Anatolii Kinakh, Nataliia Vitrenko, Leonid Chernovetskyi, and Kiev mayor Oleksandr Omelchenko.
# All the others are classified as fakes, so-called 'technical', candidates. The author would also consider Vitrenko a fake, but she did once have considerable parliamentary support.
** To Yanukovych.
Source: http://coalition.org.ua/index.php?option=content&task=view&id=119&Itemid=

neutral journalism. Payment was normally given for the journalist's agreement to fix his or her name to a pre-written article. 'Bigboards' is the local term for billboards in big cities or on highways. 'Internet' is self-explanatory. 'Election control' means election monitoring, but also the material aspects of fixing the vote. The figures for TV and radio only include direct advertisements. All candidates produced posters and leaflets; the estimates for Yanukovych are that $25 million was spent on his own materials and $10 million on the black PR attacking Yushchenko, including the notorious 'Bushchenko' series. 'Purchase of ECs', 'provocations' and bribes for voters only have expenditure marked in one column.

'Freedom of Choice's' calculations were for outputs, as it were. Many TV adverts, for example, would have been aired for free on sympathetic channels. So even Yanukovych's massive spending advantage, $392.5 million to $46.2 million, may be an underestimate. The key issue here, of course, is what the Yanukovych campaign did that others didn't do: it had a massive advantage in advertising and in paid stories planted in the regional press, and it had a larger staff. The campaign also spent money on provocations, bribes to voters and election commission officials, and 'the control and conduct of the elections'. Many of its demonstrations had to be paid for, whereas Yushchenko's supporters turned up for free.

The figures for the 'technical' candidates are interesting. Because they were fake candidates, with no pre-established support, getting them the necessary 500,000 signatures from voters was expensive. They also had a strong virtual TV and bigboard presence, but no actual real campaigning costs. Their total spend of $17.2 million can be added to the Yanukovych campaign's $392.5 million.

----

This chapter has set out to demonstrate that the amount of fraud committed on each side was not equal, and that, even at the time, it was not true that 'we have no way of knowing if he [Yushchenko] was robbed of actual victory'.[41] Protesters, who had plenty of hard evidence, never sought to question why a 96 per cent turnout in Donetsk . . . is proof of electoral fraud. But apparently turnouts of over 80 per cent in areas which support Viktor Yushchenko are not.'[42] The authorities, however, had been caught in the act. Would they pay the price?

# The Protest

The mass protests watched around the world after the Ukranian election were obviously pre-planned, but then so was the fraud that led to them. Neither is there anything suspicious about how quickly the opposition reacted. They knew what was coming and they knew they would have to act fast – Yanukovych would come within a whisker of being declared the formal winner within three days of the second round vote on 21 November. According to several sources, both sides expected demonstrations, and assumed that they would probably be bigger than the 'Ukraine Without Kuchma' campaign in 2001, but that they would attract no more than 60,000 to 70,000 protesters.[1] Pora's leaders hoped to supply 15,000 of their own.[2] Tymoshenko caused a storm by saying society was 'inadequately' prepared to protest. And it was getting pretty cold, falling from −1°C at the start of the week to −7°C at its end. The authorities expected a tent city, but they had seen those off before. They had no real contingency plans, but they assumed that the deck was sufficiently stacked and the population sufficiently cowed for them to quell a demonstration without trouble.

There had been several practice runs, dating as far back as May – particularly a big rally in July, which attracted 30,000 to 60,000 protesters. Nevertheless, numbers were never high enough really to frighten a regime that, psychologically, at least, always thought in terms of a 'Romanian scenario' as its likely end – namely the violent overthrow of the Ceausescus in December 1989 and their summary execution on Christmas Day. It could only think in terms of triumph or implosion. And before 22 November, the opposition weren't exactly massing at the gates. Even after Zinchenko took over from Bezsmertnyi, the Yushchenko team was being criticised for its passive approach, as a result of which most of the rabble-rousing had been left to Tymoshenko.[3] An estimated 70,000 welcomed Yushchenko home from Austria on 18 September, despite the fact that his absence had only been explained the day before. On 16 October, some 40,000 students from all over Ukraine turned up for a pro-Yushchenko rally in Kiev, during which they passed a mock 'no-confidence vote' in Yanukovych's cabinet. The next Saturday, 23 October, rather more, an estimated 50,000 at least, attended the 'Force of the People against Lies and Falsification' rally that ended up outside the headquarters of the CEC. The provocation with the militia (see page 82) was the kind of thing that happened all the time before the foreign media unexpectedly arrived in Kiev *en masse* in the middle of the Orange Revolution. Not surprisingly, therefore, many people expected more of the same after the decisive vote on 21 November.

### The Maidan

The Yushchenko team weren't secretly preparing for revolution. They were prepared to protest, but rather too many were expecting defeat for their plans to be wholehearted. Yushchenko could have called for protests after the first round, but he held his fire until the second (though Pora had set up a small protest camp downtown – outside the main university, UKMA, on 6 November). Quite sensibly, he knew he had to let matters take their course. Slightly more cynically, his team knew it was the steal itself – which everybody knew the authorities were planning – that would provoke protests. Yushchenko's initial call was for a limited number of protestors to assemble in Kiev's Independence Square, popularly known as the 'Maidan', when the polls closed at 8 p.m. on Sunday 21 November. The rationale at this stage was to gather for the announcement of the exit polls and to undertake a parallel count in public – and it was then assumed that the official count would take several days, if not the nineteen days taken after the first round. On the other hand, Bezsmertnyi had applied with sufficient notice for a 'concert' to be held in the square from 21 November, providing good cover for several options. The stage in the Maidan was therefore built on the Sunday – early, but for a specific purpose. The first tents – not yet actually protest tents – were also set up on the Sunday. There were twenty-five tents for each of Ukraine's twenty-five oblasts. With or without further scaled planning, the crowd that Sunday night comprised between 25,000 and 30,000 people. Some have called this 'premature protest' on Yushchenko's part, the first step in a *coup d'état*, and have accused his side of never intending to accept the official results, whatever they were. But at the time, this was a carefully calibrated move. In any case, as everyone expected a massive fraud, it would be surprising to expect the opposition simply to sit back and take it. (The Georgian protest was more controversial, as it used a partial parallel vote to discredit the official results *before* they were

Kiev, showing the main events of the Orange Revolution

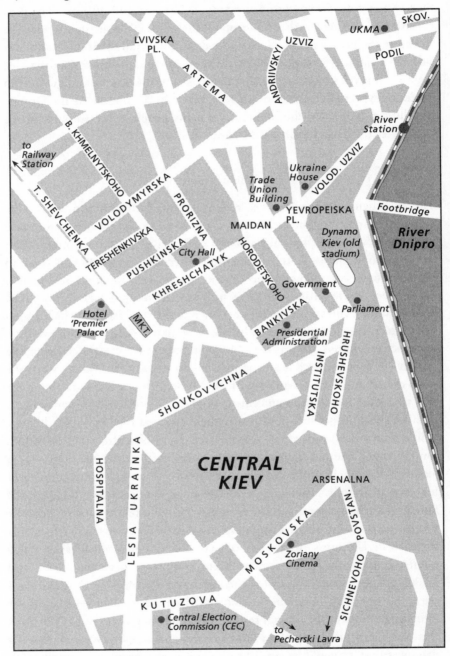

Source: adapted from Tim Burford, Hiking Guide to Poland and the Ukraine (Chalfont St Peter: Bradt, 1994).

announced.) After the Sunday night gathering, most people went home (see below). The situation was hardly revolutionary at this point.

The real surprise came on the morning of Monday 22 November. Yanukovych was pre-announced as the winner, but the Democratic Initiatives centre was printing leaflets in batches of 100,000, using the KIIS–Razumkov exit poll data to declare, 'Viktor Yushchenko Has Won! By 54 per cent to 43'. According to Zinchenko's deputy, Mykola Martynenko, 'we did not prepare for revolution . . . we asked people to defend their choice. We knew people would come, but did not know that it would be so many' (the word Martynenko used for 'defend', *vidstoiuvaty*, implies 'to stand for a long time').[4] Armed with the leaflets, an estimated 200,000 to 300,000 Kievites skipped work to crowd the Maidan and the adjoining main street, Khreshchatyk, by mid-morning. This was the moment when 'revolution' became an appropriate word, in that everybody's expectations were now confounded. The authorities had miscalculated; the masses surprised everyone with their entrance stage-left, the opposition's pessimism was abruptly challenged, and the world began to sit up and take notice. Sheer numbers already made the initial difference. Suddenly, there was a televisual event. Martynenko claimed that he had talked privately with the Kiev mayor Oleksandr Omelchenko on the Sunday evening, and that he had said: 'If you bring out 100,000 I'm with you, we'll take power in one day! If it'll be 99,000 I won't be with you'.[5] After the Revolution he joined the bandwagon soon enough, but not soon enough for some. Other reports have it that the army had admitted in private that it would defer to anything more than 50,000.

Over the next three days, numbers would be augmented by those arriving by bus and train from west Ukraine, but contrary to the later myth of their disproportionate numbers, west Ukrainians, facing either an overnight train journey or dodgy roads, were simply unable to arrive as spontaneously or as quickly as was claimed. Obviously, however, once they arrived they tended to stay longer, for practical reasons (by the end of the week, there were an estimated 50,000 from the west). Yanukovych's Donetsk team had numbers on their side in east Ukraine, but the epicentre of government, of electoral fraud, and the world media's likely point of interest was the capital, and Kiev city had voted heavily for Yushchenko in the second round (74.7 per cent, even on the official figures). Kiev businesses, small, medium and large, had grown impressively during the economic recovery since 2000, and had begun to resent the influence of the *arriviste* Donetsk elite since Yanukovych had become prime minister, muscling in on real estate and hotel deals, and on Kiev's huge new shopping mall ventures. A drunken cavalcade of

Mercedes down Khreshchatyk to celebrate Yanukovych's appointment back in 2002, with horns honking amid shouts of, 'We are the masters now', had not been a good start.

By Tuesday 23 November, the protest was properly organised, and the Maidan became the centre of events. It also became a proper name, a shorthand, sometimes even an anthropomorphised agent. The 'people' became the 'Maidan', and individual people began speaking in its name. *Maidan* is the Ukrainian word for 'square', a borrowing from Turkish. It was rarely used before 1991 – the Russian word is *ploshchad* – and took some time to catch on thereafter. As a space, however, the Maidan is symbolic of the new Ukraine. In Soviet times, it was a pedestrian and public transport thoroughfare, its underpasses notoriously grotty, the stench of stale urine fortunately masked by dense tobacco smoke. In the late 1990s, these were cleaned up, and a huge underground mall was built beneath. An eclectic mix of kitsch statuary appeared above ground. During the Orange Revolution, the sheer number of people who congregated in the area meant that the metro missed out the Maidan stop, but the mall underneath stayed open. The local McDonalds, at least, sold cheap coffee for the duration. Viewers around the world only saw the crowds above ground, of course.

Yushchenko's campaign team proved better at organising a protest than organising a campaign. Roman Bezsmertnyi came back into his own as the Maidan's main 'commandant', and Our Ukraine businessman Davyd Zhvaniia was the main practical provider of tents, mattresses, food, transport and bio-toilets.[6] He had, indeed, ensured a supply of tents before the event, which Yanukovych supporters latched on to as evidence of a plot, but in the end, there weren't nearly enough to go around. The rest came mainly from donations once the protest got going, and some from the city administration.[7] Yurii Lutsenko, the young Socialist who had been one of the main leaders of the Ukraine Without Kuchma protests in 2001, was the Maidan's political 'DJ'. Soon enough, its other DJs had massive speakers and a plasma TV screen behind them. According to Yushchenko's aide, Oleksandr Tretiakov, speaking in December, the total cost of the Maidan was UAH20 million (about $3.8 million) plus $1 million in US money, nearly all of which was made up from small donations and not a penny of which came from abroad.[8] Thousands of acts of individual kindness kept the protesters going – and were extended to Yanukovych supporters, as well. The food and shelter provided by so many individuals could not be costed. Meanwhile, two firefly websites, www.orange-revolution.org and www.2advantage.net, suggested donating money to Privatbank, part of the Dnipropetrovsk 'clan', instead. Some money, however, allegedly came from the Ukrainian-born Russian citizen Konstantin Grigorishin and from Aleksandr Abramov, whose Evrazholding group had sought to bid for Kryvorizhstal with another Russian company, Severstal.[9]

Contrary to the authorities' expectations, the numbers on the streets continued to expand. In the first three days, this was the opposition's key card; no one in authority was yet defecting to support them, despite some west Ukrainian councils voting to recognise Yushchenko as president. There was a certain falling off of the crowd at night, but not by enough to improve the authorities' physical opportunities for clearing the streets. Numbers became so large that counting was unreliable, but the organisers estimated a maximum number of half a million by the first Saturday, 27 November.[10] Yevhen Marchuk, who still had good contacts and intelligence networks, claimed there were over a million.[11] According to a poll undertaken by KIIS in mid-December, 18.4 per cent of the adult population claimed to have taken part in the protests throughout Ukraine, but this rose considerably in west (35.5 per cent) and west-central Ukraine (30.1 per cent). In Kiev, that would work out at about 800,000 people. More than half (57 per cent) of those taking part in the meetings came from large cities (defined as having a population of more than 100,000). Interestingly, despite the pictures of photogenic young people on the Maidan only 27.5 per cent came from the youngest age group of 18–29 year olds (only slightly more than this group's 22.4 per cent share of the population as a whole) and 23.7 per cent came from the 30–39 age group.[12]

The crowds now occupied much more than the Maidan, spilling over on to most of Khreshchatyk and the adjoining streets. More people did not just mean that more bodies were present. It meant that the social profile of protest got broader and broader – the sons and daughters, even the grandparents, of the militia were now on the streets. The growing numbers also allowed the leaders of the protest to broaden their tactics. The Yushchenko team deliberately sought to disconcert the authorities by planning a surprise a day – as with Tymoshenko's 'theatre of opposition' in 2002. On Tuesday 23 November, Yushchenko's symbolic, but technically meaningless, decision to read out the inauguration oath in parliament took the moral high ground. The international response, particularly Colin Powell's condemnation of the fraud on Wednesday, was more vigorous than expected, especially as the authorities had concentrated on the more ambiguous messages that had previously come from the likes of Donald Rumsfeld. The foreign response was fuelled by the emergence of transcripts of Yanukovych's team, who had been taped in the act of organising the fraud on election day. After a low point on the Wednesday, Thursday 25 November was a key day of transition, with the protestors fanning out to encircle public buildings close to the Maidan.

The opposition used a three-fold division of labour to keep the authorities off guard. Yushchenko mainly took the constitutional high ground, carefully bridging the gap between those who simply demanded that the fraud be recognised and those who demanded he be installed as president. Even after he took the inauguration oath on Tuesday 23 November, Yushchenko was mindful that the enormous numbers on the Maidan meant that his own supporters had been joined by hundreds of thousands of other voters who were more concerned with the threat to democracy in general. Tymoshenko acted as rabble-rouser, returning to a role that could have been tailor-made for her after a sometimes difficult campaign season, and Pora were more radical still. Tymoshenko often seemed rash, calling on the crowds to seize power by taking over airports and railway stations. She also set deadlines, which, when issued to the Supreme Court over impending legal decisions were particularly inappropriate. On Sunday 28 November, she felt confident enough to threaten Kuchma's physical safety. She peppered her speeches with wild talk of there being Russian special forces everywhere in Kiev, and of a rumoured 'insurrection', which she claimed had been sponsored by Medvedchuk. In December, Hryhorii Omelchenko, a deputy from the Tymoshenko bloc, claimed that weapons from the Black Sea Fleet had been transferred to Donetsk, to arm gangs who would descend on Kiev.[13] In private, Tymoshenko rowed with Bezsmertnyi, who accused her of making repression more likely.

But Tymoshenko's job was to maintain the regime's fear of insurrection. The division of labour held. Pora, meanwhile, were given their tent space, but were kept off the stage, and reserved for the potential dirty work. Both the Maidan and Pora obeyed clear rules: no alcohol; stay clear of the police; be on your guard against provocateurs; and, above all, 'do not allow a single violent act'. It was not exactly sex and drugs and rock and roll, but for some, it was two out of the three, and even two engagements were announced on the Maidan.[14] Instructions were even given on how to greet demonstrators from the other side (warmly). One of the most telegenic images of the whole Orange Revolution was of Tymoshenko placing a flower in a militia man's shield (see plate 19), deliberately recycling an iconic gesture from the 1960s. Another was when militia were seen tapping their feet to the music of one of the folk groups who were entertaining the crowd. The closest anybody came to breaking the rules was an attempted break-in at the Rada on Tuesday 30 November. However, Yushchenko and his team pushed the intruders back from the inside.

In private, during nightly debates, there were many who were calling for more direct action – namely to storm, rather than just encircle, the key government buildings. Significantly, this idea did not really originate with Pora, who had chosen a method to stick to, but with Tymoshenko and the more radical members of Yushchenko's camp.[15] There were a few sticky moments when the protests seemed to be losing momentum, but Yushchenko's restraint would, in retrospect, seem wise.

Although Pora were not on the stage in the Maidan, their tactics caught hold. Humour was everywhere and 'daily jokes' were circulated. These don't always translate well, but here goes: 'We have started to live for the better', says the government; 'We are glad for you', reply the people. People latched on to the more gullible parts of the Western media, who were echoing stories of an American 'plot', and embroidered their jackets with 'Made in the USA'. Placards showed Putin waving an orange flag. Most popular were the 'Yanukdoty', which mocked Yanukovych (jokes are *anekdoty* in Ukrainian), especially the mock-ups of his own agit-prop (see plate 4). The Maidan also developed its own language, especially the chants and slogans, which included 'We are together' and 'Together we are many. We will not be defeated!' (*Razom nas bahato. Nas ne podolaty!*) These made obvious sense, but also harked back to the lessons of 2001. 'The World is With Us' was a powerful reminder of the international media presence, that did much to restrain the authorities. In Russian, this also means 'Peace is With Us'. After the Revolution, the slogan would be coopted by phone advertisers, as *Mir Vam* ('The World to You'). Significantly, although the crowd would chant for Yushchenko and Tymoshenko long and hard, few of the slogans really moved from the general-political to the personal. One exception, the poster and T-shirt that depicted Yush-che-nko in the style of the classic Che Guevara poster of the 1960s, seemed almost gently to mock his moderation.

The three strands of the opposition were therefore weaving together well. The CEC's declaration that Yanukovych was the victor on Wednesday 24 November upped the ante, and the next day the demonstrators took over Trade Union House on the north side of the Maidan, the Ukraine House (formerly Lenin House) to the left, on Khreshchatyk, and the city hall to the right. This ensured both practical support for the protesters and somewhere to house the flood of small donations of food and clothing. Pora now came into its own. Its role was to block government buildings, the presidential administration, and even Kuchma's *dacha* outside Kiev at Koncha-Zaspa. More exactly, Pora provided 'a couple of thousand [people], no more; their job was to create an initial "nucleus" for the demonstrations; although further into the revolution Pora symbols were very popular, so many non-members would carry a sign or a yellow (or even black) bandana'.[16]

In the first week it was pressure on the streets that counted. By Friday 25 November, the authorities were beginning to lose both unity and nerve. One more nervous member of the CEC withdrew his signature approving the results, making him the sixth honest member of the CEC to rebel. If another two followed, the whole election would be legally invalid. The Supreme Court bought the opposition precious time by agreeing to review Yushchenko's appeal against the results on the Monday, and so making official recognition of Yanukovych impossible. International mediators also arrived on Friday, when Yushchenko dramatically switched tactics by calling for a new vote in December. Yanukovych countered with an offer to allow a new election in the two Donbas oblasts only. He also disingenuously suggested that as president he might make Yushchenko prime minister. Neither offer was remotely attractive. But the opposition was now back indoors.

## The Media

The revolution, of course, *was* televised, although the authorities controlled all the more popular Ukrainian channels. The main state TV channel, UT-1, reaches 98 per cent of Ukraine, but is less popular in the east, where the largest channels, 1+1 (market share one third) and Inter, which has the exclusive right to broadcast material from the Russian First Channel, are private. All three, UT-1 rather more opaquely, were controlled by the shadowy structures of the SDPU(o), and therefore ultimately, though holdings were not in his name, by the head of the presidential administration, Viktor Medvedchuk. Inter and 1+1 were vehemently anti-Yushchenko. Three other channels were controlled by the rival Pinchuk group based in Dnipropetrovsk, and were pro-Yanukovych, although somewhat less strident. Of these, ICTV is more popular in central Ukraine, STB is an entertainment channel, full of reality TV and the national strip-tease championship, and New Channel shows mainly films and family shows. A new channel backed by Akhmetov, called simply 'Ukraine', was launched in Donetsk in January 2004. The only two opposition channels were also recent set-ups; these were Poroshenko's Channel 5, although that only reached 48 per cent of Ukrainian territory, and Era, which was run by Andrii Derkach, who had previously been close to Pinchuk, but was now putting out feelers to the opposition. Era, however, only broadcast via UT-1 early in the morning and late at night, after 11 pm.

There was some discontent among channel staff before the election. Seven journalists resigned from 1+1 on 28 October in protest at their editors' particularly blatant bias. However, a more serious rebellion began on

22 November, when the chief editor had to read the news himself. Inter and 1+1 had only one reporter covering the Maidan, until he resigned on 25 November. The joke circulated that 1+1 stood for Viacheslav 'Pikhovshek [the station's notoriously biased anchor] + a cameraman'. On Wednesday 24 November, UT-1 news was busy celebrating Yanukovych's victory, but the signing translator, Nataliia Dmitruk, indicated: 'The Central Electoral Committee falsified the results of the election. Do not believe what you are told. Our President-elect is Yushchenko. I am very sorry that I had to translate lies before. I won't do it any more. I am not sure if you will ever see me again.' Viewers never did see her on the screen again, as she was promptly sacked, but she did appear on the Maidan instead. On 25 November, 1+1 started up coverage again, but promised to be objective.[17] By the weekend, therefore, the mass audience in Ukraine was beginning to see the same pictures of the Maidan as the growing international audience. In east Ukraine, however, coverage was still heavily biased – and it should be pointed out that Channel 5, despite a huge surge in its ratings, was often guilty of cheerleading.

The accusation that the media 'created' the revolution, as it supposedly had done in Georgia with the manipulation of the channel Rustavi-2, hardly stands up to scrutiny. More or less the opposite is true. Georgia had one main channel, but in Ukraine the pro-Yanukovych channels (and papers) remained dominant, though they were haemorrhaging viewers because of their failure to cover events objectively, or even cover them at all. However, there were some elements of clever manipulation. One thing the organisers of the Maidan got spectacularly right was their understanding of the power of TV images to form public opinion in the West, and, to an extent, at home. The Yushchenko team hired a satellite station so that any TV company in the world could easily obtain pictures of the peaceful but determined crowds. This ensured that the Maidan would always be the main story, the implied epicentre of events.

Another equally important media battle was won by the opposition at an earlier stage. The Yanukovych media effort was coordinated by the likes of Pavlovskii and took the typical post-Soviet approach, using the commanding heights of the mainstream media to launch blanket propaganda. Dirty tricks were produced on a Fordist industrial scale, with millions of copies of fake leaflets and posters mocking 'Bushchenko'. The opposition, however, won the battle of the internet and other alternative media hands down. It was not that Pavlovskii, Gelman *et al.* didn't use the internet. They set up a series of characteristic sites either for obvious black PR purposes (www.provokator.com.ua, and www.aznews.narod.ru, based in Russia) or for black PR masquerading as news (www.temnik.com.ua, www.proua.com, www.for-ua.com). The rival opposition network, however, won the battle for hearts and minds, including most 'opinion-formers' in Kiev. Opposition sites were groovier, funnier, more informative, and, in the last analysis, simply more honest. The new NGO sites (see pages 75–6) now interacted with the 'traditional' opposition web (www.pravda.com.ua, www.obozrevatel.com, www.obkom.net.ua, www.glavred.info), and with new satirical or blog set-ups. Internet access rose by 39.6 per cent throughout November, and continued to rocket up thereafter. Vladislav Kaskiv of Pora claimed this aspect of their work was more important than their physical contribution to blocking buildings and helping with the demonstration. He claimed that www.pora.org.ua had become Ukraine's fifth most popular site, and that the organisation had distributed a massive 70 million copies of printed materials.[18]

The opposition was also much more skilled than the old regime in posting video clips, often from camera phones, on the net – Channel 5's comic masterpiece of the Yanukovych 'egging' incident, for instance, received 90,000 hits in a week. Topical internet games were also hugely popular. These included *Khams'ke yaiechko* (a play on words, meaning 'ham and eggs', but also the 'thug's bollocks'), in which players fought a war of control over the regions of Ukraine by bombarding Yanukovych with eggs; and Dmytro Chekalin's *Veseli yaitsia* ('Merry Eggs').[19] The latter, along with the cartoon series 'Operation ProFFesor' (like many post-Soviet politicians, Yanukovych had arranged a doctorate in economics for himself, but, like Dan Quayle, famously misspelled his qualification in public), which placed Yanukovych in various satirical roles from well-known Soviet films, were both allegedly privately backed by none other than Tymoshenko.[20] There was also a web site, www.ham.com.ua, devoted to jokes about and attacks on Yanukovych, the 'big kham' (in Ukrainian, pronounced with a faint 'k'). The other side's attempted response, 'Lampa' (http://lampa.for-ua.com) was pretty lame in comparison. The opposition also texted campaign slogans to mobiles, and used them to give times and places for demonstrations. Mobiles are as popular in Ukraine as they are in the West, albeit for different reasons (the local phone network is rubbish, and it's the only way to contact people who don't have secretarial staff), but the Yanukovych camp didn't even try to target the opposition. In this sense, given technology leapfrogging, the Yushchenko campaign was as modern, even more modern or more post-modern, than any in the West.

This was one reason for the one-way traffic in cultural icons appearing at the Maidan. Eurovision winner Ruslana, for instance, was an important early performer, who also went on hunger strike and set her next video amongst the photogenic crowds (having defected from her original role as a 'cultural adviser' to Yanukovych). The Klichko brothers, Ukraine's world-champion boxers, said the right thing to the crowd about their force being with the demonstrators (they had also promised to 'train' Yushchenko for the TV debates). Torch singer Oksana Bilozir sang repeatedly, her reward was to become Ukraine's youngest-ever minister of culture in the New Year. The girl group *VIA Gra* remained bravely scantily-clad. Old favourites, such as the 1970s refugee Taras Petrynenko, performed almost every day, and were soon joined by the giants of Ukrainian rock, V-V (*Vopli Vidopliasova*, or 'Vidopliasov's Screams', a reference to how a Dostoevsky character signs his letters) and *Okean elzy* ('Elza's Ocean'). There was also plenty of folk music, from the likes of *Kobza*, for the middle-aged. The revolution's theme song, *Razom nas bahato*, was a rap, but was home-made and released on MP3.[21] Quite sensibly, the Maidan's organisers hoped to encourage as many different groups of the population as they could to stay in the square for as long as possible. Despite the cold, the Maidan remained exciting. The festival atmosphere was a wonderful way of maintaining morale, and of keeping a photogenic feed going to the world's media. Many protestors stayed there permanently, confounding the élite's disdain, and would have kept going longer if that had been necessary. Many kept coming back again and again. Some were sorry when it was all over.

## The Potential Crackdown

Not everyone was so jolly. From the very beginning, Yanukovych and Medvedchuk were pressing for Kuchma to take direct action, but most of the elite remained risk-averse. On Sunday 21 November, Yushchenko actually told the first crowds to go home for the night. This presented the authorities with an ideal opportunity to seize the Maidan, but they failed to do so. On the next night, Monday 22 November, with almost a hundred thousand people still in the Maidan, the lights were turned off, but again nothing happened. The next day, Tuesday 23 November, however, 30,000 would-be counter-demonstrators were brought by train from the Donbas and stationed outside Kiev, at Irpin. As this was reported on Channel 5, the element of surprise was presumably lost. Channel 5 also claimed many had arrived drunk. So they were stood down and sent back. Another version has it that demonstrators from the east, possibly extra demonstrators, were turned back halfway, at Kharkiv. If Kuchma had countermanded the order, then the regime was already losing its nerve, though there remained much nervous talk of another 'Romanian scenario'. The reference this time was to a notorious two-day rampage in June 1990 by Romanian miners from the Jiu valley, who were brought to Bucharest by President Iliescu to attack his opponents. As a result of the clashes, twenty-one were left dead. The Ukrainian equivalent might have involved either similar bloodshed, or a staged confrontation, providing an excuse to 'restore order'.

As early as Wednesday, when the world's media arrived in force, option one – a 'blitz' declaration of Yanukovych as the victor and the use of *agents provocateurs* as an easy excuse to disperse limited crowds (the formula that had allowed the authorities to survive the Gongadze scandal back in 2001) – was already unavailable. This was fortunate, as some in the Western press were already primed to concentrate on the 'nationalist threat' from the likes of the UNA.[22] Yushchenko was criticised by some for taking the presidential oath in the Rada on Tuesday 23 November, but his boldness had clearly unnerved the authorities. The CEC went ahead and announced Yanukovych as the winner on Wednesday, but one peculiar feature of Ukrainian law is that election results are not official until they are actually published in offic-ial papers such as *Uriadovyi kurier* ('*Government Courier*') – election time is probably the only time anyone would actually read such a notoriously bor-ing paper. The Supreme Court forbade official newspapers from publishing the results, but deputy premier and old Kuchma stalwart Dmytro Tabachnyk ordered them to be published anyway, resulting in some overnight drama as opposition deputies rushed to the *Courier*'s offices to prevent the printing going ahead. The 'Romanian scenario' seemed most likely on Wednesday 24 November, when thousands of miners marched into Kiev along Lesia Ukraïnka Boulevard. However, their destination this time was no further than the CEC, where they celebrated Kivalov's announcement of Yanukovych's victory, had a barbecue and went back to their base outside Kiev.

The authorities assumed that the worsening weather would sharply reduce the number of protesters, as it had done in 2001. It was an indication of the semi-authoritarian nature of the Kuchma regime that its first instinct was not to crack heads, but to consult the weather forecast. Throughout the first week of the crisis, the authorities were also constantly let down by their inability to put their supporters on the streets in competitive numbers, largely because of their natural inclination to pay or to coerce virtual sup-port, rather than to motivate those who genuinely believed they were right. That is, the fault was theirs. It wasn't, as some reports chose to imply, that Yanukovych's supporters were somehow inherently lazy, drunken or dod-dery. Busloads of easterners were pre-paid to come to Kiev, but they simply melted away on arrival. The authorities also suffered from doing things on the cheap. Many Yanukovych supporters were sent to Kiev with only a one-way ticket, or with their internal passport held at home to ensure 'good behaviour' – which made it difficult to buy a return ticket, and left many stranded in Kiev. (Lviv council, in the west, was also accused of using its official budget to help fund travelling protesters to get to Kiev.) The pro-Yanukovych demonstration in Kiev, held on Friday 26 November, embodied all of these weaknesses at once: it was small, it was held near the railway station, a good two miles from the Maidan, and it only lasted two days. During the roundtable discussions, Yushchenko disdainfully said to Yanukovych, when he disingenuously proposed both sides should take their protesters off the streets, 'You can tell your five thousand people to leave.'[23] Although they were often sneered at, it should be pointed out that the easterners' passive and peaceful behaviour was as creditworthy as the restraint shown on the Maidan. Yanukovych had tapped real issues of concern in east Ukraine, but his supporters sensed that something was not right and that they were being used. Both sides showed great maturity in not being manoeuvred into the conflict that some 'technologists' so desperately wanted. It takes two sides to avoid an argument.

By now, there were so many people on the Maidan that any crackdown would have been extremely bloody. As early as Monday 22 November, cars and buses had been positioned in side streets leading to the Maidan to make any assault more difficult. Some expensive-looking Mercedes were parked amongst them, though it was not clear whether this was done with the owners' permission. Two former SBU generals, Oleksandr Skipalskyi, and Oleksandr Skibinetskyi, addressed the Maidan on 25 November, promising they would not be a party to any spilling of blood. A unit of young interior ministry cadets defected on 26 November, providing great TV when they marched into the square decked in the opposition's chosen colour of orange. The gain was initially more psychological than real, but more broadly it was clear that any use of forces would meet resistance at several levels. Yushchenko's 'security chief', Yevhen Chervonenko, later claimed that he and Zhvaniia were prepared to organise a forceful response to any provocation.[24] Zhvaniia has rather more explicitly stated that this meant arms or armed units, though these were sensibly kept away from the Maidan, despite rumours of snipers being placed on the roofs. There seems to be an element of myth-making here, as more or less the opposite was claimed at the time, with Yushchenko's people constantly stressing their peaceful intent. It is well-established, however, that SBU men were in the square to monitor and liaise, but also potentially to act in its defence.

Yanukovych was certainly blowing his top in private and, according to one first-hand report of private phone calls, Putin was also applying pressure. When Kuchma rang him after the second round for advice, he started by claiming, 'Everything's normal, the elections have been won, but there's a few problems – the opposition is getting agitated, there are demonstrations, tents. So I want to discuss what to do.' To this Putin replied, 'It's up to the president of Ukraine, not the president of Russia. But in general, in theory, in such circumstances, presidents introduce a state of emergency, or there is a second variant – you have an elected president [Yanukovych], you could transfer power.' And at that moment, Kuchma made a fantastic statement – 'Well, how on earth can I hand over power to him, Vladimir Vladimirovich? He's just a Donetsk bandit.'[25] This last statement is indeed extraordinary. Some have taken it as evidence that Kuchma never really wanted Yanukovych to win. In the context, it seems more like evidence of the splits and uncertainty in the regime, as they wondered how to respond to the new situation they now found themselves in.

Accordingly, when Yanukovych raised his demands on Saturday 27 November at a key meeting of the National Security and Defence Council held away from the turmoil, just outside Kiev at Koncha Zaspa, he got short shrift from the SBU chief, Ihor Smeshko and from Kuchma too. Reportedly, Kuchma slapped him down by saying, 'You have become very brave, Viktor Fedorovych, to speak to me in this manner . . . It would be best for you to show this bravery on Independence Square', i.e. the Maidan.[26] Presumably, this was a reproof, rather than an invitation. Kuchma, by most accounts, wasn't temperamentally prepared for violence. His metier was divide-and-rule, not force, and he seems seriously to have believed he would be rehabilitated after the Gongadze affair in prestigious retirement. He had prepared a charitable foundation as a comfortable sinecure, and 'written' several books. The most famous of these, *Ukraine is not Russia*, attracted a review from Mykola Tomenko, who commented with acid sarcasm that 'the presence of Leonid Kuchma could sometimes be felt in this authors' collective' of anonymous historians, at least in the bits that were 'insignificant and more or less autobiographical'.[27]

There were several reports, however, that violent measures were seriously contemplated on the night of Sunday 28 to Monday 29 November. Shortly after 10 p.m., some 10,000 to 13,000 troops under the deputy interior minister Serhii Popkov (the head of internal forces) were supposedly mobilised and supplied with live ammunition and tear gas, and allegedly began moving towards Kiev from all points: from Petrivka (the north), Boryspil (the airport in the east) and Zhytomyr (the west). The troops were reportedly from Crimea and had been kept isolated and ignorant of events. The use of outsiders, who might be more prepared to crack heads than local troops, was a key principle from the hardliners' handbook; the tactic had been used with deadly effect in Tiananmen Square in 1989, but forgotten in Moscow in August 1991. The plans were supposedly derailed by a flurry of phone calls: from SBU chief Ihor Smeshko to key Yushchenko campaign aides Oleh Rybachuk; from Smeshko and Vitalii Romanchenko, head of military counter-intelligence, back to Popkov; from Smeshko to interior minister Mykola Bilokon; from Rybachuk to the American ambassador John Herbst, who phoned Pinchuk, who contacted Medvedchuk; and from Colin Powell to Kuchma, although this last call was declined.[28] The regular army contacted the interior ministry, to say they were unwilling to do the regime's dirty work. According to Borys Tarasiuk, 'by two o'clock we had the situation under control'.[29] One version has it that Kuchma himself gave the ultimate order to stand down (it was unlikely that Smeshko could have done so on his own), because Yanukovych had acted unilaterally in attempting to mobilise the troops. Another is that Medvedchuk gave the order to use force, and tried to make it look as presidential as possible. Popkov would have wanted to see something on paper and, given the chain of command, either man would have gone via Bilokon to start the operation. At the time, Tymoshenko blamed Bilokon. Popkov was reportedly promoted, presumably for having agreed to do nothing at the time of the revolution, but, unsurprisingly, was removed in the New Year.

Others consider that the key story on which much of this speculation is based, published in the *New York Times* in January, contained a lot of PR put out by the SBU after its alleged role in the Yushchenko poisoning became public, and after allegations of corruption involving Smeshko and others, including the covert sale of cruise missiles to China and Iran, were made earlier in January at the well-connected whistleblower site, www.ord.com.ua.[30] Oleksandr Turchynov, appointed to take over the SBU in 2005, considered that the story contained 'exaggerations'; 'not all those figures who spread [this] information about themselves carried out their obligations truly honourably. On the other hand, the influence of many honourable principled officers to avoid the spilling of blood was crucial'. He also stated that 'the order was given with Kuchma's direct consent'.[31] At the time, there wasn't the sense of crisis that there would have been if the threat had been in imminent danger of turning into reality (though it is consistent with moves being made that were doomed to fail). Neither was the sense of grievance apparent that one would expect to have surfaced in private talks with Kuchma if the Yushchenko team had suspected so much blood could really have been spilt. But, of course, as time went by and the regime did not crack down, more and more people lost their fear.

## The EU Intervention

Another factor which threw the authorities off balance was that international protest had not just been unexpectedly robust, but that it had suddenly been transformed into direct intervention. By the night of 28 November, the authorities were already between rounds of talks with international leaders, and a crackdown would have been doubly difficult. The Polish president, Aleksander Kwaśniewski, later gave a very candid, if occasionally grandstanding, account of his role in leading the intervention,[32] most probably because it was one of the few things he had to be proud of as he approached the end of his scandal-ridden second term. First, although he enlisted the support of the German chancellor, Gerhard Schröder, the Czech president, Václav Klaus, the Austrian president, Wolfgang Schüssel and the Dutch premier, Jan Peter Balkenende (the Dutch held the EU presidency at this time and were broadly sympathetic), this was clearly his initiative, although the harsh words exchanged at the Russia–EU summit in The Hague on 25 November helped to ensure that an initially reluctant Javier Solana, the EU's common foreign policy High Representative, would accompany him to Ukraine, and that the intervention would become an official EU mission. Kwaśniewski asserts that the presence of the Lithuanian president, Valdas Adamkus, was arranged at Kuchma's request, but actually Yushchenko had phoned him first, as well, because the two were old friends. Kuchma, however, was friends with Kwaśniewski and had phoned him on the Tuesday.[33] Kuchma owed him a favour because Kwaśniewski had kept talking to him during the Gongadze affair, when the West had given up, and Kuchma therefore hoped he would now play a similar role in smoothing his forthcoming retirement. Kwaśniewski, of course, advised restraint, and Kuchma therefore persuaded Yanukovych to sit down with the delegation, which initially he had been far from keen to do. Yanukovych did not want to concede victory and had to be persuaded that the EU visit was entirely separate from that of Lech Wałęsa,[34] whose supposed 'mediation' mission had ended up with him bounding on to the stage in the Maidan on 25 November to declare himself 'astounded by the sentiments and enthusiasm' of the crowd and 'profoundly certain that this will lead you to victory'.[35] Wałęsa, however, claims he also played a key role, through counselling restraint in private.[36]

Kwaśniewski's and Solana's first visit made the most difference. First, their very presence in Kiev provided the protesters with legitimacy and time, which were both vital ingredients in giving their action bite. They arrived just at the right time, bridging the awkward moment on Wednesday and Thursday, 24 and 25 November, when the opposition's protests were no longer building momentum and the authorities tried to declare Yanukovych the winner (the Poles had their first meeting with Kuchma around midday on 25 November). Kwaśniewski, who arrived the next day, also asserts that his presence helped forestall a big counter-demonstration by Donbas miners planned for 26 November. 'Nine years of contacts' meant he had mobile numbers for all of Ukraine's leading politicians, and a call to Serhii Tihipko helped to get the demonstration called off, though another version has it that it was Tihipko himself who had threatened trouble and that it was Kuchma who made the call.[37] The Donetsk group had a practical reason for paying attention: the Poles had recently decided to reopen the protracted struggle for control of the steel mill at Huta Częstochowa, which the group hoped to win in 2005. The creation in March 2005 of a joint venture between the IUD and the Polish company Ziomrex, the industrial metallurgical company, to complete this and other deals was presumably a complete coincidence, despite the competition from the Mittal group. Other targets included the Walcownia Rur Jedność pipe plant, Huta Batory steelworks, and a 50 per cent stake in a refractory plant via the Polish company Ropczyce. It would be an exaggeration to say that the Donetsk clan cared more about a steel mill than they did about the political outcome of the Orange Revolution. It would not be an exaggeration, however, to say that they cared more about their potential Polish investments than they did about the alleged Yanukovych 'issues' that they had helped to politicise, such as the Russian language and dual citizenship.

Secondly, Kwaśniewski correctly appraised the situation in Kiev. Yushchenko's team was saying it would have nothing to do with the 'bandits' in power, but its position was legally weak. Yanukovych was waving his endorsement letters from various central Asian leaders, but the authorities were physically hemmed in. As Kwaśniewski said to Kuchma, in reference to Pora trapping him in his *dacha*: 'If you are stuck in the middle of nowhere, it means you have no power.' Yushchenko had the advantage of warning that 'in a couple of days even he would lose control over the masses'; whereas Yanukovych undermined his own negotiating position by first asserting that the election was fair, and then, when Yushchenko submitted 700 appeals regarding violations in eastern Ukraine, 'submitting [7,700] appeals from western electoral districts . . . in response. As a result [Kwaśniewski calmly pointed out], we had 7,700 complaints, which [clearly] meant that the election [overall] had been unfair.' Yanukovych, moreover, was only backed up by Putin's envoy, the Duma chair Boris Gryzlov, who was often late for key meetings. After an initial tirade, mainly about hanging chads in Florida in the 2000 US election – which itself was no paradigm of democracy – Kuchma said little, while the chair of parliament, Volodymyr Lytvyn, advocated a 'political solution'. According to another Polish account, Kuchma began by accusing the demonstrators of being 'paid by Berezovskii and Soros', but then used his key aide, Serhii Levochkin, to sound out the idea of a 'packet', that is, a compromise on the election in return for constitutional reform and his own personal guarantees.[38] Previously, Kuchma had tried to trap Yushchenko with his earlier criticism of the first round, suggesting that logically that should be rerun as well.

Putin apparently rang three times during the negotiations, in frustration. The meeting between Putin and Kuchma at Moscow's Vnukovo airport on 2 December was basically a summons for a dressing-down. So the biggest achievement of the first round table on 26 November was that Yanukovych went in as president-elect and Yushchenko as his uppity challenger, but that the two men came out on an equal footing. Both sides agreed to continue the dialogue and to await the Supreme Court's decision.

The second and third round tables on 1 and 6 December were less decisive – and less constructive. At the second, Yushchenko almost made a fatal mis-step by apparently agreeing to withdraw protesters from government buildings, though he swiftly backed down when it became clear that the crowds themselves wouldn't budge. The negotiations were most notable for the fading away of the idea that the whole election might be rerun, and for the increasing prominence of the proposal to link electoral and constitutional reform. Some have credited Kwaśniewski with coming up with the idea of rerunning only the second round of the election at this time. At the third round table, given that 'Kuchma knew that it was his last chance and insisted on including the constitutional reform into the package', and that, 'Yushchenko and his supporters expected an immediate dissolution of the government, which, according to all the evidence, partook in falsifying the election',[39] the opposition was arguably out-manoeuvred. Overall, however, the EU intervention was effective because it occurred at an early stage, because it was unexpected, and because the Poles led a consensus that, with America's support, even spanned the Atlantic. Russia was certainly left wrong-footed.

### The Rada

As a result of the first round table, parliament assembled for a special session the following day, Saturday 27 November, in a totally different atmosphere to the one that had been prevalent when it had been thought that the session might be used formally to inaugurate Yanukovych. The balance of power in the Rada still favoured the government 'majority', but it was increasingly nervous and fractious. The very existence of a parliamentary opposition, however, was an advantage in Ukraine, compared to many other post-Soviet states, including Russia. In Russia, all of the four parties that won seats in the December 2003 Duma elections were backed to some degree by the Kremlin. Belarus had just organised elections in which the opposition wasn't even allowed to stand. The new Kazakhstan parliament had one opposition deputy, but he declined to take up his seat.

In Ukraine, the opposition had leverage but not control. Although the authorities' artificial and tenuous 'majority' in the Rada had temporarily fallen apart in September, it was in theory restored intact on the eve of the election. The three opposition factions only controlled 139 seats out of 450; the authorities proper had 182 and the Communists 59. Two nervously neutral groups, the 'Centre' faction set up in the spring and 'United Ukraine', set up in September, had sixteen seats each. By 27 November, the majority was beginning to break up, but there was as yet no mass defection to the opposition. The old guard preferred to reinvent itself, setting up a series of new factions with innocent-sounding names such as 'People's Will', most of which were controlled by the Rada chair Volodymyr Lytvyn, who now became a key player in the crisis.

Despite being an academic, Lytvyn had long been regarded as Kuchma's man. Lytvyn had served as chief of the president's administration through the difficult years between 1999 and 2002. His controversial appearance on the Melnychenko tapes was excused by his defenders as the necessary presence of someone constantly in the president's office, but his actual words – 'take [Gongadze] to Georgia and dump him there' (see page 53) seem to be urging Kuchma on. Melnychenko himself certainly thought of Lytvyn as a co-conspirator. Lytvyn was also fortunate to escape the procurator's attentions in December 2001, when he was accused of running a $10 million intellectual property scam with Ihor Bakai. Lytvyn also wrote an article that was both ominous in its attacks on the 'myth' of civil society and on NGOs for undermining national sovereignty, and embarrassing – as it was plagiarised from an old edition of the journal *Foreign Policy*. Lytvyn, however, retained Kuchma's support and moved on to another powerful post, heading the For A United Ukraine bloc in the 2002 elections, and his reward for its failure was to be controversially installed as chair of the Rada in May 2002. Lytvyn was also close to the Communists, having served as an aide to their last leader, Stanislav Hurenko, in 1989–91, and was therefore a key link in ensuring they played by the regime's rules.

However, once he was installed as Rada chair, Lytvyn began posing as a neutral arbiter. On a diplomatic tour throughout 2004, he allowed himself to be courted by the West, making a low-profile visit to Washington before the second round on 15 November, where he met Colin Powell, Condoleezza Rice, Richard Lugar, John McCain and Henry Hyde of the House International Relations Committee.[40] It was unclear, however, whether Lytvyn was still Kuchma's emissary at this stage, or whether the West was right to believe he could be encouraged to become a power in his own right.

On 27 November, Lytvyn stitched together a general resolution, which, after heated debate, won 307 votes out of 450 and therefore a two-thirds' majority. Only Yanukovych's Regions of Ukraine faction and the SDPU(o) dug in and voted against it. 'Oligarchic unity' had gone. The resolution was backed, or at least not opposed, by other 'clans', such as Pinchuk's Labour Ukraine, from Dnipropetrovsk. On the specific motions, 255 deputies backed a declaration that the elections 'took place with violations of the law and do not reflect the will of citizens'; 270 voted to censure the CEC; and 228 to order the president to appoint a new one. The Rada also attempted to draw up a list of new members for the CEC, but Lytvyn ruled the proposal unconstitutional. 307 deputies voted to hold a special parliamentary hearing on allegations of electoral fraud, while 279 voted against the use of force against demonstrators and 233 to order the relevant committee to prepare a new bill on repeat elections within two days, and incorporate many of the Yushchenko camp's criticisms, such as banning absentee voting and broadening domestic oversight. Parliament also voted to send Yanukovych and Yushchenko to the negotiating table. This time, 261 deputies voted in favour, but Yushchenko's supporters abstained. 271 deputies voted to reactivate the ongoing project of constitutional reform. Finally, 242 deputies urged the international community to be more circumspect in its interventions, which, as it was not defined who the Rada had in mind – Russia, Poland or America – was a victory for both sides.

After an initial euphoric reaction, when the opposition began to dream of actual victory, the way forward seemed less clear. The Yushchenko camp assumed that negotiations would now take place on the basis on the 'packet', but Kuchma kept wriggling away. One problem was that parliament had clearly overstepped its powers. Constitutionally, it was up to the outgoing president to propose a new CEC, and, it was thought, it was up to the CEC to decide whether to declare the elections invalid and move forward to a new vote. The opposition therefore upped the ante. The next day, on the

## The changing balance of power in parliament, 2004–5

| | 6/10 | 6/12 | 28/12 | 24/1 | 15/2 | 15/3 | 18/3 | 11/4 | 20/6 |
|---|---|---|---|---|---|---|---|---|---|
| **Opposition** | | | | | | | | | |
| Tymoshenko bloc | 19 | 19 | 19 | 19 | 18 | 24 | 24 | 26 | 37 |
| Our Ukraine | 100 | 100 | 101 | 100 | 101 | 91 | 81## | 87 | 89 |
| Ukrainian People's Party | – | – | – | – | – | – | 22~ | 24 | 24 |
| Socialists | 20 | 20 | 20 | 21 | 24 | 25 | 28 | 29 | 27 |
| PIEU (Kinakh) | – | – | – | 14# | 15 | 15 | 17 | 17 | 15 |
| Centre | 16 | 15 | 14 | 14 | 12 | 12 | – | – | – |
| | | | | | | | | | |
| **Lytvynisty** | | | | | | | | | |
| People's Agrarians (satellites) | – | 20 | 29 | 32 | 33 | 30** | 30 | 32 | 39 |
| United Ukraine | – | 17 | 21 | 22 | 22 | 22 | 22 | 21 | 19 |
| Union | – | 17 | 17 | 16 | 15 | 13 | 13 | 14 | –+ |
| Democratic Initiatives | – | 14 | 14 | 13 | 14 | 14 | 14 | 14 | 11 |
| No Faction | 18 | 41 | 47 | 28 | 33 | 31 | 33 | 34 | 40 |
| | | | | | | | | | |
| **Authorities** | | | | | | | | | |
| Communists | 59 | 59 | 59 | 59 | 59 | 56 | 56 | 56 | 56 |
| Regions of Ukraine | 64 | 61 | 61 | 56 | 54 | 54 | 53 | 52 | 50 |
| SDPU(o) | 40 | 33 | 30 | 27 | 23 | 21 | 21 | 22 | 20 |
| Labour Ukraine | 30 | 18 | 18* | 14 | – | – | – | – | – |
| NDP | 16 | 16 | – | – | – | – | – | – | – |
| Democratic Ukraine | – | – | – | 14 | 16 | 18 | 18 | 19 | 20 |
| Republic | – | – | – | – | – | 10 | 11 | 11 | – |
| United Ukraine | 16 | – | | | | | | | |
| Union | 18 | – | | | | | | | |
| Democratic Initiatives | 14 | – | | | | | | | |

\* On 23 December Labour Ukraine and the NDP formed a joint faction temporarily to survive, then split again to create Democratic Ukraine (Pinchuk) on 20 January, and Republic on 1 February, which only lasted until 6 April.

\# The faction Industrialists and Enterprise Bosses – People's Will, 'Will of the People' for short, was established on 21 January.

\*\*Lytvyn's People's Agrarian Party became the People's Party on 1 March.

\#\#Our Ukraine's numbers dropped when the new government was formed, but rose again after the Centre faction was dissolved into it on 18 March.

~ Our Ukraine also lost members to the Ukrainian People's Party (Kostenko), established on 16 March.

+ 'Union' was dissolved on 31 May 2005, with most members joining the Tymoshenko bloc.

Source: regular updates from www.rada.gov.ua/depkor.htm

evening of Sunday 28 November, they set up a 'Committee of National Salvation', headed by Yushchenko. On Monday, it issued four demands for Kuchma to meet within 24 hours. They were: that he dismiss Yanukovych as prime minister; immediately respond to parliament's proposal to set up a new CEC; fire the governors of Kharkiv, Donetsk and Luhansk oblasts, implicitly for their role in the 21 November fraud, but, in the words of the final resolution, more generally to take action against 'separatists' in southeast Ukraine, who now clearly felt the tide was turning against them.

On Tuesday 30 November, the Rada seemed to be backsliding. The Communists sided with the oligarchs to secure a vote of 232 to reverse Saturday's condemnation of the election and the CEC. Only 196 votes could be found to dismiss the government. Disingenuous offers and blatant sabotage options were hinted at in private. Kuchma was now arguing that 'neither [man] can unite Ukraine', and, on 1 December, Yanukovych suggested that both main candidates should withdraw. For a brief moment Serhii Tihipko threatened to enter the race in his stead, but this option assumed the Supreme Court would grant the authorities six months or so to prepare a new campaign. It also ignored the fact that Tihipko's PR blitz in the spring had never really lifted his ratings, despite costing millions. The ploy only served to undermine Yanukovych further – Tihipko had been his campaign manager, after all. He was now replaced as campaign manager by none other than Andrii Chornovil. Yanukovych presumably meant to demonstrate that he had supporters from both east and west Ukraine, but in fact he succeeded in yoking himself to a fake nationalist, while simultaneously complaining about Yushchenko's phantom nationalism in an election where most agreed that the issue had moved on.

The opposition responded by raising the tempo of the demonstrations once again. After several attempts, the Rada finally voted the next day, Wednesday 1 December, to dismiss Yanukovych as prime minister. However, it faced a technical difficulty. Only 222 votes could be found for the direct motion, in part because there were very real doubts about the constitutionality of the move. According to the 1996 Constitution (article 87), 'the issue of responsibility of the Cabinet of Ministers shall not be considered . . . within one year after the approval of the programme of Action of the Cabinet', which had last been done in March 2004. The Rada therefore voted, rather disingenuously, by 229 to 8, to overturn the March vote, 'the consequence of which', it claimed, 'is the resignation of the government'. Except that it wasn't. Given the constitutional weakness of the opposition's position, Kuchma for the time being ignored the motion and the demand that he form 'a government of national accord'. Thanks to Pora *et al.*, on the other hand, Ukraine didn't really have any government, or at least not one that could issue orders from its offices.

### 'Separatism'

On Sunday 28 November, east Ukrainian leaders gathered at a special conference in the Donbas mining town of Severodonetsk (just north of Stakhanov, named after the champion miner), which demanded a referendum on the federalisation of Ukraine.

Kharkiv governor, Yevhen Kushnariov, made most of the more radical statements, but this was clearly a Donetsk-led affair, and there were demonstrations in Kharkiv against him. The other clans largely kept their distance. Nor was it a particularly spontaneous outburst of local anger. Yanukovych arranged for two planeloads of foreign journalists to be flown in, and swiftly out again. Apart from general rhetoric about reviving the 'Donetsk–Kryvyi Rih Republic' of 1918 (then a tactical manoeuvre by the Bolsheviks), or setting up a republic of 'New Russia' (in the sense of *Novorossiia*, the Tsarist name for the broad sweep of territory from Odesa to Kharkiv), the one practical result was a referendum on local autonomy, which was briefly scheduled to be held in Donetsk on 9 January 2005, but cancelled as soon as compromise was reached in Kiev on 8 December. This was hardly radical, even in comparison to 1994, when Donetsk had held its own mini-'referendum' on federalism and Russian language rights. Crimea, the only region with an ethnic Russian majority, which had briefly flirted with real separatism during a six-month crisis in 1994, was largely quiescent.

Ukraine was never 'on the brink of civil war'.[41] Yanukovych's words during the round table talks indicated the artificial nature of the protests, when he said he would be happy to tell his supporters: 'Go home to your families, we will have a legitimate legal process, we will take the issue to the negotiations table, and then all the turmoil in the regions will disappear after that. Yes, all the turmoil in the region will disappear, in the East, in the South, and everything that unfolded will disappear when we calm the people down and tell them to calm down, that everything will be taken care of, so you can just live your lives.'[42] The inflaming of the separatist issue was also designed to frighten moderates away from the Maidan, and to allow Kuchma to pose as a neutral arbiter against the 'greater evil'. The ploy certainly succeeded in briefly changing the tone of much of the coverage in the West.[43]

It was less successful, however, in that it led to Ukraine's leading newspaper, *Dzerkalo tyzhnia* ('Mirror of the Week') directly accusing Kuchma of organising, or at least ordering, the rally,[44] though it also seemed in part a response to 'Moscow schemes'. The Moscow mayor Yurii Luzhkov was the star turn at the rally. The four-point proposal issued by Kuchma through the National Security and Defence Council (NSDC) on 28 November showed what he had in mind. In addition to accelerated dialogue and a promise not to use force, it said, Yushchenko should agree to remove demonstrators from government buildings 'in return' for the rescinding of all 'illegal' decisions by local authorities (i.e. the 'separatist' councils in the east, but also potentially including the recognition of Yushchenko as president by some councils in the west) – a blatant attempt to gain a concession by graciously withdrawing a problem Kuchma had himself created in the first place. The 'patriotic part' of the SBU responded with a threat to take legal action against 'separatists' on 30 November.

It was not that the issues surrounding separatism weren't real. It's just that this time they were being fanned by cynical local leaders whose local control was then so strong they assumed they could easily put whatever genie they released back in the bottle. They also knew that if they lost, it would be somebody else's mess to clean up.

## The Court

The fact that both sides left so much up to the Supreme Court hearings that began on 29 November is hard to explain. The most likely possibility is simply that the authorities were over-confident. At the 1 December round table, Kuchma had stated hubristically that: 'Unfortunately, the Supreme Court does not have a right to acknowledge the election as invalid. Our law is multidimensional, and it is likely that our judges will provide us with some recommendations so that in the future the CEC, and the parliament, and the president could implement them.'[45] Kwaśniewski had suggested televising the hearings, and Medvedchuk assumed the courts were safely under his control. Ukrainian courts had no great reputation for their independence, and just to make sure that this would not change, the authorities had launched a general pre-election clampdown on relatively independent judges,[46] most notably attempting to repress judge Mykola Zamkovenko, who had freed Tymoshenko from prison in March 2001. He received a two-year suspended sentence in September 2004 for delivering judgements 'without considering the evidence'.[47] Crucially, however, the SDPU(o) had most control over the local courts, as that suited their business purposes, whereas Kuchma controlled the Constitutional Court, one of Ukraine's two 'highest' courts.

The other, the Supreme Court, is the highest civil court, and had not been so necessary to control in the past. The authorities also seemed to have forgotten that they had previously crossed swords with the Supreme Court during the 1999 election, when the court chair, Vitalii Boiko, criticised the CEC for not even following its own procedures (the court enforced the reinstatement of four minor candidates). Boiko, who gained a reputation for independence – which, according to Kuchma on the Melnychenko tapes, meant he was an 'underhand bastard' who needed dealing with – was replaced in 2002, but he had helped set the court on a relatively professional path.[48]

On Friday 3 December, the Supreme Court's decision unexpectedly broke the political deadlock. It dropped all pretence of equivocation, and of 'equal fraud on all sides', and squarely blamed the authorities. The CEC had announced Yanukovych's victory without considering outstanding legal appeals, but, more fundamentally, the court declared that 'during the conduct of the runoff vote there were [mass] violations of Ukrainian law', especially with 'the formation and checking of voters' lists' [the notorious absentee voting], and the 'unlawful intrusion into the electoral process' of government officials. Provisions for counting and writing 'the reports of district election commissions' [the government's now notorious computer fraud], the court diplomatically declared, were violated. Finally, 'access to the mass media did not accord with the principle of equal access'. Therefore, the court concluded, 'the violations of the principles of the electoral law ... exclude the possibility of credibly establishing the actual results of the expression of the voters' will in the country as a whole'.[49]

Both the Kuchma and the Yanukovych camps had assumed that the court, even if it agreed with Yushchenko's case, would stop at that, and throw the problem back into the lap of parliament or the international round table. However, the court radically short-circuited the political process by ordering its own explicitly political solution – a repeat of the second round on 26 December. This would not be a new election open to all comers, or a rerun in the Donbas only. Neither would it be an election without Yushchenko or Yanukovych, as the latter had disingenuously proposed. The court's decision could not be appealed. The verdict completely changed the political game. It seemed that Yushchenko's supporters no longer had any incentive to support the compromise being worked out at the end of the week, which was offering Yushchenko a new second round in return for accepting the longstanding package of constitutional reform (i.e. reduced presidential power) after a one-year interval. Tymoshenko was now arguing that the opposition's victory was inevitable without any further concessions. One opinion poll predicted that Yushchenko would win by 56 per cent to 40. The other side did not cave in immediately, however. The regime had, as yet, no 'exit strategy', and had not exhausted its negative potential. Kuchma in particular, although deeply discredited as a politician, still held sufficient powers as president to act as a roadblock to further progress. He had not yet agreed to dismiss the government, and his proposals for the new CEC looked rather like the old CEC. He could still veto any bill or package of bills passed by parliament, even if it fell into the hands of the opposition.

The authorities' range of sabotage options was now narrower than it had been, but it was still formidable. They could pull Yanukovych out of the repeat vote, turning it into a 'plebiscite, not an election',[50] and so deprive Yushchenko of the moral victory he still needed. They could also urge a boycott in east Ukraine, close the opinion poll gap with sufficient fraud, or, alternatively, make their fraud so obvious that the Supreme Court might invalidate yet another election. The authorities blocked parliament's attempt to pass a new election law to establish fairer process on Saturday 4 December, as a result of which parliament was initially adjourned for ten days. From 5 December, protesters' numbers began to grow again. One final push was still needed.

In private, however, Kuchma was putting out feelers about his desire for immunity and financial security. At the time, the first seemed to be no real problem, as Yushchenko's camp had offered it several times already. In the long term it would become more problematic, however, as he got no concrete promises on paper. The second was also possible, unless he got too obviously greedy. He had already asked to keep his *dacha* and his yacht. More difficult was Kuchma's reported demand that Yushchenko drop his threat to reverse controversial privatisations that benefited his supporters, such as the notorious sale of the giant Kryvorizhstal steel mill in June. However, one thing was clear: Kuchma's obvious self-interest undermined the more serious threats he was making via his entourage.

## The Compromise

Parliament sat again on 8 December. When the Orange Revolution was over, Our Ukraine put out a booklet called 'Seventeen Days, Which Changed Ukraine', assuming that the protests, which began on 22 November, ended with some kind of final victory on 8 December. Others would argue that the revolution continued until the third vote on 26 December, or until Yushchenko's inauguration on 23 January – or even that it is still not over and will have to go on for years. Radical critics, who at the time included Tymoshenko, also argued that Yushchenko gave in to his natural instinct for compromise and gave away too much just when victory was in sight, and that Medvedchuk won in the end.

Things looked different at the time, however. The Supreme Court judgment mandated a new election, but no one knew if it could be held on time. Technically, the process could be dragged out for ninety days. Kuchma was still refusing to create a new CEC and sign a new election law, and without a clean third round the opposition might be no further forward. The Zoriany team might no longer be at work, but without new authorities overseeing the count under new rules, all of the other voting 'technologies' could be reapplied. Kuchma's meeting with Putin on 2 December was most notable for Putin's veiled threat that: 'A re-vote could be conducted a third, a fourth, a twenty-fifth time, until one side gets the results it needs.'[51] The threat was not so much of indefinite delay, as of a stalemate resulting from the authorities clinging on to their vestigal 'administrative' power. The Severodonetsk meeting was also clearly a marker; the issue was not real separatism now, but the threat that the authorities might exploit the issue if they didn't get the exit strategy they wanted. And the longer Kuchma refused to form a new government, the more damage would be done to the economy, which faced both macroeconomic risks such as trade disruption, confidence in the currency and so on, and increasingly obvious plunder by the more unscrupulous members of the old guard. The opposition wanted to do things legally, but they didn't have a majority in parliament. More exactly, their near majority had been taken away from them in 2002.

The regime was losing its fragile unity, but only a handful of figures such as Oleksandr Volkov had at this stage defected to the Yushchenko camp. The likes of Pinchuk, Akhmetov, Yaroslavskyi and the host of smaller figures (it was estimated that a staggering 300 out of 450 Rada deputies were dollar millionaires) wanted to wash their hands of the hard-line scheming of Medvedchuk and Kliuiev, but their main priority was their own survival. Medvedchuk's constitutional reform project was therefore revived with a transformed purpose, which was no longer that of forcing a would-be president Yushchenko into a cul-de-sac of limited power, but of transforming the Rada into a safe haven for the old elite, which would, it was hoped, feel less like a retirement home and more like a business club. Yushchenko could swallow constitutional reform; he had promised it to Moroz, and his aides believed he would now be a revolutionary president unbound by Lilliputian restraints, and that whatever concessions were made would be won back by victory in the Rada elections due in 2006.

Deputies therefore voted for a 'packet' on 8 December: constitutional reform along with a new election law, local government reform and

Kuchma's final agreement to dismiss the discredited prosecutor general and chair of the Election Commission. The 'packet' was voted on as a whole, and received 402 votes out of 450. Significantly, most of the enthusiasm was on the government's side. All the then 'majority' factions voted in favour of the 'packet', but this included only 78 out of 101 members of Yushchenko's Our Ukraine bloc, and only one out of nineteen of Tymoshenko's supporters. Tymoshenko herself did not vote, on principle. More mysteriously, neither did Yushchenko, although he was present in parliament at the time. Kuchma and Lytvyn signed the 'packet' in the Rada's main hall, there and then, supposedly to demonstrate national accord, but their haste also demonstrated the extent of their relief. More practically, the opposition simply did not trust Kuchma. In private, he might sign the Constitution bill and forget about the other measures. He had certainly ratted on many other similar deals in the past.

The way forward to a new election on 26 December, and to what all sides assumed would be Yushchenko's inevitable victory, was now clear. The CEC was reconstituted with a new chair, the respected Yarolsav Davydovych and four new members. On 15 December, the 225 TECs and 33,000 individual Polling Station Commissions (PSCs) were reconstituted on a streamlined, bipartisan basis, with equal representation for Yushchenko and Yanukovych supporters. It would also now be impossible to dismiss any member within two days of the new vote (many of Yushchenko's 'trustees' had been booted off at the last minute in the previous rounds). That said, the Yushchenko team didn't have enough 'trustees' to staff all the commissions in the time available, and often had to rely on students. Several stable doors were bolted to prevent the more obvious 'technologies' used in the previous rounds. Much tighter restrictions were placed on the issue of Absentee Voting Certificates (188,000 rather than 1.5 million), on voting with mobile ballot boxes, and on the printing of surplus ballot papers – the last was a normal feature of most elections, but not with the millions of extra copies produced in previous Ukraine elections. Absentee voting would be restricted to the 'category one' infirm, disabled or injured, who were actually immobile. Much more information would be required from the CEC to track the voting summation process, although unfortunately not down to the PSC level. The CEC would also have to publish this information in the mass media.

The constitutional reform bill, technically number 4180, was supposed to resemble the package agreed between Yushchenko and Moroz, but was actually a close copy of the one that had failed in April. Amendments have to be passed twice, at consecutive Rada sessions. The Constitutional Court had to pretend not to notice. The changes made by the bill were due to take effect on 1 September 2005, if the necessary reforms to the system of local government were made by then (these mainly stipulated that local leaders should be directly elected, rather than appointed by the president, as they had been since 1994). If not, bill 4180 was to take effect from 1 January 2006, regardless. Under the new system, parliaments would serve for five years rather than for four. The president's powers to dissolve parliament remained limited. The next parliament would be wholly elected by proportional representation on national party lists, and the barrier for representation would be lowered from 4 per cent to 3 (this confirmed a proposal passed earlier in 2004). Elected deputies would serve a so-called 'imperative mandate', meaning that if they were elected, say, as Our Ukraine or as a Communist, they would have to remain as such or lose their mandate. This provision had long been backed by the opposition and was designed to stop the constant splitting and reinvention of factions that has plagued Ukraine since independence. Critics said this measure would make deputies too dependent on authoritarian party leaders, that power would pass to backroom cliques rather than to parliament as a whole. In addition, Deputies would be unable to take other well-paid positions, or serve simultaneously in the government. The first provision was not well-defined, but was a good idea, although it produced an unseemly row when Oleh Blokhin, the successful national football coach who also served as a deputy for the SDPU(o), having been first elected as a Communist, was forced to resign in March. (Blokhin was arguably the USSR's best-ever player. He won the European Cup Winners' Cup twice with Dynamo Kiev and was named European Footballer of the Year in 1975. He won 112 caps for the USSR and scored 42 goals – both records.) The second provision was a bad idea that negated the basic idea of party government.

The new deputy corpus was supposed to form a 'coalition of deputy factions', that is, a majority. If they didn't, this would allow the president to dissolve the Rada (previously, his main theoretical power had been to dissolve it only if the Rada failed to begin a given session within thirty days – which was never likely, even with Ukraine's long holidays). However, it was unclear how the formation of a majority was to be formally recognised. Neither was there provision for one party to form a majority by itself. Most importantly, however, the government was now more accountable to that majority, instead of mainly to the president, as it had been in the past. For example, the government would now resign as a matter of routine when new parliamentary elections were held. However, the detailed provisions setting out just who was accountable to whom were somewhat contradictory. The Rada would propose candidates for prime minister, and the president would propose the actual prime minister to the Rada for approval. The Rada would have clearer powers over the National Bank, members of the CEC and state Executive Agencies. It would appoint half the Constitutional Court, rather than one third – with the president appointing the other half. Although the president would appoint the procurator and the head of the SBU, the Rada would have stronger powers of approval and dismissal, especially in the case of the head of the SBU. The procurator remained an over-mighty agency; its powers were even expanded to include 'supervision of the observance of human and citizens' rights and freedoms [and] the fulfilment of laws ... by the public authorities'. The rule of law would depend on the good faith of the incumbent, and the question of whether there would be any witch-hunt after the Orange Revolution would depend on the authorities' self-restraint.

The overall composition of the government, plus the heads of the State Property (privatisation) Committee and the TV and Radio Board, it seemed, would be up to the prime minister, subject to the confirmation of the Rada, but the president would still propose the ministers of defence and foreign affairs. Parliament's censure powers against individual ministers would be much stronger, raising the prospect of wars of attrition against reformist ministers or stronger sectoral lobbying of others. Indeed, the reform strengthened parliament more than it did the government. There were still technical problems of 'dual subordination'; that is, the president's and prime minister's responsibilities still overlapped, and continuing turf wars between the two were likely. In plainer terms, it was a little bit clearer, though not completely clear, who was in charge.

Overall, the president seemed likely to lose power after 2005 or 2006, but it was not clear to what extent this would happen. What are technically known as 'semi-presidential regimes' are marked by the circumstances of their emergence as much as by what the formal Constitution says. Ireland, for example, has an elected president, but the premier (Taisoeach) has all the power because this is the office the 'founding father', Eamon De Valera, chose to occupy. Yushchenko was likely to retain a similar status as hero of the revolution and survivor of the poisoning. Our Ukraine expected to do well in 2006, both because of a coat-tails effect, and because it did well in the proportional side of the 2002 elections (it came first with 23.3 per cent, and had the 2006 rules been in place then, Our Ukraine, the Socialists and Tymoshenko would have won half the seats, the Communists a quarter and the government a quarter).

Both Yushchenko and Moroz had campaigned on the platform that a more parliamentary republic would improve Ukrainian democracy in the longer term, and make the Ukrainian system more like that of 'normal' countries such as Poland and Romania. It was far from clear, however, that the package was the best that could have been negotiated, or even whether improvements could not have been made under the existing system. Ukraine has certainly suffered from over-mighty presidents in the past. More 'normal' channels of accountability were potentially clearer in the longer run, from the electorate to a parliamentary majority to a more responsible government, but Ukraine now had a charismatic president who was not likely to cede power if his anti-corruption campaign had not taken effect in, potentially, a mere nine months.

### The Third Round

The day we can't get our hands on the ballot boxes before
the vote is counted we're done for.

Esteban Trueba, the conservative senator in Isabel Allende's
*The House of the Spirits.*[52]

The 'seventeen day' perspective was right, however, in that the main political drama was now over, and Yushchenko was an assured victor in the 'third' round. The campaign was a retread. After the 8 December agreement, local elites outside the Donbas foreswore the more blatant types of abuse of 'administrative resources'. The level of fraud declined sharply, if not to zero, and most of the fraud was still in the east. Russia backed off. Money disappeared. Most important of all, there was no real popular anger in the east mobilising against Yushchenko and 'Orangism'. But there was plenty of passive resentment.

On 26 December, Yushchenko triumphed with an official 52 per cent of the vote, against 44.2 per cent for Yanukovych. The KIIS-Razumkov poll had Yushchenko leading by 56.3 per cent to 41.3 (this was later adjusted to 55.3 and 40.6). Social Monitoring adjusted its 'methodology', and showed Yushchenko even further ahead, by 58.1 per cent to 38.4 per cent. Residual 'administrative resources' clearly worked in Yanukovych's favour, retrospectively justifying the 8 December agreement to some. On the other hand, the problems with absentee voting disenfranchised many pensioners (see page 150), who were more likely to be Yanukovych supporters (not overwhelmingly however; according to one poll, Yanukovych was only ahead by 44.5 per cent to 40.9 per cent amongst the over-sixties, perhaps because it was Yushchenko who had originally paid off their pensions in 1999–2001).[53] Absentee voting was supposed to be restricted to the 'category one' infirm, disabled or injured, which had the undesirable side-effect of either forcing many of the less disabled, but not particularly mobile, elderly out of their homes, or denying them the vote. The Constitutional Court sought to reverse this change on the very eve of the third round, on 25 December (not a holiday in Ukraine, which celebrates Christmas according to the old Orthodox calendar), but this was undoubtedly too late for many to apply.

Overall, however, Volodymyr Paniotto of KIIS estimates that only 2 per cent of the exit poll discrepancy was attributable to fraud, and that the rest was due to difficulty in sampling certain populations (such as prison, and army voters), and to some Yanukovych supporters being more wary of pollsters after the second round.[54] More fundamentally, however, despite the turmoil of the Orange Revolution, there was no landslide of votes to Yushchenko. The vote on 26 December was remarkably similar to the 'real' vote on 21 November before it was obscured by the election fraud. This may help convince the Yanukovych electorate, in the long run, that the result wasn't 'stolen'. It may also help Ukraine to develop a healthier long-term balance between the new authorities and a still vigorous opposition.

Turnout was down 4 per cent at 77.3 per cent, but there was no mass boycott in the east. The Organisation for Security and Cooperation in Europe/Office for Democratic Institutions and Human Rights (OSCE/ODIHR) and the Committee of Voters of Ukraine both reported polling 'closer to European standards'.[55] The latter also claimed most violations that did occur were still in the eastern regions, in Donetsk and Sumy. Despite widespread claims of intimidation from the Yanukovych camp, his vote held up more or less in the west, only falling by a few points, rather than being squeezed to an implausible minimum. This made it very difficult for a now very embittered Yanukovych to build a strong case to contest the results, especially as so many elements from the outgoing administration had made their peace with the Yushchenko team.

Detailed local results were now in the plausibility zone. In east Ukraine there was again a heavy vote for Yanukovych, but not an absurdly exaggerated one. Turnout in Donetsk was claimed at only 86.9 per cent (as compared to 97.6 per cent the previous time), and the Yanukovych vote at 93.7 per cent (as compared to 97.2 per cent). In Crimea, 81.2 per cent voted for Yanukovych and 15.4 per cent for Yushchenko, though this was largely due to the influence of the local Crimean Tatar electorate (see pages 90–1). Yushchenko won 32 per cent in Dnipropetrovsk, 27.5 per cent in Odesa and 43.4 per cent in Kherson. The build-up of his vote in the east and south over the three rounds was gradual but significant.

On the other hand, there was no doubting the depth of the regional division, even in the re-run vote. Not only did Yanukovych still win every oblast in the east and south, and Yushchenko every oblast in the west and centre, but their respective margins of victory were huge. If the US election in 2004 showed a divided country with only half a dozen states actually 'in play', arguably not a single region in Ukraine was actually really competitive. The closest oblast was Kherson, where the two men were still 8 per cent apart.[56] In this respect, Ukraine was apparently more divided than in the election of 1994, when Kuchma had beaten Kravchuk with a similar regional split, but not with such massive votes in their respective strongholds. More fundamentally, though, Yushchenko had changed the political map by consolidating the centre and winning civic-issue voters in the east and south, i.e. those voting negatively against the old authorities. The latent regional question, moreover, had been artificially emphasised, though once this had happened, the real sentiments and resentments simmering away in the east were bound to become a problem.

----

Like many skilfully negotiated compromises, more than one side came out of the Orange Revolution thinking it had won. They were not all right. There were some clear losers – in fact, the toll of mysterious deaths soon began to pile up. Yanukovych was unlikely to remain a player for long, and Kuchma's retirement plans were on hold. The moderate revolutionaries thought they had won what they needed by not being too revolutionary. The Yushchenko team was confident it could shrug off the concessions made on 8 December, while the more radical revolutionaries in Pora had their doubts. So did Tymoshenko, but her position would soon be transformed. Did the elite get the exit strategy it wanted? Only time would tell.

# 8

# The Aftermath

Revolutions normally begin after the headline events that launch them. As Ukraine moved into 2005, many in the old elite thought they had pulled off a great survival stunt on 8 December. The new government, however, proved surprisingly radical, determined not to let the dust settle before 2006. A political and economic clean-up was promised. Several key figures from the old regime fled, or died in suspicious circumstances. On the other hand, it seemed unlikely that Ukraine would stage some great cathartic trial, or 'Truth and Reconciliation' process, like South Africa after apartheid.

In Brussels in February, President Yushchenko declared that he wanted the Gongadze affair solved within a month or two. That seemed highly unlikely after the former interior minister, Yurii Kravchenko, shot himself on 4 March just hours before he was due to give evidence. Kravchenko's first shot went up through his chin and out; the second was more effective, straight through the right temple. His suicide note to his wife read: 'My dear. I'm innocent. I'm sorry. I've become the victim in political intrigues of President Kuchma and his circle. I'm leaving with a light heart. Farewell.'[1] A few days before, the gangster Nesterov had been injured in a grenade attack at his 'safe' apartment. Oleksii Pukach, the other key suspect in the Gongadze affair, was reported to have fled to Israel. Kuchma himself was questioned, as was Lytvyn, though this was only cursory, as he still seemed too powerful to be investigated thoroughly. The trail of evidence seemed to stop with Kravchenko, although several of those who actually organised the murder were now in custody. Another apparent victim in June 2005 was Ihór Pluzhnykov, who owned 71 per cent of the Inter TV channel, and who died from a mystery illness at the age of 46 in a Czech health spa, allegedly poisoned for his willingness to move Inter away from the SDPU(o) to circles more sympathetic to the new authorities. Pluzhnykov voted the SDPU(o) line in parliament several times after his death, as his grief-stricken colleagues used his electronic voting card.

The new authorities barely mentioned the Pandora's Box of the remaining Melnychenko tapes. Melnychenko, meanwhile, was losing credibility through his entanglement with Berezovskii, who sought to use the tapes to lever himself into political influence in Kiev, and through stories alleging that Melnychenko had tried to sell the recordings elsewhere. In April 2005 Berezovskii threatened to present his version of the tapes, but was alleged to have sought out 'conversations of Kuchma with Yushchenko and Tymoshenko, in which they look much worse than they claim to be',[2] and to have attempted to shed better light on Kuchma or anybody else who might pay him.[3] Yushchenko's poisoning continued to be investigated, but again with only underlings in the dragnet.

It seemed more likely that several members of the Zoriany team would – or should – end up in jail. In February 2005, a libel case filed by Medvedchuk against Rybachuk for 'exposing' the Zoriany tapes was thrown out by a Kiev court. In April, prosecutors reopened the investigation into the death of Viacheslav Chornovil in 1999. By spring 2005, Serhii Kivalov, former head of the CEC, former oligarch, Ihor Bakai, former interior minister, Mykola Bilokon, former Sumy governor, Volodymyr Shcherban, and former Odesa mayor, Ruslan Bodelan, were all on the run. Leonid Kuchma, Serhii Tihipko and Rinat Akhmetov all went on long holidays, during which they no doubt shared their critics' thoughts about whether they should return. The likes of Viktor Medvedchuk continued to brazen it out.

### Busy Bankivska

As well as covering its back over the Gongadze affair, the outgoing administration (which in Ukrainian is often referred to by its location, on Bankivska, 'Bank', Street, in the same building that once housed the Central Committee of the Communist Party of Ukraine) persuaded Yanukovych to initiate a lengthy appeals process, while they settled last-minute accounts and destroyed as many documents as they could. The election observer mission from Russia and the CIS, which had noticed nothing untoward in the previous two rounds, now found that pro-Yushchenko leaflets and all-things orange were now everywhere on election day. Yanukovych's appeal was undermined not by its triviality, however, but by its sheer size, which was obviously designed with delay in mind. Yanukovych's team submitted no less than 621 volumes of printed documents and 233 audio and video cassettes.[4] Many of the complaints they made were identical to one another. Yushchenko would not be officially inaugurated until 23 January.

Meanwhile, Yushchenko complained that the outgoing powers were organising a flurry of 'barter deals in the energy sector, reimbursing VAT to structures close to Kuchma–Yanukovych, dispensing them licenses, forming retrospective privatisation agreements, setting up fictitious joint enterprises for undertaking questionable financial operations and so on',[5] such as doling out long-term leases on lucrative commercial buildings in Kiev and entire enterprises elsewhere. Ihor Bakai helped transfer ownership of Kuchma's favourite winter *dacha* in the Carpathian mountains to an off-shore company, even though it was owned by the state.[6] Brezhnev's old Crimean *dacha* Hlitsyria (Wisteria) was sold to the Russians via a children's charity. In total, Bakai was involved in suspect transfers – including that of the Dnipro Hotel in Kiev to 'Mad Max', Kurochkin for UAH92 million ($18 million) – allegedly amounting to UAH319 million (about $60 million).[7] Bakai fled to Russia. The outgoing presidential administration was accused of issuing two hundred passports with aliases for other members of the old regime. One and a third billion dollars left the country in November and December. On 15 December, Medvedchuk made a secret flight to St Petersburg,[8] but this seems only to have been to inform Putin that the game was up. Several of Ukraine's most popular sanatoria were also disposed of. Bakai also specialised in decrees that changed investment conditions after sale; i.e. that reduced or eliminated the amount that buyers had promised to pump into their new purchases.[9] In March the new finance minister, Viktor Pynzenyk, accused the old authorities of hiding UAH17 billion ($3.2 billion) in budget funds. Several huge projects had been allegedly plundered, at least in part, including $700 million for the new Kiev bridge over the river Dnipro, $480 million for rebuilding the Kiev–Odesa highway, and a $107 million credit to Kuchma's old rocket factory, Pivdenmash.[10]

Another complex scheme involved the Russian energy giant Gazprom, which used to organise the export of gas from Turkmenistan to Ukraine. From December 2003, however, it seemed complicit in the creation of fictitious companies to provide nominal 'transport services' in return for hundreds of millions of dollars. First was Eural Trans Gas, which allegedly divided its cut of 13.7 billion cubic metres as follows: 50 per cent to Gazprom, 30 per cent to Oil and Gas of Ukraine and 20 per cent to the mobster Semion Mogilevich. Its replacement, RosUkrEnergo, was half-owned by Gazprom-bank and by 'Raiffeissen Investment AG', with the latter again allegedly serving as a front for Ukrainian oligarchs such as Ihor Bakai and Yurii Boiko. Despite the lost revenue, Russia allowed the scheme to continue throughout 2004 to fund Yanukovych's campaign. Eural Trans Gas admitted a gross profit of $220 million. Other estimates were twice as high, as gas supplied by Turkmenistan at $44 per thousand cubic metres could be resold in Central Europe for $119 or more. Money was also siphoned out of Ukrmorport (the State seaports agency) and Ukravtodor (the highways agency).

Kuchma finally accepted Yanukovych's resignation as prime minister on 5 January, but replaced him with the equally controversial Mykola Azarov, whose sole significant act in office was to steer through Kuchma's 'retirement package' on 19 January. Azarov secured Kuchma the right to continue drawing a full presidential salary rather than pension (with index-linking potential), to use state *dacha* number 72 and its staff, as well as providing him with two cars and four drivers, free travel (except taxis, which he hardly seemed likely to need), free medical care for himself and his wife, half off his electricity bill (a particularly curmudgeonly demand), and an adviser and two assistants, all of which were to be paid for from the state budget for the rest of his life. This was in addition to the three-storey building for his 'Ukraine' Foundation which had already been provided by the state.[11] Not surprisingly, the new government was soon trying to undo this overly-generous offer.

## Maintaining Momentum

On the other side of the fence, the role of conscience of the revolution was initially shared by Tymoshenko and Pora. Roman Bezsmertnyi, the camp 'manager' on the Maidan, thought the protestors could disperse after the second version of the second round on 26 December, but Tymoshenko encouraged them to stay on until the inauguration (and was threatening to bring them back by March). Three trucks and a minivan arrived to gee up the remainder on 15 January, but they stayed put. Bezsmertnyi accused Tymoshenko of 'blackmail'.[12] More serious by far was the leaking of the secret part of the 'Force of the People' agreement signed by Tymoshenko and Yushchenko back in July 2004 (see plate 22). Clause one of the agreement promised Tymoshenko first shot at the premiership, and not just as a token gesture. Yushchenko would use the 'force of his personal moral authority' to ensure that Our Ukraine deputies would join the Tymoshenko bloc to support her candidacy 'in full'. Clause two promised that a precise 55 per cent of government posts would go to Our Ukraine and 23 per cent to the Tymoshenko bloc (the Socialists were not party to the agreement); clause three stated that the remaining 22 per cent 'is reserved . . . for securing the formation of a new parliamentary majority', that is, for distributing to any new allies from the old regime. Clause seven promised that the two sides would decide 'together' how to 'normalise the situation in the electronic mass-media market'. Most interestingly, clause eight of the deal promised a big purge of the old guard bureaucracy and that the two parties to the 'Coalition will confirm the securing of the regions [to Kiev] with the leaders of the political and staff structures of the Coalition'.[13] When the new government was drawn up in February, despite several predictions to the contrary, Yushchenko was not forced to include any of the more odious figures of the Kuchma era. He had his doubts about Tymoshenko, however.

Come January, Tymoshenko was busy shafting her rivals for the premiership with old-style methods. Petro Poroshenko's candidacy was undermined by stories about his links with Mykola Azarov, an old Donetsk kingpin, and by a 'special operation', which made out that he was trying to bring back the old guard into the new government. Poroshenko's invitation to Azarov to visit the Maidan was a big mistake. According to the gadfly journalist Kost Bondarenko, himself something of a hired gun, Poroshenko had talked secretly with Kuchma 'at the height of the Orange Revolution', who had offered him the premiership and the backing of the necessary 'majority' factions, if he backed the constitutional reform package – as indeed happened on 8 December.[14] However, this may all have been black PR, or may have been orchestrated by Tymoshenko, who declared on 4 January on Channel 5 that 'people, who have business, should not pretend to a place in the [new] government'. Poroshenko was perfectly capable of responding in kind, and it was even rumoured that he and Tymoshenko were already spying on one another (once in government, Poroshenko controlled the National Security Council, while Tymoshenko took charge of the SBU – see below). Tymoshenko, however, still got the benefit of the doubt. Her nomination to the premiership on 24 January, Yushchenko's first full day in office, therefore elicited opposite reactions in Ukraine and in Russia and the West. Despite her business past and her still unexplained wealth, in Ukraine she was seen as *more* likely to take on the oligarchs than a safer choice such as Poroshenko or Anatolii Kinakh. Oleksandr Moroz was never a serious candidate, as Yushchenko's inner circle has never considered him a serious economist. Nevertheless, the decision to nominate Tymoshenko startled many, especially because it was made public on the day Yushchenko made his first bridge-building trip to Moscow.

This was all reminiscent of the politics 'made in the corridor' of old. Tymoshenko could still behave like a big Bolshevik in a blouse. The first scandal to hit the new government also raised the odd eyebrow, when the justice minister Roman Zvarych, who had been born in New York to

Ukrainian refugees, was accused of self-interest in voting against a measure to ban oil re-export from Russia. (His wife, Svitlana, was deputy director of a company, Oil Transit, which was involved in such traffic to Slovakia.) Zvarych accused the politician-businessman Ihor Yeremeiev of creating the scandal by suggesting his wife transfer her oil to his company, Halychyna, so he could claim a dubious VAT refund. Both sides planted stories in the press and internet under pseudonyms. Zvarych clearly had enemies, because a second story appeared a month later (via an anonymous letter to www.pravda.com.ua) claiming that both his MA and PhD from Columbia were fictitious – or rather that he had failed to complete either.[15] While fictitious degrees from Kiev or Moscow were common enough amongst politicians, telling less than the truth about 'real' degrees from abroad was thought to be a more serious offence – as was the appointment of a justice minister who had no law degree. A third story claimed Zvarych was actually a bigamist.

Several of the new government's measures were slipshod, and ran roughshod over various laws, even over the Constitution.[16] Yushchenko continued Kuchma's habit of issuing secret decrees, producing forty in his first two months in office. More generally, much was done in haste, as neither the new president nor prime minister had a programme of action ready for inauguration day. This was no great sin, just further evidence that their victory had been a surprise to many.

Tymoshenko was also criticised for welcoming some strange allies, such as the veteran (presumed ex-) oligarch, Oleksandr Volkov, who was now drumming up support for her nomination in the Rada – though Yushchenko had insisted that no money should change hands. Pora, on the other hand, set itself up for a second phase in its activity by declaring itself the 'Cerberus of Democracy'. It promised to collect a register of election promises, to help in the 'objective investigation' of the deaths of Gongadze and other journalists such as Ihor Aleksandrov (the director of TOR TV and Radio Company in Sloviansk, Donetsk, who was beaten to death with baseball bats in 2001), to draw up a list of those who had falsified the elections and a more general blacklist of their supporters, and to press for full redress for all those who had lost their jobs or otherwise suffered for opposition activity in the elections. Most ambitiously, Pora called for all state servants to be released and rehired on a competitive basis.[17] (By June, 18,000 had actually been replaced.) A formal winding-up ceremony was held on 29 January in the Hotel Rus. Andrii Yusov was tasked with setting up a party on the basis of Yellow Pora, although some also talked of setting up some kind of international watchdog, tentatively entitled the Centre in Support of

Weak Democracies. Allegedly, Pora had money left over from the winter. Significantly, it now posed as the party of young entrepreneurs, and of 'small and medium' business.

## Out With the Old, In With the New?

On 4 February 2005, a day late, Tymoshenko was confirmed as Ukraine's new prime minister, with a record-breaking 373 votes out of 450. The Communist Party was the only significant force to vote against her, and the three deputies who broke ranks to vote for her were promptly expelled. The other two parts of the 'new opposition' largely backed Tymoshenko, with only five Social Democrats abstaining or absent (though these included Surkis and Satsiuk), and only eight abstentions from Yanukovych's Party of Regions. Fears that up to a third of Our Ukraine deputies might not back Tymoshenko – either because of concern at her courting of Yanukovych's supporters, or because they were annoyed at being jumped by the secret deal – were not borne out. Tymoshenko could magnanimously afford not to vote for herself.

As the July agreement had promised, the new government was a coalition, but with some new members. The Socialists were now on board, as was Anatolii Kinakh's mini-party, and one or two independents. The Socialists had three ministries: agriculture, interior, and science and education. The interior ministry guaranteed the party a high, potentially populist, profile, especially as the new minister was the youthful Yurii Lutsenko, who promised a big purge of personnel and tangible improvements in everyday life via a bonfire of controls and more honest traffic cops. Agriculture was a mixed blessing. The countryside was the party's natural fiefdom, but anything remotely resembling the market reform the sector so obviously needed would alienate large numbers of their supporters. Another Socialist, Valentyna Semeniuk, was given the powerful position of being in charge of the State Property Fund, that is, the privatisation committee. Semeniuk, who looked like a Soviet grandmother, was actually a Communist deputy until 1995 and had been a staunch opponent of all privatisation in the past – which raised interesting questions about the new government's commitment to *re*privatisation (see below).

Tymoshenko was prime minister, but her namesake bloc had few other prizes, though Tymoshenko made her mark in the 'force' ministries, placing a civilian intellectual, Anatolii Hrytsenko, at defence, and close ally Oleksandr Turchynov as head of the SBU. In his previous job as head of the Razumkov Centre, Ukraine's premier intellectual think-tank, Hrytsenko had been an articulate advocate of defence modernisation and rapprochement with NATO. Turchynov would ask difficult questions both about the Yushchenko poisoning and about the SBU's attempts to whitewash its role in the Orange Revolution. But the clearest sign of the times, and of Tymoshenko's working methods, was the appointment of Mykola Syvulskyi, who had been arrested when working for Tymoshenko back in 1998 (see page 21), as Chief of the Auditing and Inspection Commission – in other words as Tymoshenko's hired gun to clean up corruption in government and state industry. Oksana Bilozir at Culture was part of Tymoshenko's choice, part glamour rival.

Yushchenko's supporters, on the other hand, monopolised the four powerful deputy premierships. Anatolii Kinakh, Yushchenko's successor as prime minister from 2001 to 2002, represented the Party of Industrialists and Enterprise Bosses, and was in charge of maintaining links with industry while simultaneously delivering the new clean-up message. Yushchenko's faithful servant, Oleh Rybachuk, led a powerful new post dedicated to 'European Integration'. This position was so powerful, in fact, that although Borys Tarasiuk became foreign minister as expected, he was somewhat peeved to be subordinated to Rybachuk, who was to lead a drive to upgrade relations with the EU (though Rybackuk's enemies soon responded by ignoring the drive). Mykola Tomenko was deputy premier for humanitarian affairs – that is, the sensitive area of mass media relations. Tomenko had been head of media relations for Kiev city council from February 2000 to March 2001, during which period he had been distinctly proactive, launching one brand-new paper, *Hazeta po-Kyivsky*, and changing the format of two older papers, *Khreshchatyk* and *Vechirnii Kyïv*. (The latter was changed twice.) After 2002, he served as head on the Rada's committee of freedom of speech and the mass media. As so much of the media was hostile to Yushchenko and Tymoshenko, critics predicted that the old system of *temnyky* (weekly orders on news management) would be replaced by 'Tomennyky', and that maintaining media freedom would be a key test. The appointment of Taras Stetskiv, a professional politician with no media experience, to head the national TV company raised a few eyebrows. On the whole, however, the government planned to proceed by morphing the existing UT channels into a new public service broadcaster, a 'Ukrainian BBC', rather than by unleashing some kind of monopoly commission against its opponents' channels. Several papers, on the other hand, seemed likely to fold, as they had been run as loss-making political projects by various oligarchs. Lastly, Tymoshenko's foe, Roman Bezsmertnyi, was made deputy premier in charge of the difficult job of administrative reform.

President Yushchenko declared that his new government 'will not steal' and that business would be kept out of politics. Ukraine was still not the West, however, and new ministers with business interests were not exactly expected to set up blind trusts to run their affairs. Nevertheless, in addition to Tymoshenko, with her often-questioned past, all of Our Ukraine's key financiers had key jobs. Petro Poroshenko was made head of the National Security and Defence Council on the same day Tymoshenko was appointed premier, though it was unclear whether he had relinquished control of any of his substantial interests. Davyd Zhvaniia was made minister for emergency situations. The most obvious potential conflict of interest concerned Yevhen Chervonenko, who ran a transport business, but now also headed a reduced transport ministry that had been a hot-bed of corruption in the past. Volodymyr Shandra became minister for industrial policy, while Yurii Nedashivskyi, an ally of Zhvaniia's, headed Enerhoatom, Ukraine's atomic energy industry.

All eyes were on whether the 'new oligarchs' would resist the temptation to make good the undoubted losses their businesses had suffered over the past two to three years. Outside the government, Konstantin Grigorishin was pressing for the return of 'his' *oblenergos*. Technically, if this were to be effected, it would not count as reprivatisation, as Grigorishin was still the majority shareholder. Viktor Medvedchuk, the cuckoo in this particular nest, was the one sending in the security guards, to create the appearance of a scandal and hold on to his ill-gotten gains. Initial signs overall were mixed. There may not have been a new reign of universal virtue, but there was a potential critical mass of people prepared to play by the rules.

Petro Poroshenko signalled his dissatisfaction that few of his supporters had posts, but he was given considerable power at the National Security Council, including control over issues that had little to do with security, such as the judiciary and auditing other government departments, as well as a big say in personnel. He even interfered in foreign policy, devising a ham-fisted plan to settle the separatist conflict in Moldova, which the Moldovan authorities initially chucked straight in the bin (see page 196). He was also able to build himself a mini-empire of four governors in and around his native Vinnytsia. In general, however, Yushchenko's gubernatorial appointments were bold; nearly all the new men were representatives of the parties in the Kiev coalition rather than the local powers-that-be, with only a few Lytvyn supporters as handovers from the Kuchma era. Yushchenko and Tymoshenko had given a clear signal that they would not tolerate the so-called 'bureaucratic separatism' that made the headlines in December.

Radicals were kept away from the key education and culture ministries, to allay fears of forcible Ukrainianisation amongst former Yanukovych voters. On the other hand, the most striking feature of the new government was that it contained no major politician from the east. Although Tymoshenko, Rybachuk, Kinakh *et al.* were all born in the east, they no longer represented it politically. Most of the twenty-three new ministers were from central Ukraine, and only four were from the west. The new government was also extremely youthful, with an average age of forty-four. Ukraine was now promised the elite turnover it had missed out on in 1991.

### Early Steps

Yushchenko had balanced his allies with skill, which was at least better than Kuchma's habit of balancing the clans. Although Tymoshenko was prime minister, the overall balance within the government was towards Our Ukraine's pragmatic business wing. In contrast to her stint as deputy prime minister in 1999 to 2001, Tymoshenko had little power over the economy. Her economic approach remained instinctively populist, however, and there were soon tensions within the government.

The first of these occurred over the so-called 'reprivatisation' issue. Hundreds of enterprises had been sold in controversial fashion under Kuchma. Yushchenko had criticised the way this had been done, rather than the fact that it was done, and had therefore called not for them to be renationalised, but for the state first to buy them back and then to arrange for resale via open competition and a fair price. The new Cabinet signalled its radical intent by immediately ruling for a complete reprivatisation of the most controversial recent example, the giant steel mill at Kryvorizhstal, which had been sold for half-price ($800 million, despite a foreign offer of $1.5 billion) to leading oligarchs Viktor Pinchuk and Rinat Akhmetov during the election campaign, rather than simply demanding a higher payment from both. Tymoshenko talked of 'three thousand' reprivatisations, but this soon turned out to be rhetoric for domestic consumption. The actual list was likely to be much closer to Yushchenko's alternative suggestion of 'thirty', though the threat of retrospective justice taking precedence over property rights still caused jitters amongst potential investors in the West. According to one leading commentator, the 'winners are not strong enough to start a major war of redistribution'.[18] Oleh Rybachuk promised that there would be no replay of the notorious Yukos affair in Russia (Yushchenko took offence in Moscow when Putin tried to claim both were anti-oligarch crusaders). All cases would go through the courts and would involve full repayment first. Rybachuk even intimated that the eventual list would include some cases involving businessmen now on the government's side. The list's appearance was constantly delayed, however. On 27 April, Yushchenko showed his frustration by demanding the Cabinet publish it within ten days. They didn't. But a list of twenty-nine companies was leaked in May, which included Kryvorizhstal and some other infamous cases such as Rosava and Oranta, which was one of four companies that were Russian-owned, the others being Zaporizhzhia and Mykolaïv Aluminium, and Ukraine's largest petrochemical company, Lukor.

If reprivatisation were to be confined to a few high-profile cases, as seemed likely, the old oligarchs might not lose too much. It was even possible that Pinchuk and Akhmetov might be able to buy Kryvorizhstal again, if they agreed to pay something over $1.5 billion for it. There was an argument that their old assets might actually be worth more in the long term, with World Trade Organisation (WTO) membership and the EU opening some trade doors to the 'new Ukraine'. The various groups faced very different prospects, however. Pinchuk had been trying to advertise his new respectability for some time, and the SDPU(o) empire was likely to collapse, so the key question was about the future in Donetsk. The Donetsk clan's main hidden weakness was that its export profits were dependent on subsidised inputs of coal and electricity, although it was highly unlikely that the new government would touch these before the 2006 elections. Its main hidden strength was its international ambition. The Akhmetov group already had business interests in west Ukraine and was seeking to expand in Poland (see page 139) and Hungary, where the IUD had bought the Dunaferr metallurgical plant in December 2003 and DAM steel in July 2004, in an attempt to duck under the EU tariff wall. The government claimed there was no witch-hunt against oligarchs in general. On the other hand, it was claimed that Akhmetov was milking his businesses for dividends and that Pinchuk was preparing a flash sale including his Ukrsotsbank. It was also rumoured that the Kharkiv group had put Ukrsibbank up for sale. This could be a sign either of distress, or of the need for cash in the reprivatisation process.[19]

The new Cabinet also faced difficulties in the wider economy. It soon trumpeted its successes in raising taxes and customs duties, but there were some signs of serious budgetary deterioration, with UAH2.1 billion in domestic borrowing in February alone, half the planned amount for the whole year.[20] The 2005 budget passed in March was blatantly populist, with a 50 per cent increase in welfare spending and in public sector wages, back-dated to the start of the year, including a trademark Tymoshenko measure providing a tenfold increase in payments to new mothers, UAH3,384 at birth and UAH5,113 in the next year (some $1,500 in total, which would be thought generous in some parts of the West). Tymoshenko argued that implementing Yanukovych's campaign promises as well as Yushchenko's was a necessary bridge-building measure with east Ukraine. Inflation, however, was already 12.3 per cent by the end of 2004. The new government also faced sharply rising fuel prices, which Yanukovych's PR machine had warned would happen in the autumn, safe in the knowledge that Russian exporters had agreed to forgo following rapidly rising world crude prices upwards until the election was over. In January and February, as winter bit, they went sharply up. Tymoshenko raged at collusive 'price-fixing' and in April tried to cap fuel prices. It was only possible to do so by allowing the exchange rate to appreciate from UAH5.19 to UAH5.05 to the dollar, so as to cancel out rising import prices. Domestic dollar holdings took a theoretical hit of $250 million, much of which belonged to the new middle class.

The government sharply cut several taxes, including VAT from 20 to 15 per cent, gambling that it could close the gap with rising expenditure via a revenue surge as businesses moved out of the black economy. Sensibly, its projected reprivatisation revenues remained small, at UAH6.75 billion ($1.2 billion). On the other hand, the government was determined to scrap all tax privileges, which it estimated had grown under Kuchma (or grown again since Yushchenko had been ousted as prime minister) to cost the economy UAH8.7 billion ($1.55 billion) annually. Tymoshenko also ordered an audit of all the state businesses under new management, such as Oil and Gas of Ukraine after Bakai, the railways after Kirpa and Ukrtelekom after the Zoriany team. She clearly hoped money could be saved if these sieves could be prevented from leaking. This was obviously an election budget, the success of which depended on whether the projected revolution in business culture turned out as promised, particularly as some businesses were being hit pretty hard. Tough measures, whether cuts in social subsidies or coal subsidies, were not on the agenda until the election was over.

### East and West

Ukraine's underlying linguistic and regional divisions are real enough, if latent. I gained a certain notoriety in the 1990s for pointing this out.[21] The divisions may have been artificially brought to the fore in 2004, but there is no disputing the fact that they were dramatically apparent in all three rounds of the election, even if it seemed likely they might subside again thereafter. The new government contained few real Ukrainian nationalists. In fact, Yushchenko's strategy for the 2006 election seemed to rely on his new centrist mega-party, allowing the nationalists to run on their own. On the other hand, the new government contained no real easterners. Several of his new governors in the east were replaced within months, most notably Lytvyn's close ally Serhii Kasianov in Dnipropetrovsk. Yushchenko also faced problems in Zaporizhzhia, Poltava, Transcarpathia and Chernivtsi. Yushchenko's first post-election visit to the east was for a speech in Donetsk on 10 February 2005. His all-guns-blazing assault on local corruption and those who had disrupted his campaign visit in November 2003, when posters depicting him giving a Nazi salute had been put up, built no bridges.[22] (In contrast, when Tymoshenko had appeared on the Donetsk-based Ukraïna TV channel in December she had worn the orange T-shirt of the local club Shakhtar.)

It was widely assumed that Yushchenko's reception in 2003 had been organised by Borys Kolesnykov, chair of Donetsk council and local head of Yanukovych's party, Regions of Ukraine.[23] It was often said in the Donbas that Akhmetov looked after economics, Yanukovych looked after politics and that Kolesnykov took care of the 'other stuff'. In other words, he was a racketeer. In April 2005, Kolesnykov was arrested, but there was confusion over what he was actually charged with. According to one version, it was for extorting shares from Donetsk's largest multi-storey shopping centre, 'White Swan'. According to another, he had personally ordered three assassination attempts. According to a third, it was for his central involvement in the 'separatism case', i.e. for helping to organise the December 2004 meeting at Severodonetsk. There were certainly legitimate suspicions that Yushchenko bore a grudge against Kolesnykov.

The former governor of Dnipropetrovsk turned chair of the local council, Mykola Shvets, was also taken in for questioning in April over the irregular finances of the Tavria resort complex on the Crimea coast. Then the head of the Crimean cabinet of ministers, Serhii Kunitsyn, was forced out, allegedly because of the dossier that the SBU had quietly placed in front of him in private. A local court overturned the 2002 election of alleged arms smuggler Ruslan Bodelan as mayor of Odesa (he was supposedly involved in illicit traffic to the 'Dnister Republic' and with the *neftemafiia*, or local 'oil mafia'), and replaced him with Eduard Hurvits, who leant towards Our Ukraine but also had alleged links to organised crime. Former Sumy governor, Volodymyr Shcherban, who had left a trail of corruption throughout his various jobs in east Ukraine, was charged with extortion. Former Kharkiv governor, Yevhen Kushnariov, was also in the firing line, and Viktor Diadchenko, former governor of Transcarpathia, was charged with faking the result in the controversial Mukachevo election in April 2004.

Clearly, a higher proportion of investigations were against politicians and businessmen based in the east than against those from other parts of Ukraine. Hryhorii Surkis was accused of a bizarre transfer of UAH6 million from the football club Dynamo Kiev to Kuchma's charitable fund, but he was almost an honorary easterner. Optimists claimed that a cleansing of the stables was a necessary condition for the rebirth of democracy in the east, and that 'protest' rallies in support of the victims were once again artificial, carefully-costed affairs. On the other hand, the arrest campaign gifted the old guard the kind of propaganda that could keep resentments high. Oleksandr Yefremov, the former governor of Luhansk, was hauled in for questioning over the 'separatism' saga, but it was far from clear that arrests were the best way to deal with what was basically a political issue. Crucially, the campaign, and the fact that it seemed to be orchestrated, cast doubt on the independence of the new legal team. It was also not yet accompanied by any symbolic concessions to east Ukraine, particularly as regards language policy and relations with Russia. Yushchenko was widely reported to have drawn up a decree 'On the Protection of Citizens' Rights to use the Russian Language', but it remained in his desk. 'Exporting' democracy and civil society eastwards after 2004 might prove no less difficult than 'exporting' the Ukrainian language eastwards after 1991.

## 2006

If the new authorities could consolidate their gains at the Rada elections due in 2006, then their slogan of '1+5' years of stable progress might become reality. One option was for the Yushchenko camp to create a single party, but every part of the Our Ukraine coalition wanted to be its nucleus. The parties with stronger organisations were reluctant to stand them down. Running several parties would satisfy all ambitions but hamper the main cause, which was to maximise Yushchenko's coat-tails effect. He could only anoint one vehicle. The dream scenario would be a broad coalition with Tymoshenko at number one, and 40 per cent of the vote. Step one was the creation of a pro-presidential super-party on 4 March, dubbed People's Union – Our Ukraine, organised by Bezsmertnyi. Unlike Yeltsin and both previous Ukrainian presidents, Kravchuk and Kuchma, Yushchenko agreed to be the honorary head of the new party. It reflected the balance of power in the new government, so the more nationalist groups such as Rukh and the People's Party seemed likely to stay out. Moving to a more centrist position was obviously sensible, especially with most of the rival centrist parties who once backed Yanukovych imploding so spectacularly. Whether Yushchenko was allying with the right centrists was another matter. Yushchenko let it be known that the new vehicle would need two stabilisers, Tymoshenko on one side and Lytvyn's People's Party on the other. Lytvyn, despite being the most questionable hangover from the Kuchma period, was allowed to sit on a parliamentary report into the Gongadze affair. The People's Party's head in the Rada was Ihor Yeremeiev, with whom justice minister Roman Zvarych had recently crossed swords. There were murmurs that the new mega party's leaders, Bezsmertnyi, Yekhanurov and Poroshenko, were rather too old guard, and even that it had begun to act as 'the party of power' rather than a 'party in power'. Petro Oliinyk, the new governor of Lviv oblast, had, for example, 'encouraged' local bureaucrats to join. Pora openly mocked the new party as 'For A United Ukraine, Mark 2'.

In part, the new party was designed to compete with Tymoshenko's rising popularity, or to lock her into a common front, but it was an open question whether she would eventually appear on its list. Tymoshenko was obviously on the way up – even numerically. In 2002, Our Ukraine won five times more seats than the Tymoshenko bloc. The secret part of the July 2004 agreement set a ratio of 55 to 23 per cent; the negotiations before the formation of the 2005 government were based on a formula of 50 per cent to Our Ukraine, 25 to BYuT and 25 per cent to the Socialists. While Yushchenko's supporters talked of a minimum of 30 per cent in 2006, Tymoshenko's team were certain she could now win 20 per cent. Tymoshenko's bloc was also rapidly re-expanding in the Rada, with several surprise recruits, including Oleksandr Abdullin, a colleague of Tymoshenko's old rival, Ihor Bakai, and Oleh Lukashuk from the SDPU(o). In May she swallowed the 'Union' group whole, and in June she took on board the notorious businessman-fixer-politician Vasyl Khmelnytskyi, who had financed the fake 'Green' Party in 1998 and the fake 'Women' Party in 2002. Professional oppositionist Stepan Khmara flounced out of the bloc in claimed disgust. Other recruits seemed attracted by Tymoshenko's political dynamism. Lev Biriuk, who had been number 76 on the original Our Ukraine list in 2002, was promoted to a vacant seat after (most of) the new Our Ukraine ministers resigned their seats and defected to Tymoshenko within days.

Tymoshenko was also now the ironic beneficiary of the constitutional reform package. Whispers that maybe it should not be implemented after all now came mainly from the presidential camp. Tymoshenko had lodged an appeal against it with the Constitutional Court back in December, and some now talked of calling a referendum on the issue. Both leaders enjoyed high approval ratings. By March 2005, they were basically level-pegging. Yushchenko's balance of positive over negative ratings was + 39.5 per cent,

Tymoshenko's was + 37.6 per cent, and the government's overall ratings had also gone up. An impressive 47.4 per cent considered the country was moving in the right direction, and only 21.1 per cent said it was heading in the wrong direction. This was a dramatic reversal of the situation just before the Orange Revolution in September 2004, when, despite record economic growth, only 26 per cent considered Ukraine to be on the right track, and 54 per cent described it as on the wrong track.[24]

Tymoshenko was also widely rumoured to be making a deal with the Donetsk clan. In any country other than Ukraine this would make no sense, but in Ukraine, each needed the other. Despite her colourful reputation, Tymoshenko needed money, though this time for campaigning, not for herself, and for their part, the Donetsk group still had ambitions in all-Ukrainian business and in the West. The most intriguing new governor was Vadym Chuprun in Donetsk, who had headed the local council in 1992–4, but, more importantly, had just served as ambassador to Turkmenistan. He was therefore link-man to do a deal with the energy interests in the region. As premier, Tymoshenko appeared to maintain a hands-off attitude to Akhmetov – at least it was apparent there would be no attempt to run down Ukraine's enormous coal subsidies before 2006.

The Socialists were likely to run on their own. Traditionally, they do well in central Ukraine, but it seemed that this time they were aiming at the relative vacuum in the east. Oleksandr Moroz introduced a bill in the Rada to upgrade the Russian language to a second official language, and in March 2005 made a bizarre trip to Moscow, where he made very strange bedfellows with the Russian nationalist party Rodina, signing a cooperation agreement to 'promote the socialist ideal in both states' (*sic*) with the party leader and Russian presidential hopeful Dmitrii Rogozin. There was even talk of the Socialists using the education ministry to make history textbooks reintroduce the Soviet term 'Great Patriotic War' for World War Two. Several leading Socialists were already itching to go into opposition, especially Moroz, who was not in government, solely because they could see no one else doing the job.

The Communists hoped to recover to something like the 12.7 per cent their Russian equivalents won in 2003, if not the 20 per cent they themselves won in 2002, but may have done themselves permanent damage by handing their electorate so passively over to Yanukovych in 2004. The SDPU(o) were in free-fall. Given the dynamics of a parliamentary election and the post-revolutionary realignment, it was most unlikely that there would be any east Ukrainian 'front' capable of capturing the 44 per cent Yanukovych won in the third round. Yanukovych himself was likely to be dumped as the

Donetsk clan strove to reinvent itself, despite optimistically relabelling his website as www.ya2006.com.ua. Local political culture doesn't like losers. The Industrial Union of the Donbas (IUD) had already deserted him financially; Akhmetov was busy drawing in his horns, and plotting a relaunch with Andrii Kliuiev behind Yanukovych's back.[25] Yanukovych's opposition 'coalition', launched on 13 April, again showed a disastrous preference for fake allies, including both fake leftists such as Vitrenko and Bazyliuk and fake rightists such as Korchynskyi, who would be inexplicable bedfellows in any non-virtual world. The Donbas, however, was the one Ukrainian region where the local machine seemed certain to survive, under whatever new label it chose. The short-term prospects for the old 'Party of Regions' remained good. Its polling rating of 20 per cent or just below, however, probably reflected east Ukrainians restating their preference from the 2004 elections, rather than its real long-term prospects.

Elsewhere in east and south Ukraine, local elites were already setting up a series of small regional parties with new 'brand' labels that were unlikely to ally with the Donetsk group. These included New Democracy (Kharkiv), Democratic Ukraine (Dnipropetrovsk, the old Labour Ukraine) and the People's Will (the old National-Democratic Party, NDP). The Rada chair, Lytvyn, had at one time seemed most likely to lead a coalition of the formerly powerful (the NDP *et al.*) and win something like the 11.8 per cent that For A United Ukraine won in 2002, but either this would now go to the new Yushchenko mega-party, or it was up for grabs. The one wild card was who would win the support of alienated east Ukrainian voters, of whom there were undoubtedly many.

----

In short, there was every chance that the new mega-party might win a majority at the next elections. With Tymoshenko on board, it might win even a two-thirds' majority. The opposition was fragmenting. Many business groups were reluctant even to go into opposition, and the old guard was ineffective in its new role, stubbornly reluctant to abandon the methods that had lost them the 2004 election, though no less than the American National Democratic Institute promised to help Yanukovych operate more effectively as an opposition leader. The introduction of a fully proportional system for the first time in 2006 would over-reward the main parties with big chunks of the vote and punish the smaller fragments. Short-term circumstances favour Ukraine more than they had Yugoslavia–Serbia after 2000, whose own post-revolutionary tandem of Koštunica and Djindjic lasted barely two years.

The great compromise made on 8 December might turn out not to be so important after all, but expectations of what can be achieved will only increase in the event of a second victory in 2006, and the balance of power between Yushchenko and Tymoshenko will undoubtedly change. It was not impossible to imagine Tymoshenko seeking a populist majority on her own, in alliances with the Socialists and others. A whispering campaign against her began as early as April 2005, but, given her popularity, the president would be foolish to allow her so easily into opposition.

On the other hand, the 2006 elections would undoubtedly be the last outing for the broad coalition that had coalesced by the end of 2004, made up of the old right, Yushchenko, Tymoshenko, the Socialists, the Lytvyn group and other defectors from the Kuchma regime, and all the various parties' respective business supporters, but this is perfectly normal. Like Solidarity in Poland or Sajudis in Lithuania, a broad civic coalition dedicated solely to a change of power cannot be expected to last forever; and a normal politics of ideological division will always eventually return to the surface.

# The International Implications

Even if the Orange Revolution ultimately disappoints expectations at home, there can be no doubt that it has profoundly changed the international environment. It has challenged the regional slide into semi-authoritarianism, forced Russia to rethink its role in the world, and will, it is hoped, prompt Brussels to re-examine its policy on Europe's institutional expansion. It has helped to shift the balance of power within the EU, not decisively but perceptibly, from the 'old' Europe in favour of the new members from central and eastern Europe which were admitted in 2004, and those due for entry in 2007 (Romania and Bulgaria). The Orange Revolution also promised to change the balance of power within the post-Soviet world, with Ukraine taking up a more active leadership role, pulling several other countries in its wake, and perhaps inspiring them to their own version of Orange Revolution. Ukraine and its leaders now have an international PR profile, which in the modern era makes them players in global politics for the first time. After the poisoning, Viktor Yushchenko was a genuine hero in the eyes of the world, and Yuliia Tymoshenko had real glamour. In February 2005 it made sense for Hilary Clinton to drop in and shake hands with them, in order to bolster *her* image at home. Kiev hosted the fiftieth Eurovision Song Contest in May 2005. Even the football team is doing well at the time of writing (June 2005), heading the European champions, Greece, in a difficult group, to qualify, for the first time, for the World Cup finals in Germany in 2006.

## Russia's Excuses

Given its lopsided intervention, Russia had most to reassess. Russia's view of the Orange Revolution was first that it should never have happened because, it claimed, there was equal fraud on both sides in the election. In Gleb Pavlovskii's words, 'everywhere the administration acted in the interests of the "regional hero" – in the west and centre for Yushchenko, in the east for Yanukovych. There has been a great fuss about the large number of Western observers, but it was clear beforehand that they would ignore violations in the group of regions "for Yushchenko" and only fix on violations in the east.'[1] More dramatically but even more implausibly, Pavlovskii claims to have suffered from 'electoral idiotism', from playing the game just too damn fair [sic]. 'Opposition circles', he alleges, 'weren't preparing for elections. They were preparing to take power in the form of elections'. The Yanukovych side was simply unprepared for their *coup d'etat*. 'If we had had the power to consult our Ukrainian partners on preventative counter-revolution, and not just elections, then this misfortune wouldn't have occurred', continues Pavlovskii. The sub-text here seems to be that the Yanukovych side just assumed that 'administrative resources' would guarantee it victory. Pavlovskii doesn't spell out exactly what 'preventative counter-revolution' means.

Pavlovskii also refers to orange as 'the colour of children's diarrhoea',[2] and dismisses the Ukrainian Revolution as 'a Kiev city revolution, if you like – a national-populist revolution of the middle ranks', comparing it to Paris in 1968, which is a pretty major misreading of recent French history.[3] Alternatively, and obviously contradictorily, he claims that Yushchenko was only the 'president of the Galicians'.[4] Pavlovskii also blames Kuchma for his inaction – and here the sub-text is much clearer: 'If Yeltsin had conducted himself in 1999 like Kuchma here, then Moscow would have boiled over some time in October [1999] and Putin would never have become president.'[5]

As well as fraud (greater than their own) the Russians blamed manipulation from abroad (greater than their own). Some blamed spies and mountains of US money, seeing the US playing the same zero-sum 'great geopolitical game', and trying to create a 'cordon sanitaire' around Russia. According to Sergei Markov, Russia was simply outspent by America and Poland (sic).[6] More interestingly, Pavlovskii blamed the 'new revolutionary technologies of the globalisation era', a tacit admission that some of his methods might be old hat, and that new media technologies and Western soft power could undermine the Kremlin's normal techniques of control.

It was also an article of faith amongst some Russians that Boris Berezovskii was involved. The website www.compromat.ru alleged a direct link between Yushchenko and Berezovskii (supposedly via Oleksandr Zinchenko or Oleksandr Volkov), with Berezovskii helping with PR in the West, and pledging $20 to $30 million for fifteen seats on the Our Ukraine list for 2006.[7] His emissary, Dmitrii Bosov of the Trans World Group, supposedly met Volkov in Kiev on 17 October 2004 to smoothe the deal.[8] The internet businessman Demian Kudriavtsev and a number of unnamed

Israelis supposedly helped with Yushchenko's PR. Davyd Zhvaniia was supposedly also linked to Berezovskii via the Georgian Badri Patarkatsishvili,
another tycoon disliked by the Kremlin, who announced his intention to
move to Ukraine in March 2005. One website summed up this way of thinking with an article ironically entitled 'The Orange Revolution: Made in
Russia'.[9]

Berezovskii had invested in Ukraine in the mid-Kuchma era, before his
exile from Russia in November 2000 made this more difficult. He is supposed to have invested in businesses that dovetailed with his Russian interests, namely the Inter TV channel and the Zaporizhzhia Aluminium
Combine. It was far from clear, however, how many of these interests
remained active, apart from the Ukrainian edition of Kommersant.
Berezovskii's 'Civil Liberties Foundation' was also known to be helping
Mykola Melnychenko in exile and aiding the transcription of his tapes,
although it was not clear that this was intended as an anti-Russian act.
Nevertheless, Marat Gelman suggested that Berezovskii's alleged involvement provoked Putin to block Yushchenko, though perhaps this is simply a
convenient cover story for his own failings. 'Of course, he [Putin] couldn't
allow that, in the case of a Yushchenko victory, Berezovskii would move
from London to Kiev and open a TV company somewhere in Luhansk [in
Yanukovych territory in the far east, but bordering Russia, broadcast-wise]
and start to broadcast anti-Putin propaganda to Russia.'[10] Berezovskii
declared his intention to move to Ukraine in February 2005, but even
Zhvaniia poured scorn on the idea. More generally, it was argued in Russia
that 'the confrontation revolved around which of the two moneybag clans
could lay its hands on big money and big resources' – an idea that also
found an echo in the West.[11]

Everyone, of course, blamed the candidate. In fact, Pavlovskii would later
claim that his team had done remarkably well with such poor material:
'From the beginning of the year, [Yanukovych's] support quadrupled. After
[what we did for] Putin, this is a phenomenon. I don't see any failure from
our side'.[12] But Pavlovskii also admitted that he hadn't investigated the
alternatives: 'we weren't interested in discussions amongst the Ukrainian
elite, around the formula of Kuchma's successor and [who should be the]
candidate of the existing powers'.[13]

## Russia's Response

In essence though, Russian political technologists such as Pavlovskii 'sold
Putin a false bill of goods'.[14] Their view of Ukraine was half-true, but not

true enough; which is why their work for Yanukovych had often backfired (see page 89). Their view of the Orange Revolution was more radically skewed, much of it a classic projection of their own faults on to others. After Yushchenko's victory, the Kremlin had to decide whether to continue to work within the same world-view, or to mend and make do. Russia hadn't 'lost' Ukraine, of course. Certain options had been foreclosed, but the most likely of these – Yanukovych's Ukraine as an increasingly criminalised satrap dependent on Kremlin favour and 'political technology' for its survival – was no loss to anybody.

In December and January at least, before Yushchenko's inauguration, hardline Russian voices were still predominant. On the existential question, it was hard to let go of the 'two Ukraines' line spun so enthusiastically by the technologists, even if it was now only a partial truth.[15] The nationalist intellectual Aleksandr Dugin argued that the split between the two coincided with the 'clash of civilisations', the struggle between the Russian world and the West, although the 'war on the Dnipro' as he put it, never quite got going.[16] Konstantin Zatulin, the director of the CIS Institute, argued: 'If Ukraine, even if independent, does not have special, allied relations with Russia, its fledgling statehood can easily be turned into an anti-Russian bridgehead, and it will eventually be transformed into a second Poland . . . a historico-cultural project, which is alien to Russia.'[17] This kind of zero-sum thinking, however, and in particular the assumption that Ukraine would transform itself overnight from one of Russia's closest allies to one of its most bitter enemies, was wide of the mark. It also mistook the phantom opponent for the real. The radical west Ukrainian nationalism that Yanukovych claimed to be fighting against in 2004 was a paper tiger, and Yushchenko had been carefully steering the 'national-democratic' movement in a more centrist direction since 1999. Yushchenko was certainly radically Westernising, whereas Russia has historically veered between emulating the West and rejecting it, but that was insufficient to make Ukraine and Russia polar opposites.

Without Ukraine, Russia would yet be the biggest country in the world, but it might still feel psychologically cramped. Russians have never felt comfortable with an exclusively ethnic identity. Even if not explicitly imperial, Russian thinkers such as Aleksandr Dugin have argued that the 'Russian idea is a Grand Idea . . . not the idea of one nationality alone – as for example the Ukrainian idea'.[18] But there were many forms that a 'Grand' Russian identity could take, and for many Russians the 'East Slavic' option was becoming a more attractive alternative to a Soviet, Eurasian or seemingly empty civic identity. Without it, they would have to choose one of the other, less attractive, options. Or as another political technologist, Marat Gelman, put it: 'now after the Ukrainian events the imperial project has just vanished', so where would all the imperialists go? [19]

Russians also claimed that, without Ukraine, European Russia would be defenceless. Its access to the south, to the Black and Mediterranean Seas, and its flanking influence in the Caucasus would all be circumscribed. In April 2005, the new Ukrainian foreign minister, Borys Tarasiuk, said the 1997 agreement granting the Russian Black Sea Fleet basing rights in Sevastopil for twenty years would most likely not be renewed in 2017. The previous month, Kiev had protested when Russian special forces from Chechnia landed to 'rest' in the Crimea. Some even called it 'invasion'. Without Ukraine, Russia would not have been able to stage the 'dash to Pristina', the brief attempt to challenge NATO's occupation of Kosovo in 1999.

The new Ukrainian leadership occasionally seemed guilty of rubbing Russia's nose in its unfortunate reversal, but in the short-term, this was probably a necessary antidote to a lingering reluctance to treat Ukraine as fully sovereign. On a visit to Germany in April 2005, Putin claimed that, 'If Ukraine joins the Schengen zone, it will create a certain problem. As far as I know, no less than 17 per cent of Ukraine's population is Russian. This would mean splitting the nation the way Germany was divided into East Germany and West Germany'.[20] The statement was conditional, and it referred to ethnic Russians, but it did not help.

Russia's reversal in Ukraine was not just cultural and geopolitical. The Kremlin's biggest fear had to be that the Orange Revolution would succeed in making Ukraine's political and business culture 'more European'. In February 2005, Yushchenko appointed the old-time Russian liberal Boris Nemtsov as adviser. He promptly invited private Russian business to invest in Ukraine, as it supposedly couldn't operate in Russia. 'In Russia business is being squeezed to a dead stop, it can't cope with such a severe bureaucratic dictatorship', he claimed.[21] Economically, the main result of the Orange Revolution was the likely death of the Single Economic Space agreement, initialled in 2003 (at least in its original form), which was in any case only ever a framework 'heads of agreement', and never actually implemented. Ukraine was no longer interested in a common currency or tariff zone, but its alternative idea of a free-trade area was of potential benefit to all.

Pavlovskii began to talk of making good on 'preventative counter-revolution' at home, while building links with the 'new opposition' abroad. 'During the electoral campaign in Ukraine there was an underestimation [by Russia] and low level of cooperation between Russian society and Ukrainian NGOs. We will try to avoid such an underestimation in the future . . . Mr

Yushchenko will certainly not be regarded by us as a person with exclusive rights to interpret the position of Ukrainian society, political, and non-governmental organisations,'[22] he wrote. Russia, in other words, would intervene again in 2006 and if necessary in 2009, to 'thwart the consolidation of the two parts of Ukraine on an anti-Russian platform'.[23]

The first indications were that Russia would indeed continue to use the same 'political technology' methods abroad, and its first test came with the Moldovan elections held in March 2005. Since 2001, Moldova has been the only European state to be ruled by a party that actually calls itself Communist, although the label is somewhat nominal. Although originally pro-Russian, the party has grown into a party of Moldovan statehood, and earned the Kremlin's wrath by rejecting the November 2003 'Kozak memorandum' for federalising the country, that is, for institutionalising the breakaway 'Dnister Republic' in the eastern part of Moldova. (The plans for this were drawn up by Dmitrii Kozak, then deputy head of the Kremlin administration.) Attempting to force out the Communists, the Kremlin first found and funded a proxy, the 'centrist' Democratic bloc of Moldova (actually a very motley crew of opportunists), and then set up a fake party on the left, Patria-Rodina, to try and catch the Communists in a pincer movement. On the day, the Communists won 46 per cent, the Democratic bloc 28.5 per cent and Patria-Rodina 5 per cent. Although their majority was reduced, the Communists survived to dominate the new parliament with fifty-six seats against the Democratic bloc's thirty-four, and eleven for the only other party to gain representation, the pro-Romanian Christian-Democratic People's Party (6 per cent of the vote was necessary to win any seats). The overall result, then, was more or less a draw. The Kremlin didn't get what it wanted, but there was no local Orange Revolution either (see below).

Arguably, however, this was because the plan to oust Voronin was drawn up before the Orange Revolution began, and because the momentum that had already been established carried them through. Elsewhere in the former USSR, Russia pulled back, most notably in Kyrgyzstan (see below). More serious potential conflict looms in Belarus in 2006, when presidential elections fall due in September, and in Armenia, where the fraudulent elections held in 2003 threaten to unravel retrospectively. In both countries, Russia thinks of itself as a long-term cultural, economic and geopolitical stakeholder, and is unlikely to stand back.

The Kremlin has also continued to use the same 'political technology' methods at home, where its first instinct is to clone and control. With copycat versions of Pora appearing in Russia, the Kremlin's *éminence grise*, Vladislav Surkov, has set up a rival youth movement, dedicated to defending the established order, called *Nashi* ('Ours'). Anti-Kremlin liberals immediately dubbed them the *Nashisti*, ironically the very same propaganda nickname the Russian political technologists had given Our Ukraine. The Kremlin's version of political competition in the 2007 Duma elections seems likely to involve spinning off three pocket parties from within the current loyalist mega-party, United Russia: a Kremlin 'liberal' party instead of Yabloko, a Kremlin 'nationalist' party capable of drawing away the safe elements from the likes of Rodina, and a Kremlin 'state-socialist' party to draw away the safe elements from the Communists.

How much of this is just bluster? It remains to be seen whom Russia will support at the next Ukrainian elections in 2006 and 2009 – and between times – but in the medium term, it has readjusted pragmatically enough. 'Plan B', maintaining links with all sides, had always been possible in any case, given the extent of Ukraine's economic linkage to Russia and Yushchenko's more than friendly attitude to Russian capital when he was prime minister from 1999 to 2001. When President Yushchenko invited leading Russian businessmen to Kiev in March 2005, the result was like a stampede in a sweet shop. There was just so much money potentially to be made, and too many opportunities in the reprivatisation process to miss out. Nevertheless, the prospect of the Russian economic elite, tamed domestically after the Yukos affair in 2003, taking part in, and even adapting to, Ukraine's 'new business culture' was deeply worrying to the Kremlin – just as Kiev's religious and cultural innovations in the seventeenth century had originally been anathema to Moscow. So was talk amongst liberal Russians of the possibility of the Orange Revolution helping Russia's return to Europe, with post-revolutionary Kiev reprising the role it played in the seventeenth century of the 'window on Europe' for the whole east Slavic world.[24] Some also talked of Ukraine filling the missing role of a 'bridge' between institutional Europe and Russia, though it was doubtful that either party was interested in such a role.

## Orange for Export?

The new Ukraine also sold the idea of revolution to the surrounding region. A first effect was arguably to tip the scales in the Romanian election on 12 December 2004. Despite its promise of EU entry in 2007, Romania under Ion Iliescu was in many ways similar to Ukraine under Kuchma, with ex-Communists in power, and serious problems of crony capitalism and corruption (though Iliescu had briefly ceded power to the unsuccessful liberal Emil Constantinescu from 1996 to 2000). As had happened in Ukraine, and arguably helped by Ukraine's example, the new model centrist Traian Băsescu edged out Adrian Năstase, the candidate of *ancien régime* continuity by 51.2 per cent to 48.7.

There was no regime change in neighbouring Moldova in March 2005, because there were no real opposition forces. All sides, including the ruling Communists, tried to depict themselves as somehow 'orange'. Iurie Roşca of the Christian-Democratic People's Party was the first to shift his party's campaign colours and parade under photos of himself shaking hands with Yushchenko, although he was not the most natural partner for Our Ukraine, as he represented the pan-Romanian rather than the patriotic wing of Moldovan politics. Ukraine's everpresent Eurovision star, Ruslana, sang for the Communists. The fact that the Democratic bloc managed to convince both Russia *and* America of its credentials as a viable opposition party is only testament to the skill of its leaders' opportunism.

In Belarus, Lukashenka dismissively ruled out any idea of popular revolution, whether it was 'rose, orange or banana . . . or pink' (gay).[25] 'All these "flower revolutions"', he stated in his 2005 state of the nation address, 'are in reality no kind of revolution at all. Just plain banditry in the guise of democracy.'[26] Lukashenka could thank his lucky stars that he had organised rigged elections to his puppet parliament and a referendum on changing the constitution to expand his term just *before* the Orange Revolution, on 17 October 2004. Just to make sure, he appointed Viktar Sheiman, who was allegedly responsible, as chair of the Security Council, for the 'disappearances' of several key opposition figures in 1999, as his chief of staff in December 2004.

President Askar Akaev of Kyrgyzstan was also initially determined to prevent any franchise revolution, dubbed locally the 'lemon' (traffic light) or 'tulip' revolution, by the would-be Pora clone KelKel ('New Epoch'). His ouster in March 2005 bore some superficial similarities to the Orange Revolution, most notably in the boomerang effect of ineffective election fraud on mobilising the opposition. Nevertheless, there were serious differences. It was far from clear that the opposition had really won; neither was the extent of fraud clear. Different estimates gave the opposition five or six, but no more than ten, out of seventy-five seats. As in Ukraine, the Eurasia Foundation financed an exit poll for the first time (www.kyrgyzpoll.org), but, with few mass parties, it only covered individual constituencies, and only questioned the announced results in a few of these. There was no united opposition, which was more regional and clan-based than in Ukraine, and the opposition had few financial resources – in Kyrgyzstan, most of these were controlled by Akaev's son Aydar and son-in-law Adil

Toygonbaev. Most importantly, the amount of popular violence and simple looting in the capital, Bishkek, made it more doubtful that the new regime would stick (and if the violence was orchestrated by *provocateurs*, this was another fate Ukraine had managed to avoid). In 2004, the US spent $50.8 million in Kyrgyzstan, including $12.2 million on democracy assistance.[27] The undoubtedly powerful American ambassador, Stephen Young, tipped to move on to Taiwan, was reported to have given a private speech in which he urged the destabilisation of the outgoing regime, and the use of Kyrgyzstan 'as a base for advancing the process of democratisation in Tajikistan, Kazakhstan and Uzbekistan, and limiting Chinese and Russian influence in the region'.[28] Unfortunately, the document outlining his 'speech' seemed to be a forgery. One obvious consequence of the Ukrainian precedent, however, was that this time Moscow stayed out of events. Ukraine offered to mediate instead.

Nevertheless, the contagion effect could still be felt in Kazakhstan and Belarus, where elections were due in 2006, and retrospectively in Armenia, where a potentially strong but still disunited opposition was still smarting from an election fraud similar to Ukraine's in 2003. They hoped for US support to oust local strongman Robert Kocharian, but precisely because this would be retrospective (Kocharian would be able to stay in office until 2008), there was concern that this might look manufactured. One opposition leader, Victor Dallakian, actually said, 'We will choose the right moment for carrying out regime change as a result of a popular movement.'[29] In Belarus and Kazakhstan, the opposition parties were potentially stronger than they seemed, given the authorities' constant game of divide-and-rule but, of course, they would have to overcome such tactics in order to grow in strength. In none of the three countries did the regime yet seem on its last legs. All had relatively strong security apparatuses that still seemed loyal.

The other central Asian states and Azerbaijan were much more autocratic. Unless the benign international environment (stemming from the war on terror in central Asia, and oil in Azerbaijan), that had so far limited foreign interference in these countries were to change, they would either survive, implode or organise elite successions. Significantly, however, after the Orange Revolution (and after Iraq and the 'Cedar Revolution' in Lebanon) American rhetoric was now more consistent in backing democracy in Azerbaijan. Russia was not an autocracy, but 'directed democracy' was much more firmly entrenched there than it was in Ukraine. The liberal opposition groups who hoped to appropriate the Ukrainian brand were neglecting the need to improve their own image and to compensate for their past unpopularity first. After the Orange Revolution, however, Russia was much less likely to organise an uncontested succession or extension of Putin's power in 2008.

Yushchenko caused a considerable stir in April 2005 by declaring in Washington that he would work with America 'to support the advance of freedom in countries such as Belarus and Cuba'.[30] In Belarus, this could be a joint action, as the US Congress passed the Belarus Democracy Act in October 2004. Joint action in Cuba was not particularly likely, but the fact that Washington valued Ukraine's endorsement was testament to how much had changed. The world's press was now full of reports on countries as diverse as Lebanon, Ecuador, Nepal and Iran that mentioned the Ukrainian example either to confirm or deny the potential for change. The *Christian Science Monitor*, for example, published an article on 'Why Zimbabwe is Not Ukraine'.[31]

Even if it did not deliberately export revolution, post-Orange Ukraine was set to assert itself in the post-Soviet world, pulling others in its wake by force of example and even serving as an alternative pole of attraction to Russia. Ukraine was particularly likely to ally with the old states of the Polish–Lithuanian Commonwealth – Poland, Lithuania, and, it is hoped, one day, Belarus and Moldova – which historically had close relations, and with Turkey, with whom relations were historically all too close. The new geopolitics of oil and the burgeoning relationship with Georgia under Mikhail Saakashvili also meant a new emphasis on the so-called GUAM group (Georgia, Ukraine, Azerbaijan and Moldova – Uzbekistan left in 2002), which was first launched in 1997 but was largely moribund as a result of Russian pressure in the later Kuchma era. It was formally revived at a summit in Chişinău, Moldova, in April 2005, with the presidents of Lithuania and Romania in additional attendance, despite Russia now attacking it as an 'orange belt' along its vulnerable south-western flank.

### The West's Role in the Revolution

Russia's accusations of illegitimate or excessive Western interference found an echo in certain circles in the West, some of whom argued that the entire Revolution was 'made in the USA', as some sarcastic banners on the Maidan had it. It was alleged that 'Yushchenko got the Western nod, and floods of money poured in to groups which support him'.[32] The critics' attempt to draw 'attention to the degree of funding by the US and other western governments for the campaign',[33] normally centred in on a figure of $65 million over two years to back the Ukrainian opposition.[34] Some saw any spending as illegitimate or inherently partial. On 7 December, US Congressman Ron Paul of Texas, a libertarian Republican and critic of the Iraq war, speaking before the House International Relations Committee quoted President Bush saying 'that "Any election (in Ukraine), if there is one, ought to be free from any foreign influence." I agree with the president wholeheartedly,' he continued. 'Unfortunately, it seems that several US government agencies saw things differently and sent US taxpayer dollars into Ukraine in an attempt to influence the outcome.'[35] It was also often alleged that monies were 'funnelled through' US organisations such as Freedom House and the Carnegie Foundation,[36] as if these were extra monies. This is normally how the process works.

American spending was indeed substantial, albeit actually on a declining trend. A lot of detailed figures follow, as an antidote to the vague assertions of America's critics, as well as numerous websites, so readers can check information for themselves. The official figures are that all US government agencies spent $280.48 million in aid to Ukraine in the fiscal year 2002, including $157.92 million under the 1992 Freedom Support Act. The latter included $74 million through USAID, and $25 million for the US State Department Public Diplomacy programme.[37] In 2003, funding for democracy support was cut substantially, by about a third, because of US anger over the Kolchuha affair (Washington believed President Kuchma was guilty of illicitly supplying a hi-tech radar system to Saddam Hussein on the eve of the invasion of Iraq). Overall funding was now $227.48 million, with $55.11 million for democratic reform programmes.[38] The figure for the fiscal year 2004 was $143.47 million, including $34.11 million for democracy assistance.[39] The equivalent figures for the United Kingdom Department for International Development's overall annual budget in Ukraine was £6.5 million, only a small proportion of which went on democracy assistance.[40] George Soros's Renaissance Foundation spent $1.65 million between autumn 2003 and December 2004, supporting the 'New Choice 2004' and 'Freedom of Choice' coalitions of NGOs, and providing very detailed accounts.[41] Considerable sums were also raised privately by the Ukrainian diaspora and by supporters of the Orange Revolution; it is harder to give an accurate sense of how much was raised in this way, but it is possible that it was several million dollars. In Chicago, for example, home to one of North America's largest Ukrainian communities and the original home of Ukraine's new first lady, Katherine Chumachenko, $363,000 were raised.[42]

The critics also listed various reprobates who were guilty of receiving the money. Freedom House administers the Polish-American-Ukrainian Cooperation Institute (PAUCI), which is funded by USAID (www.usaid.kiev.ua), and, through PAUCI, a variety of Ukrainian NGOs.

PAUCI's grants are all listed publicly at www.pauci.org/en/grants/grant. One argument was that the Ukranian recipients were inappropriately political. One Ukrainian NGO criticised by Ron Paul and others was the International Centre for Policy Studies (ICPS, www.icps.kiev.ua), set up in 1994, because Yushchenko was a member of the board. However, the whole point of the ICPS is elite dialogue, which is why regime stalwarts such as Serhii Tihipko were also on the board. ICPS itself claimed that 'the only ICPS–PAUCI project [in this period], worth US $4,500, was aimed at researching and developing methodology for designing regional small business development programs and had nothing to do with any election campaigns'.[43] Another NGO on the list was the Centre for Political and Legal Reforms (www.pravo.org.ua), run by two Rada deputies, Serhii Holovatyi and Ihor Koliushko, and which was set up in November 1996 with the not particularly sinister aim of promoting constitutionalism, i.e. promoting the better working and actual observance of Ukraine's own constitution after it was passed in June of that year. The National Democratic Institute funded similar works, running legal seminars and supporting the Committee of Voters of Ukraine, which has also received help from the Eurasia Foundation. The National Endowment for Democracy (NED) supported the Laboratory of Legislative Initiatives and its excellent publication of academic reference, *Parlament* (Ukrainian spelling, but www.parliament.org.ua), and the website first set up by Hryhorii Gongadze, www.pravda.com.ua. The NED and the US Embassy Public Affairs Section helped fund www.telekritika.kiev.ua, a site devoted to media analysis and media bias monitoring, which was hugely popular amongst Ukrainian journalists. The Institute for Sustainable Communities, based in Vermont, had a $11 million federal contract to help bring about a 'fundamental cultural shift' in Ukraine, as the organisation puts it, 'from a passive citizenry under an authoritarian regime to a thriving democracy with active citizen participation'. Leslie J. McCuaig, Ukraine project director, accepted that 'It has become particularly tricky to walk a very thin line.'[44] In May 2004, the Virginia-based private management consultancy, Development Associates, Inc., was awarded $100 million by the US government 'for strengthening national legislatures and other deliberative bodies worldwide'. According to the organisation's website (www.devassoc.com/devassoc/index.html), several million dollars from this went to Ukraine in advance of the elections.

In late December 2004, the Ukrainian ministry of the economy released details of two contracts, pointing out that the CEC and USAID had signed a Memorandum on Mutual Understanding in March 2004. As a result, two non-partisan projects, 'Citizens' Role in the Elections in Ukraine' (budget

$3.674 million) and 'Promoting Election Organisation in Ukraine' (budget $4.481 million) heavily benefited the CEC, the Rada and all the main political parties, including many of the fake ones.[45] In other words, a large proportion of foreign funding went to the government side – as it should.

In election year, Freedom House, along with the National Democratic Institute and the International Republican Institute (IRI) helped to fund election monitoring by the European Network of Election Monitoring (ENEMO), which was strongly critical of the 21 November poll.[46] Eight Western embassies (the US, the UK, Canada, Netherlands, Switzerland, Norway, Sweden and Denmark) and four NGOs (the NED, Charles Stewart Mott Foundation, Eurasia and George Soros's Renaissance Foundation) helped fund the exit polls conducted by KIIS, the Razumkov Centre, SOCIS, and the Social Monitoring Centre (though only the first two remained in the consortium after the first round). Dick Morris, a former adviser to Bill Clinton, admitted to a clandestine meeting in an unnamed East European capital with members of Yushchenko's team, at which he advised them that a big exit poll would not only be useful in helping to minimise fraud, but that it might also help to bring protesters out on to the streets if it indicated an obvious steal.[47] Despite the assertion by some that this meant that a manufactured projection would replace a 'real' count, the opposite was the case. The official results were fixed and the rival exit polls were fixed, but the exit poll by KIIS–Razumkov was the only fair game in town. It cost $24,700 in round one and $31,000 in round two – which, frankly, was money extremely well spent.[48]

Finally, the Open Society Initiative, and the Citizen Participation in Elections in Ukraine programme, run by Freedom House, the National Democratic Institute (NDI) and the International Republican Institute (IRI), along with the German Marshall Fund and the Canadian International Development Agency, provided support for the youth organisation Pora. However, Pora's own accounts claim this only amounted to $130,000 in total – as against €5 million in small donations 'in kind' – from local sources.[49] Similar support for Znaiu has already been mentioned (see pages 75–6). More general seminars for youth activists had been run in 2002–3, supported by the Alfred Moser Foundation (Netherlands), the Westminster Foundation (UK) and the Fund for European Education (Poland).[50] Many of those trained later ended up in Pora. Freedom House also helped train election monitors in Crimea in August 2004. Contacts began in March 2003, and in April 2004 eighteen Ukrainian activists went to a seminar in the Yugoslav town of Novi Sad. Otpor's Aleksandar Maric was a frequent visitor to Ukraine until he was eventually denied re-entry on 12 October.

According to Maric, 'We trained them [Pora] in how to set up an organisation, how to open local chapters, how to create a "brand", how to create a logo, symbols, and key messages. We trained them in how to identify the key weaknesses in society and what people's most pressing problems were — what might be a motivating factor for people, and above all young people, to go to the ballot box and in this way shape their own destiny.'[51] However, unlike the more direct support for Otpor in 2000 (where the US spent $41 million on the 'operation'),[52] possibly for Zubr in Belarus in 2001, when much money went missing, [53] but not for Georgia's Kmara in 2003,[54] there is not yet any evidence of extra covert payments to Pora. It would be interesting if there were, but the ball is in the critics' court.

USAID also funded Znaiu. The Washington PR firm Rock Creek Creative helped set up a 'Friends of Ukraine' network on behalf of the Global Fairness Initiative linked to Bill Clinton; a conference on 'Ukraine in Europe and the World' in Kiev in February 2004, which was attended by Yanukovych, Yushchenko and the likes of Václav Havel and Madeleine Albright; and the corresponding website www.ukraineineurope.com.[55] In Germany, the Friedrich Ebert Foundation (www.fesukraine.kiev.ua) and Centre for Applied Politics have funded many of the same causes.

So what? None of this is especially problematic. On the whole the West was doing exactly what it should have been doing in Ukraine, though arguably not doing enough. 'Our money doesn't go to candidates; it goes to the process, the institutions that it takes to run a free and fair election,' as the State Department spokesman, Richard Boucher, said.[56] The West was promoting its own values. It may not always live up to them itself, but that does not mean it is wrong to try to help other countries live up to these values. The West has nothing to apologise for. America decided to provide *more* money after the Orange Revolution, an extra $60 million in the fiscal year 2005 (though this was later cut to $33.7 million). It would be wrong to claim that the line between supporting fair process and supporting a particular candidate can always be drawn, however. Several websites, such as www.pravo.org.ua, had prominent links or endorsements ('We recommend') to Yushchenko's site at www.razom.org.ua, which was certainly inadvisable, however much he was closer to their aims, but this is a million miles from the instant insinuation that $65 million directly funded Yushchenko's campaign. At least the West is aware that a line should be drawn somewhere. Normally, the left (and many of the critics were on the left) is proud of the West's spending on international aid, and constantly urging it to spend more although, quite rightly, Britain, for example, does not have a department for 'aid' any more, but one for 'international development', instead. Supporting good government helps ensure that the money is well spent.

Moreover, the idea that Pora was the revolution and that the revolution followed some kind of US script is wide of the mark. It is true that the demonstrators were highly organised, but they were organised by Ukrainians, who were mindful of what had happened in Ukraine in 2001, when the 'Ukraine without Kuchma' protests had failed because the organisers couldn't build a wide enough coalition and put sufficient numbers on the streets. The protesters' ranks had included too many questionable 'nationalists', with too many *agents provocateurs* in their ranks. Staged confrontation with the local police gave the authorities the excuse they needed for a crackdown. In 2004, therefore, Pora was kept off the main stage. There is evidence that Pora was helped directly by similar organisations in Serbia, Georgia and Slovakia, and by thousands of small donations. It was also funded by Davyd Zhvaniia,[57] and by another local businessman, Valerii Borovyk. But it seems grossly naïve to criticise the opposition for taking money from both local businesses[58] and from the West.[59] They needed money from somewhere; without it, they would have lost. Left-wing critics seem to imply that parties that might improve the lot of the poor should remain mired in poverty themselves. Moreover, the first source made the Ukrainian opposition less dependent on the second. The West helped more with method than with money, and there was never the slightest chance of the opposition outspending the regime and its Russian backers. In any case, as one third of the €540 million loan provided by Deutsche Bank in 2004 for building the new Dnipro railway bridge was apparently unaccounted for, the West may have inadvertently financed either Heorhii Kirpa's Italian bank accounts or Yanukovych's campaign to a much greater extent than they helped Yushchenko.[60]

To put it another way, one could imagine something like the critics' fantasy scenario happening in Belarus in September 2006, when President Aliaksandr Lukashenka comes up for re-election. In April 2005, Condoleezza Rice stated fairly directly that America wanted him out of office.[61] However, for a decade Lukashenka's domestic poll rating has been remarkably stable, between 40 and 50 per cent – way ahead of any rival, but, of course, not enough for a guaranteed majority. Lukashenka therefore frequently resorted to ballot-stuffing when necessary. Over the same period, the traditional opposition polled only 10 to 15 per cent, but was strongest in Minsk. Did the US really want to call the 2006 result before the actual election, which could well see Lukashenka winning a clear plurality and faking a majority? Would the US then support protest by a minority in the capital, possibly in front of the world's cameras, against what Rice dubbed 'the last remaining true dictatorship in the heart of Europe' (so-called because there was no doubt that Lukashenka's methods were often brutal)? The point here is to make the enormous contrast with Ukraine. In Ukraine, the authorities could not win a majority, but the opposition did. There was a genuine mass movement to overturn the fraud that attempted to conceal this fact. The West criticised the fraud only after it was perpetrated. The two scenarios look very different to me.

That said, as even Pavlovskii tentatively recognised, the West's role in Ukraine was both direct and indirect. 'Soft power', the pulling power of perceived prosperity and the general ambience of life *à la européenne*, also played a role in the Ukrainian Revolution. The efforts of local NGOs were free-riding to an extent on general globalisation processes and the pulling power of Western capital and political institutions, providing them with a multiplier effect to offset the crude cash spending advantages of the incumbent regime. 'Joining the club' of the EU, NATO and WTO can be a very powerful implicit promise, and one which only 'anointed' candidates can claim to deliver. On the other hand, the West has no reason to be ashamed of the pulling power of democratic ideals and liberal culture, and it was not caught doing anything more heavy-handed. As far back as November 2001, Yushchenko was reportedly wined and dined in Washington by the Bush administration, paid for by the NED. But nothing more substantial has yet been proven, and it is up to the critics to provide evidence.

As they turned out to be so wide of the mark, it seems wrong to spend too much time on the failings of sections of the Western press, except to say that their constant desire to change the story was impatient, imprudent and wrong. It was morally unacceptable to say that there was equal fraud on both sides, or that the Orange Revolution was just a battle of élites rather than of political cultures. These were precisely the myths propagated by the Ukrainian authorities' highly paid 'technologists' in their attempt to keep the old regime in power. The Western media all too often echoed the myth of an inevitably and fatally divided Ukraine[62] that the same Russian technologists had laboured so carefully to construct. Finally, and possibly worst of all, there was far too much gainsaying on the critics' side, and far too little evidence and considered argument. The 'real story' does not suddenly appear just because some journalist decides to write it. Many of the Western harpies had the dubious honour of leading the news on the most partisan local channels, and of being reprinted in the press and on websites such as www.zadonbass.org.[63]

## The EU

There were others in the West who did not exactly welcome the Orange Revolution with open arms. Having been bounced by Poland into its dramatic intervention, a large part of the EU now seemed determined to insist that nothing had changed. The Poles were talking up the prospects of Ukraine's eventual full membership, but the president of the European Parliament, Josep Borrell Fontelles, a Spanish Socialist, in private attacked Polish and Lithuanian interference, which, he said, was 'acting under the influence of the United States'.[64] Even the mainstream EU position, which argued that the time was not right for symbolic declarations,[65] was a brush-off. Yushchenko, however, quite rightly realised that just after the Orange Revolution was exactly the time for symbolic declarations. Ukraine had a limited window of opportunity to make its newly prestigious presence felt, and it pursued a twin-track policy, signing up for an amended three-year Action Plan in February 2005, while focusing on what might then happen in 2008, in order to keep the process moving forward, even though the Action Plan again put the ball back in Ukraine's court. It was again up to Ukraine to deliver.

Yushchenko explicitly rejected the old tongue-twister term for Ukrainian foreign policy, 'multi-vector-ness'. 'I don't like this word,' he said: 'It's associated with the politics of President Kuchma, which caused problems in the East and an unintelligible position in the West.'[66] Ukraine still had plenty of friendships to maintain, but its foreign policy was now uni-directional, in so far as integration with the West was now its overriding priority. Ukrainian diplomats, especially Borys Tarasiuk and Oleh Rybachuk, began telling the West what it had long professed to want to hear: that Ukraine would now be predictable and credible, would deliver on its promises, and would maintain a ten-year programme to become 'EU-compatible', without, as often under Kuchma, periodically threatening to run to Russia instead. In the past, it was suspected that even the old opposition were playing lip-service to 'European values' as a means of joining the club. Now they had demonstrated European values in action: above all, those of civil society, peaceful demonstration and institutional continuity amidst peaceful change. Yushchenko explicitly stated that the new Ukraine's overriding recommitment to democratic values and the rule of law made the EU a more important target for it than NATO, and quite sensibly sought to play the 'procedural' game. In other words, he would aim to downplay high-flown rhetoric about Ukraine's crucial contribution to European history, and quietly get on with the job of reform. The 1999 EU 'Common Strategy' on

Ukraine had stressed that all doors were open. Any European country which fulfilled the criteria (the so-called 'Copenhagen Criteria' drawn up in 1993) was a potential member. In return, Ukraine wanted the EU to drop the term 'neighbourhood' from its vocabulary, and to drop any idea of a 'Russian veto' on Ukraine's European Choice.

A rather different position was taken by the European parliament, which, on 13 January 2005, passed a resolution by 467 to 19 that called on 'the Council, the Commission and the Member States' 'to meet the expectations and hopes raised by the European Union's close involvement in the peaceful Orange Revolution', and 'to consider, besides the measures of the Action Plan within the framework of the European Neighbourhood Policy, other forms of association with Ukraine, giving a clear European perspective for the country and responding to the demonstrated aspirations of the vast majority of the Ukrainian people, possibly leading ultimately to the country's accession to the EU'.[67] This may have been a high-water mark of sorts. Apart from Poland and Lithuania, most EU states have no well-defined historical attitude to Ukraine – which means they are more likely to be swayed by changes in Ukraine itself. Northern and New Europe, plus often Portugal, which has a large community of new Ukranian migrant workers, form a loose group of eleven in favour of a broader relationship, while Mediterranean countries naturally tend to look to the south. France is the most hostile to eventual Ukranian membership, Germany a key swing state.

Ukraine thought it had missed the EU boat after the ten new members, Poland, Lithuania *et al.*, were admitted in May 2004. It thought the Orange Revolution had put its ambitions back on track. The resounding rejection of the EU constitution in France and the Netherlands in May and June 2005 seemed to derail them again. No one could pretend this was good news for Ukraine.

Ukraine's path to NATO seemed more straightforward, given its previous history of successful cooperation under the Partnership for Peace scheme and the 'Charter on a Distinctive Partnership', signed between NATO and Ukraine in 1997. Admittedly, this had been taken as far as it could in the late Kuchma era, and Ukraine's NATO partners were now keen to move beyond joint exercises to a new era of in-service reform and technical upgrade to ease military compatibility. This would cost money, but Ukraine was confident that talks about membership might start as early as 2008. During the campaign, Yushchenko had already promised to lower military service to twelve months (nine months for graduates) as a first step towards creating a fully professional army by 2010. At the April 2005 NATO summit in Vilnius, Ukraine was offered an 'Intensified Dialogue' on Ukraine's aspirations to membership, if not yet on membership itself, and it was assumed the dialogue would get more intense once the March 2006 elections were out of the way (NATO still has a bad image in east Ukraine). Ukraine has a lot to offer NATO, heavy military transport planes in particular, but NATO basing in Ukraine might be a different story – provocative to Russia at the least.

### Poland and 'New Europe'

Poland's leading role in the EU mission to Kiev confirmed its vital importance to Ukrainian foreign policy. Despite an often troubled past, mutually warm relations now extend across the political spectrum in both countries. The right wing had buried several hatchets in the 1980s, when Solidarity and Rukh activists exchanged influence and ideas. At the time of the Orange Revolution, Poland was still governed by the main ex-Communist party, the SLD (the Union of the Democratic Left, which was in office from 1993 to 1997 and from 2001 to 2005), but this helped former Communists such as President Aleksander Kwaśniewski (1995–2005) and Marek Siwiec, head of the National Security Bureau from 1997, to cosy up with the likes of Kuchma, *and* to point the way ahead. When he headed the EU mission to Ukraine, Kwaśniewski brought a symbolic message about how the old guard can survive a round table process and ultimately prosper. Business relations were good.

The pro-Ukrainian position in Poland was therefore unlikely to be disturbed by the change of government that was likely in 2005. Some of the right-wing parties, such as the League of Polish Families and the populist Samoobrona ('Self-Defence'), harboured elements that dwelt on the Polish–Ukrainian confrontations of the past (the sixtieth anniversary of the 1943 Volyn massacres, for instance, touched many raw nerves), but the mainstream alternative, the anti-corruption Law and Justice (Prawo i Sprawiedliwóśc, usually referred to as PiS) and the neo-liberal Civic Platform, were, if anything, more romantically pro-Ukrainian, largely because the new Ukraine fitted the Polish world-view. According to one Polish commentator:

> Ukraine, central Europe and the US share a common interest in the Ukrainian revolution's success: first, because all three share the same fundamental belief that liberal democracy is better than authoritarianism, including in its capacity to ensure stability; second, because they recognise that a liberal, independent, western-oriented Ukraine is the only long-term guarantee that Russia too will slowly start to shift in the same

direction. The victory of this political fellowship and strategic perspective will mark the final defeat of the classic Franco–German, 'old European' view that the only way to deal with Russia is to flatter its leadership while ignoring or finessing its authoritarianism at home and imperial reflexes abroad. Even before Ukraine, it had been clear that this strategy was a failure: now, Russia needs from the west the language of liberal Anglo–Saxon democracy, not of continental *raison d'etat*.'[68]

Somewhat more bluntly, in the words Kwaśniewski is supposed to have used, 'for every great power Russia without Ukraine is better than Russia with Ukraine'.[69]

The Russian version of this view, propagated by the likes of Sergei Markov, is to imagine a Polish plot 'to become the patrons of the whole of Central and Eastern Europe',[70] and to regret the failure to play the 'Polish card' more vigorously before the second round: 'I told them [the Yanukovych team] to use anti-Polish rhetoric.'[71] (Lukashenka in Belarus was preparing a rabidly anti-Polish campaign for 2006.) In a historical perspective, anti-Polish propaganda played a big role in cementing east and central Ukrainians' loyalties to both imperial Russia and to the new Soviet state in the 1920s. On 2 December Mikhail Leontev of Russia's Channel One (formerly ORT, Civic Russia TV) cast doubt on the suspicious 'enthusiasm of Ukraine's Polish and Lithuanian brothers to act as mediators in the post-election conflict'. 'The motives of the Poles to [act as mediators in] Ukraine is transparent from Ukrainian history. The Poles have always been very active in Ukraine and today especially so ... They want to appear as the Great Poland, and to do so is possible only on the bones of Ukraine.' Russia was therefore simply reprising its seventeenth-century role of defending Ukraine, and President Kuchma, like the seventeenth-century Cossack leader Bohdan Khmelnytskyi, was 'the great balancer between Russia and the West'.[72] Russia, in other words, was again guilty of putting hard geopolitics before the politics of political culture.

Poland had also shown a good understanding of how the EU actually works. Before becoming a member in May 2004, Warsaw had to endure Jacques Chirac's patronising comments about the New Europeans being 'infantile' and 'missing a good opportunity to stay quiet' or keep their counsel (*de se taire*) over the Iraq war. Once inside, they could behave like the French and lead policy by the nose. Ironically, Ukraine could never afford to be as categorically anti-Russian as some of the New Europeans, but its basic instincts were clearly more in tune with its Western neighbours. Having dreaded the possibility of a hard border descending in the West after May

2004, there was now an obviously symbiotic relationship: Ukraine needed the east European lobby in Brussels and the east Europeans now found their foreign policy voice given extra weight. The new Ukraine naturally tends to have similar concerns to other east European countries. These include: a post-imperial emphasis on sovereignty; a post-communist suspicion that Russia is parleying economic power in the region for political power, a historical mistrust of great-power pragmatism, a tendency towards idealism as an antidote to historical marginalisation, which America is currently seen as embodying and Brussels abandoning for a narrowly technocratic method; and the corollary view that membership of the EU is a cultural achievement and not just a question of GDP per capita. With a much more recent experience of occupation and empire than most of Old Europe, most of New Europe is more prone to compromise rather than coercion; but there is also the experience of Munich and Yalta, an instinctive dislike of authoritarian states, such as Iraq under Saddam, and the argument that the threat of force still plays a role in international affairs. New Europeans, in Robert Kagan's formula, are more like the Americans from Mars than the Eurocrats from Venus,[73] although given some of the paradoxical effects of the 1975 Helsinki Accords, there is much more instinctive respect for international law. Given the burgeoning relationship between Yushchenko and Georgian president Mikhail Saakashvili, Kiev could also usefully help clear up New Europe's backyard by reviving the part historical, part geopolitical idea of its central position in a Baltic–Black Sea alliance of like-minded states, including Poland, Ukraine, the Baltic States, Georgia, it is hoped Moldova and also it is hoped one day Belarus.

### Ukraine and America

That said, the distinction between Old and New Europe is often overdone, as is New Europe's often simplistically strident anti-Russianism. West Ukrainian nationalism is more anti-Russian than most, but the west Ukrainians are not the new masters in Kiev. Nevertheless, Ukraine shares the empathy for Washington that is currently much greater in Warsaw or Budapest than it is in Paris or Berlin. The ease with which Washington shrugged off Ukraine's gradual troop withdrawal from Iraq in 2005 showed that it could welcome the Orange Revolution from a broader perspective. According to one neo-conservative, Radek Sikorski, 'The Iraq contingent is a small price to pay for [Yushchenko keeping his promise to withdraw]. Ukraine can be helpful elsewhere.'[74] The American reaction was partly to do with the power of media and personality politics in the

US, but the Orange Revolution was also brilliantly timed to take advantage of fashionable democracy domino theory. More narrowly, some Cold War veterans and neo-conservatives welcomed anything that weakened Russia.

Michael Ledeen of the American Enterprise Institute greeted Yushchenko's final victory as a 'happy day . . . for those of us who have long preached the power of democratic revolution' and, conversely, had condemned America's past folly of 'alliances with "friendly tyrants"'.[75] These comments were difficult to fault, as were those of Ledeen's colleague, Radek Sikorski, who heads the AEI's New Atlantic Initiative, which is 'dedicated to revitalising and expanding the Atlantic community of democracies', and was set up in 1996:

> Europe came close in 2004 to seeing a new curtain dividing it from north to south. Had the fraudulent result of the Ukrainian elections stood, the continent's geopolitical division would have gelled and the window of liberty in the former USSR would have closed. The line from the Barents Sea in the North, to the Black Sea in the South, along the eastern borders of Norway, Finland, the Baltic States, Poland, Slovakia, Hungary, Moldova, and Romania, would have marked a division between democracies to its west, and post-Soviet 'managed democracies', that is to say kleptocratic dictatorships, to its east.[76]

In his 2005 inauguration speech, President Bush declared that: 'The survival of liberty in our land increasingly depends on the success of liberty in other lands. The best hope for peace in our world is the expansion of freedom in all the world . . . So it is the policy of the United States to seek and support the growth of democratic movements and institutions in every nation and culture, with the ultimate goal of ending tyranny in our world.'[77] Bush was also fond of the catchphrase, 'democracy is not America's gift to the world, but God's gift to humanity'. As a self-proclaimed 'values-based' politician, Yushchenko was comfortable mimicking the same rhetoric, and that of some of Bush's predecessors, in a masterful speech to Congress, during which he echoed Ronald Reagan's famous Berlin speech in 1987 to say: 'We do not want any more walls dividing Europe, and I'm certain that neither do you. . .Please make this step toward Ukraine. Please tear down this wall.'[78] Ukraine was well-placed to exploit the sometime contradiction between the universal principle of democracy for all and the realpolitik with which it is sometimes applied. There was no storm of protest after the blatant fixing of the 2003 Azerbaijani election. America has downplayed its democratisation policy in 'frontline' states such as the 'Stans' of central

Asia. But Ukraine's new leader provided a perfect PR opportunity to advertise the success of the democracy export drive: he was articulate, brave and European. Not only was he granted a joint address to both houses of Congress in April 2005, with elderly senators chanting his name, but the vice-president, Dick Cheney, wore an orange tie in support.

More pragmatically, others welcomed Ukraine to the American-led 'Supra-national Mega-coalition' of the civilised world against its opponents.[79] At one time, Ukraine had threatened to fall on the wrong side of this divide, as the Kuchma coterie grew notorious for selling arms to Saddam Hussein's Iraq, as well as to China and Iran, and, supposedly, even to the Taliban. My Ukrainian friends wondered aloud if Ukraine might be the next to be included in Bush's 'axis of evil' list after his 2002 State of the Union address. Ukraine is also close to many areas of current American concern, such as the New Europe, central Asia and Georgia, and the potential 'new democracies' of the Middle East and the Levant. It could also help clean up some local 'rogue states' or quasi-states, most obviously the separatist 'Dnister Republic' in neighbouring eastern Moldova, a neo-Soviet wonderland and cesspit of corruption, which Kuchma and successive interior and customs ministers had helped prop up by participating in that corruption. Ukraine also has a role to play in local energy geopolitics, although hardly one important enough to support assertions that the Orange Revolution was all about oil.[80] Kiev hopes to find partners to reverse the recently constructed Odesa–Brody line, so that it would flow from south to north, as originally intended, to carry Caspian oil to Poland via Płock and Gdańsk and beyond. (In 2004 Kuchma had authorised 'reverse use', allowing Russian companies to supply a trickle of oil to Mediterranean countries.) Russia might also benefit from the new arrangement, via the proposed €2 billion German-Ukrainian-Russian energy consortium (Oil and Gas of Ukraine, Gazprom, and Ruhrgas). Long-term, it is hoped to extend the link eastwards to Central Asia or even Iran.

At the time of writing, the Orange Revolution is less often situated in reflex anti-Russianism and *schadenfreude*,[81] though it has certainly emboldened many critics of Russia's less than perfect democracy. Richard Holbrooke, assistant secretary of state under Clinton, argued for a rapid invitation for Ukraine to join NATO (within two years), but added a rather celebratory reference to 2004 as Putin's *'annus horribilis'*.[82] Voices such as Pat Buchanan's, who asked 'What are we up to in Ukraine?', have also been somewhat isolated.[83]

----

Ukraine's *annus mirabilis* continued into 2005. Although progress was uneven at home, Ukrainians took immense pride in Yushchenko's every visit to Brussels, Washington or Davos. There was much hope of a new virtuous circle. Under Kuchma, Ukraine had grown diplomatically semi-isolated, and its domestic habits got worse. Brussels and Washington were reluctant to open the door until Ukraine internalised Western values in politics and business, and Ukraine was unwilling to reform until some kind of opening was made. The Orange Revolution in itself won Ukraine a higher regional profile; the more it lived up to its promise, the more effective a regional player it would be. And real international partnership with the West could reinforce the reform impulse at home. Balancing the relationships with Washington and Brussels might prove difficult, however. As a 'new democracy', Ukraine looked more towards America, as 'new Europe' it looked to the EU.

Ukraine is not a natural great power, or even a slumbering giant. Even Leonid Kuchma liked to repeat the myth that the Ukrainians, 'in contrast to the Russians, are a benign and absolutely non-imperial nation'.[84] Ukrainian leaders have always cut their cloth with more skill. But under Kuchma, the foreign policy élite acted all too often as though the world owed them a living. Under Yushchenko, Ukraine promised to raise its game. Russia destroyed the illusion of its local veto power by its ham-fisted intervention in 2004, and it is open to speculation what the New, New Europe might look like in ten years' time.

# 10

# Conclusions: Revolution Number 5

After the Warsaw Pact revolutions of 1989 and the collapse of the USSR in 1991, Ukraine was third in a new wave of revolutions, after Yugoslavia in 2000 and Georgia in 2003. The Yugoslav and Georgian revolutions were also against quasi-democratic or semi-authoritarian regimes, but were arguably unique in other respects. Both were war-torn and supposedly 'failing' states. Outside intervention was important in Belgrade and probably crucial in Tbilisi, where both the West *and* Russia accepted Shevardnadze had to go. Ukraine's Orange Revolution was of a different type. And, because it was much larger than Georgia, commentators could immediately talk of Ukraine as a new trend-setter, not just a one-off.

But was it actually a revolution? Was there a change of regime? Or was it just a 'revolt of millionaires against billionaires',[1] a coup staged by 'rentier democrats' bankrolled by US dollars, as its critics suggest? Every revolution has its fellow-travellers. A split in the old regime is probably a *sine qua non* for a successful transfer of power. But this was no palace coup, and it took real people power to challenge the Ukrainian system, which was much stronger than the eleven-year Shevardnadze regime. There was certainly no bloodbath, no Terror, no set-piece storming of public buildings, though revolutions often have to be non-revolutionary in order to succeed. Ukraine's negotiated path to peaceful settlement stood in marked contrast to Kyrgyzstan or even Georgia – certainly in contrast to the bloody events and suppression of protests in Uzbekistan. Neither was it yet clear if the Orange Revolution would initiate a true social revolution, famously defined by Theda Skocpol as 'rapid, basic transformations of a society's state and class structures . . . accompanied and in part carried through by class-based revolts from below'.[2] This book was written too soon after the events for the longer-term perspective to be clear. It remained to be seen whether the undoubted generational change and apparent initial sense of purpose in the new government would usher in long-term social and economic change.

Nevertheless, the self-proclaimed Orange Revolution can be accepted as profoundly revolutionary in several key senses, and I have been happy to use the term. First, there was a revolution of expectations. What was supposed to happen did not happen; the attempted election steal failed. Second, there was a real desire for regime change, not just for a new president. The mood in the Maidan did not just indicate support for Yushchenko or Tymoshenko personally; it was the articulate anger of a people finding their voice. It was often said that Yushchenko might disappoint, but that he could always be replaced after five years. If Yanukovych had become president, there might have been no such chance. The cross-class support that some bizarrely see as suspicious is exactly what regime change needs. Students wanted a change in political culture, the poor wanted a change in political culture, and small and medium-sized businesses wanted a change in political culture. As Anders Åslund put it after visiting Kiev at the time, 'the demonstration didn't seem to have any class identity at all. Hardly any names of businesses, parties, or organisations were to be seen. No one talked about social or economic issues. This was pure politics.'[3] The regime was split, so powerful governing interests wanted a change in political culture too. The key sentiment was 'kick the bastards out', and that is what revolutions are all about. Some in the new government were often guilty of fighting dirty (Tymoshenko), of empire building (Poroshenko), and, perhaps, of failing to define and police the hazy line between politics and business (Ihor Kolomoiskyi's Privat Group allegedly hoped to become 'Orange oligarchs'), but the prospects for rapidly transforming the behaviour of the state and the relationships between the citizens and the state were good. The poisonous atmosphere of the old regime had gone. Perhaps the biggest test would be whether 'political technology' had really met its match, and whether or not its ugly methodology would be used again in 2006. A second key test would be whether the new authorities would refrain from using 'administrative resources' in 2006.

Thirdly, the epicentre of this change in political culture, for the first time in modern Ukrainian history, was in Kiev and in central Ukraine.[4] Even in August 1991, Kiev had been relatively quiet (I was there). The Orange Revolution was neither led by the West nor by west Ukraine. Electorally, it was Yushchenko who rode this civic mood, winning broader support across Ukraine, uniting the west and centre, the Right Bank and the Left, and winning sufficient anti-regime protest votes in parts of the east and south, such as Mykolaïv (once again, there is a useful contrast with Belarus, where the opposition has just not been able to broaden its political and geographical base). It was Yanukovych who looked like the regional politician, and the

Russian 'technologists' who had completely missed this change of mood. It wasn't just Yanukovych from Donetsk that they couldn't sell nationally, but Yanukovych's and their own authoritarian culture. Ukraine was therefore a profoundly different country in 2004 than it had been even in 1991. All previous elections had been 'the west (of Ukraine) versus the rest', with the west a natural minority. Now central Ukraine was on board, and at the wheel.

The reasons for this were complex. Yushchenko was undoubtedly helped in the second and third rounds by the Socialists, who are largely a party of rural central Ukraine. The rural paper, *Silski visti* ('Village News'), which had survived a campaign to close it, was broadly pro-Yushchenko in the second and third rounds, having also supported Moroz in the first. More fundamentally, rural Ukraine had changed culturally and socially since 1991. In the nineteenth century, the peasantry had been the main support base, or target constituency, of the national movement. But the Great Famine of 1932–3 and the imposition of the ruinous collective farm system had broken its back as a social force. In 2004, however, it responded warmly to Yushchenko's rebranding of the national idea, which mined older traditions, not of ethnonationalism, but of Christian rhetoric and traditional values. Cynics pointed to the presence of agribusinessmen such as Petro Poroshenko in Yushchenko's camp, who supposedly 'delivered' the rural vote, but the changing social conditions in the countryside since the reform of the collective farm system, which had begun in December 1999, were much more important. More exactly, the reform had been complied with most fully in west and central Ukraine, so that rural voters there were less dependent on what used to be the almost feudal power of the collective farm bosses. They were dependent on them to a certain extent, however. They still needed state money for the harvest and leasing payments for land shares, and, often enough, basics such as petrol for farm machinery. However, banally but crucially, the 2004 election was late, especially the second and third rounds. The Orange Revolution had been shrouded in snow. The harvest was already in, and payments had already been made. Rural voters could, for once, vote in relative freedom.[5]

In contrast to Yushchenko's value-based campaign, which helped consolidate a new version of the 'national idea', the Russian political technologists sold a largely negative message to eastern and southern Ukraine. The anti-nationalist and 'Bushchenko' campaigns attempted to play on the locals' sense of what they were not, but Pavlovskii, Markov *et al.* were captive to the myth of an ersatz Russia, and were incapable of selling east Ukrainians a positive sense of their alternative Ukrainian identity – one that might have better motivated them to collective action in support of Yanukovych or some other candidate. Yanukovych's alternative campaign colours of blue and white were all very well, but they carried little real symbolism. They were really only the colours of 'The Party', Yanukovych's Party of Regions. Southeast Ukraine remained sullen and alienated after the election, but, despite the publicity given to the regional split during the Orange Revolution, it was possible that Ukraine might come out of the election *more* united than before. Yushchenko had shown how to bring the west and the centre together (and if the authorities won again there was a real possibility of alienation growing in the former Habsburg west, which saw itself as trapped in a mire of post-Soviet corruption and unnaturally cut off from its central European past), and he had a potential message to sell further east. Commentators had always agreed that twenty-first century Ukraine was too ethnically, linguistically and culturally fragile to build a nineteenth-century *Volksstaat*, and that a 'civic' identity was the way forward. But under Kuchma, this had been an empty box. A civic identity might involve some pride in the *cives* for its political institutions (as we were taught in post-war Britain), its success in constitutional engineering and in building a stable democracy (post-war Germany), or for a generous welfare state (Scandinavia), the creation of a multi-ethnic melting-pot and land of opportunity (America), or for an active citizenry, building its own future. Under Yushchenko there was finally some real chance of Ukraine building some combination or selection of the five, of putting some real content in the empty box.

Fourthly, there was a dramatic revolution against the regional trend towards semi-authoritarian quasi-democracy, that began in Russia with Yeltsin's shelling of the Moscow White House in 1993 and with his deeply-flawed re-election in 1996, and, nearer to home, with the election of Kuchma in Ukraine and Lukashenka in Belarus in 1994. But the post-Soviet form of semi-authoritarianism is peculiar. The local states have inherited a formidable apparatus of 'administrative' control (though they do not always choose to use it), but are also paradoxically weak in many respects, even in terms of their conventional repressive capacities, even though these seem effective enough to journalists who have been imprisoned, or to demonstrators who have been beaten. Indeed, in the 1990s many of the successor states, Ukraine included, were expected to fall apart. What local élites have therefore rebuilt is in a sense a substitute for a workable state, a short-cut means of retaining power, an edifice of illusion – or what I have called elsewhere 'virtual politics'.[6] Unlike traditional authoritarian states, the point is not to trap the population in some kind of repressive box, but to trap them in the perception that they are trapped in some kind of box – in other words, to convince them that there is no alternative.

Ukraine's Orange Revolution was therefore the first revolution within and against this system of virtual politics. Post-Soviet states are not so much fragile, as vulnerable to key segments of the population turning off message, or switching channels to another message. In Georgia in 2003, a tired regime was unable to sell the population any *dramaturgiia* to justify its hold on power (Shevardnadze had previously twice arranged convenient victories against the pliable local Communist leader Dzhumber Patiashvili in 1995 and 2000). In Ukraine in 2004, the authorities' Russian 'technologists' tried vigorously to sell a particular myth of east versus west, and the nationalist 'threat'. Enough of the population bought it to polarise the election, but not enough to guarantee victory. The key tipping point in the Orange Revolution was therefore not only Yushchenko's ability to shift the electoral balance between Ukrainian east and west, but also the emergence of a large number of people who rejected the idea that the election was about regional politics, and who simply stood up in the Maidan and said the real issue was something else. First of all, there was a protest against fraud, an attempt to prove that, in the words of the Orange anthem, *Razom nas bahato*, 'We aren't beasts of burden; we aren't goats.' Second, it was a protest against the rotten system of government that had implemented this fraud, and the hope that something better would take its place. And for all its bluster, and despite the fact that Yushchenko was poisoned to stop him winning, the state showed its real weakness when sufficient numbers defied it. In this sense, the Orange Revolution definitely could be exported in the future, although other neighbouring regimes were somewhat stronger, or just more authoritarian in their response to protest.

Finally, in a comparative perspective, the style and method of the Ukrainian revolution was genuinely novel. Most notable was the radical use of the internet and other alternative media. For ten years, parties and politicians throughout the world have used the net to advertise themselves, to raise money and to build a support base, such as Howard Dean in 2004, but in Ukraine in 2004, the internet was used to combat the hegemony of the official mass media (in Pora's words, 'to kill the TV within yourself'), and to generate ideas, a style of acting, and a critical mass. As with 'flash' demos in the West, Our Ukraine, Pora *et al.* also used internet and texting technologies to coordinate action. The internet was not as well-developed as this in Belgrade in 2000. Access was limited politically and financially in Belarus in 2001, and by a comparatively underdeveloped network in Georgia in 2003. In Ukraine in 2004, however, the audience was larger and more attuned to multi-media possibilities. The NGOs all had innovative sites that interacted; there were a number of blogs that became well-read; and even official sites such as Our Ukraine's www.razom.org.ua helped the number of readers to rise enormously. Some estimates are that the total audience went up as much as ten-fold.[7] Westerners who tuned in or logged on, including those looking for feeds for news reports, seem overwhelmingly to have visited opposition sites (several of which had English versions) rather than the Yanukovych alternatives, which was another factor in cementing Western solidarity against the fraud, and, often enough, for Yushchenko.

Another factor was the explosion in humour. The Orange Revolution was possibly the first Situationist revolution, as Situationists have normally amused nobody but themselves. The Maidan's rules of (non-) engagement helped create a non-violent but aggressive opposition stance. Humour and a festival atmosphere also helped to express the population's loss of fear, and served as a prophylactic against provocations. These were frequent and potentially serious, but, unlike in 2001, they were now easily recognised and ignored. In 2001, a cynical regime had triumphed over a protest movement that, perhaps naively, assumed the Gongadze-Melnychenko scandal was so damning the regime would simply collapse or fall on its sword. In 2004, the crowd was now more sophisticated than the regime, which 'relied on primitive people for its provocations'.[8]

## Future Scenarios

So what next? An immediate political revanche was extremely unlikely given the pseudo-legalistic nature of Yushchenko's takeover of power, the extent to which Yanukovych's fraudsters had so obviously been caught in the act, the disarray of the new opposition, and some local élites' habits of deferring to new leaders. Politicians from Donetsk, who defended their 'boss' until the end, now hailed the new boss. Russia's role in 2006 was likely to be more exploratory than vengeful. Neither was a covert revanche likely, as with the Yugoslav old guard's complicity in the assassination of Zoran Djindjic in March 2003. Even if Tymoshenko was supposed to play Djindjic to Yushchenko's Koštunica, despite Pavlovskii's dark hints that he wouldn't wish to see Tymoshenko meet the same fate as Zhurab Zhvania,[9] the Georgian premier who was supposed to have died by accident, from a kitchen gas leak in 2004. The irreconcilable opposition still talked of stealth tactics, such as encouraging protests over rising fuel prices and plotting to reintroduce the majoritarian voting system, but clearly it lacked the strength to tackle the new government head-on.

Nor was it likely that Yushchenko would end up like Georgian president Mikhail Saakashvili, with no opposition and hardly any independent media. Yushchenko's opponents were in short-term disarray, but had too many resources and too big a potential electorate. Unlike Georgia, Ukraine is a big country which will always be relatively diverse. Yushchenko was not a natural autocrat – indeed, he used to be criticised for being too timid. Nor were there more ruthless figures behind him, preparing to seize power. There was no October Revolution round the corner. Tymoshenko might have behaved differently in the same position, but that is why Yushchenko is president and she isn't.

More prosaically, the new authorities might do just what they promised, so that Ukraine might settle into a normal politics of struggle and setback. Given how bad the old regime had become, Yushchenko would retain popularity for a while just by standing still. But his advisers were already daring to talk of a two-term presidency, and of what they would need to have delivered by 2009.

And what of Yushchenko's health? Medical experts had no real previous cases to draw on. One school argued that Yushchenko looked as bad as he did because the body deals with poisons of the type used against him by forcing them out through the skin, and that this showed that his defences had done their job. With treatment, they said, his facial 'acne' would disappear within two to three years. Another school of thought argued that the internal damage to his organs was likely to be considerable, especially as dioxin's half-life is seven years. On the other hand, Yushchenko the president now seemed a stronger man than Yushchenko the candidate. Some attributed this to his surviving the poisoning, but it was also the more general redemption of a man whose personal cavalry had symbolised the nation's rebirth. Ukrainians did talk in these terms – but they were also reluctant to place all their hopes in one man. Yushchenko faced the challenging job of bridging the contradiction. His time-keeping was still woeful, but he seemed more dynamic. When he faced big initial choices, he often went for the more radical option, particularly in appointing Tymoshenko, but he also slapped her back down on occasion. The division of labour between the two would define the future. It had worked well in the past. In the 1999 to 2001 government, Yushchenko fronted the reforms and international negotiations while Tymoshenko acted against the oligarchs. During the 2004 election, Tymoshenko took the radical role and allowed Yushchenko to appear more presidential. The relationship was now potentially unbalanced by the secret deal and by Tymoshenko's rising popularity. Keeping her ambition in check might prove Yushchenko's most difficult task to date. A Ukraine more dominated by Tymoshenko would certainly be revolutionary, but would also be more populist, like Evita without Péron.

Poroshenko and Tymoshenko also constantly rowed, but represented different aspects of the same problem: excessive compromise with the old regime and the excesses of 'anti-oligarchic' populism. Yushchenko normally took the middle ground, but the middle ground needed to be stronger.

----

Some old habits died hard. It was unrealistic to expect political culture to be transformed overnight. But it was also crazy to start claiming that nothing had changed, or to write off Yushchenko and Tymoshenko's efforts after only a hundred days.[10] Despite some tactical missteps and necessary compromises, the new leadership has at least tried to put its policies into long-term focus. In ten years' time, Ukraine *could* have become a very different country indeed.

# Notes

## Chapter One

1. Yanina Vas'kovskaia, 'Kak Yushchenko ssylali na krainii server', *Novaia gazeta*, no. 89, 2 December 2004.
2. Remarks by Ruslan Kniazevych in testimony to the Supreme Court, 2 December 2004, www.ukrpravda.com/archive/?4122-6-77.
3. Vasyl Koval and Yurii Butusov, 'The Presidential Administration Consultant: "According to Our Data, Yushchenko Led the Election All the Time Of the Vote Count"', *Dzerkalo tyzhnia*, no. 52, 25–30 December 2004.
4. The findings can be found in English at www.exitpoll.org.ua/index.php?lang=eng.
5. Author's interview with Oleksii Solohubenko of the BBC, 2 February 2005.
6. 'How Yanukovych Forged the Elections. Headquarters' Telephone Talks Intercepted', 24 November 2004, www2.pravda.com.ua/en/archive/2004/november/24/4.shtml. Translation somewhat adapted from the original Ukrainian. The original transcripts were published as 'Yak Yanukovych fal'syfikuvav vybory' on the *Ukrains'ka pravda* website in three parts. Part one appeared on 24 November 2004 at www2.pravda.com.ua/archive/2004/november/24/4.shtml, followed by part two on 25 November at www2.pravda.com.ua/archive/2004/november/25/4.shtml; and part three on 26 November at www2.pravda.com.ua/archive/2004/november/26/3.shtml. The tapes themselves can be found at http://maidan.uar.net/audio.
7. In 1973 Medvedchuk served two months for assault. His connections in the local *komsomol* secured his early release. Given the black PR spewed out by Medvedchuk's TV channels about Yushchenko and the 'Nashisty', it is ironic that Medvedchuk's father is alleged to have served in the *Arbeitsamt* (Employment Office) during the Nazi occupation, the bureau that rounded up Ukrainians for slave labour in the Third Reich. See Dmytro Chobit, *Nartsys. Shtrykhy do politychnoho portreta Viktora Medvedchuka*, (Kiev: Prosvita, 2001).
8. Yurii Butusov, 'Ide poliuvaniia na "krotiv", ide poliuvannia!', *Dzerkalo tyzhnia*, no. 51, 18–24 December 2004.
9. Yuliia Mostova, 'Tumannist Yanukovycha', *Dzerkalo tyzhnia*, no. 25, 26 June–2 July 2004.
10. Calculation by the Committee of Voters of Ukraine; see www.ourukraine.org/newsletter/issue58; 24 November 2004. This analysis is in English and contains an excellent map showing just how and where turnout went up in the second round.
11. Dmitrii Marunich, 'Georgii [Heorhii] Kirpa: "chelovek-lokomotiv"', 18 March 2003, www.glavred.info/?art=7143927.
12. 'Ukraine: Prime Minister Assaults Minister of Transport', 7 December 2004, www.prima-news.ru/eng/news/news/2004/12/7/30513.html.

## Chapter Two

1. See www.compromat.ru/main/kuchma/yanukovich_a.htm; Vadim Vavilov, 'Krestnyi otets Yanukovych', *Nezavisimaia gazeta*, 18 June 2004, www.ng.ru/ideas/2004-06-18/ 10_yanukovich.html.
2. *BBC News online*, 24 November 2004, http://news.bbc.co.uk/1/hi/world/europe/ 4038803.stm.
3. See the article at www2.pravda.com.ua/archive/2004/november/19/7.shtml.
4. 'V 1993 godu Kuchma uchastvoval v pokhishchenii DM 12 mln', 18 September 2000, www.compromat.ru/main/kuchma/varex.htm; and 'Allegations about "death squadrons" operating in Ukraine', 3 April 2002, http://prima-news.ru/eng/news/news/ 2002/4/3/9366.html.
5. Oleksandr Bilets'kyi, 'Donets'kyi "Shvets"', *Dzerkalo tyzhnia*, no. 45, 22–28 November 2003.
6. 'Rinat Akhmetov. Chast I', 28 October 2004, http://rupor.info/full.php?aid=1445&c =0053B5.
7. Dmitrii Midich, 'Mova po fene', *Profil*, no. 33, 13 September 2004.
8. Theodore H. Friedgut, *Iuzovka and Revolution. Volume II: Politics and Revolution in Russia's Donbass, 1869–1924*, (Princeton: Princeton University Press, 1994), p. 152. (Donbas is the Ukranian spelling.)
9. Ivan Lozowy, from an unpublished letter to the *Spectator*, via *The Ukraine List*, # 289, 28 November 2004; Ivan Kolos, 'Bombs and Smashing Heads', 20 October 2004, www.tol.cz/look/TOL/section_blogs_single.tpl?IdLanguage=1&IdPublication =22&NrIssue=4&NrSection=2.
10. See the map showing death rates reproduced at www.faminegenocide.com/resources/ famine_map.html.
11. See the book-length attack, with its own website, at http://kniga.temnik.com.ua; and the story at www.provokator.com.ua/d/2004/12/02/132137.html.
12. *Financial Times*, 28 January 2000 and 31 March 2001. See also the IMF statement at www.imf.org/external/np/sec/nb/2000/NB0015.HTM.
13. A summary is still available at www.imf.org/external/np/sec/nb/2000/nb0026.htm.
14. Mel'nichenko, *Kto est' kto. Na divane prezidenta Kuchmy* (Kiev: 2002), p. 28.
15. The fullest available biography of Tymoshenko can be found at www.elitprofi.com.ua/ olig/tymoshenko.shtml.
16. See the story in *Komsomol'skaia pravda – Ukraina*, 4 February 2005, at www.kp. kiev.ua/2005/02/04/doc51499/.
17. Matthew Brzezinski, *Casino Moscow*, (New York: Touchstone, 2002), p. 137.
18. Oleg El'tsov, 'Gazovaia printsessa Ukrainy', *FreeLanceBureau*, 28 September 2000, also available at www.compromat.ru/main/kuchma/printsessa.htm.
19. Kost' Bondarenko, *Atlanty i kariatydy*, (L'viv: Kal'variia, 2000), p. 96; Raymond Bonner, 'Ukraine Staggers on Path to the Free Market', *New York Times*, 9 April 1997.
20. Yurii Zushchik, 'Zhenshchina s proshlym', *Korrespondent*, (Ukraine), 19 February 2005, p. 21.
21. Mel'nichenko, *Kto est' kto. Na divane prezidenta Kuchmy*, pp. 19 and 23.
22. 'Tymoshenko accused of stealing $1 billion', *Kyiv Post*, 8 February 2001.
23. Navi Abdullaev, 'Russia Adds Fuel To Fire in Ukraine', *Moscow Times*, 9 August 2001.

## Chapter Three

1. 'Speech of L. Kravchuk on Ukrainian TV (19 August 1991)', in Les Taniuk (ed.), *Khronika oporu*, (Kiev: Vik-Dnipro, 1991), pp. 102–3.
2. Vasyl' Kremen, Dmytro Tabachnyk and Vasyl' Tkachenko, *Ukraïna: al'ternatyvy postupu. Krytyka istorychnoho dosvidu*, (Kiev: ARC-Ukraine, 1996), p. 465.
3. Anatolii Ben', *Syndykat*, (Kiev: Pravdy i sudu, 2004), p. 58.
4. Mykola Semena, 'Leonid Hrach: dos'e ochyma opozytsiinoho zhurnalista', dated no more exactly than '2003', www.glavred.info/mission/ ?man=1054724489&art =1054897155.
5. Serhiy Rudenko, 'Serhiy Tyhypko: A to Z', 18 December 2002, *www.glavred.info/ eng/?art=63687812*; Alexander Gorobets, 'Ukraine's Anti-Mafia Against Lazarenko #2', 16 January 2002, http://english.pravda.ru/main/2002/01/16/25709_.html
6. The Germans only held out for four days when the Red Army returned in 1944.
7. Alexander J. Motyl, 'Structural Constraints and Starting Points: The Logic of Systematic Change in Ukraine and Russia', *Comparative Politics,* vol. 29, no. 4 (July 1997), pp. 433–447.
8. Peter Byrne interview with Vladimir Malinkovich, http://www.s95451559. online home.us/test2/archives/008152.html.
9. Sasha Volkova, 'Brainy Don i Kuchma', 25 May 2004, www2.pravda.com.ua/ archive/?40525-4-new.
10. John Thornhill and Charles Clover, 'Why are the Slavs Poor?', *Financial Times*, 21 August 1999.
11. *Wprost*, 20 October 2002.
12. *Ukrainian Weekly*, 31 October 2004.
13. Kost' Bondarenko, *Atlanty i kariatydy z-pid "dakhu" Prezydenta,* (L'viv: Kal'variia, 2000), pp. 45–6.
14. Ivan Lozowy, 'There Will Be Only One', *The Ukrainian Insider*, vol. 3, no. 2, 8 October 2003, via *The Ukraine List*, # 215.
15. Evgenii Bulavka, '"Boikie" rukhovtsy vystupili v roli predvybornogo rupora?', 10 January 2002, www.part.org.ua/index.php?art=34206533.
16. Kost' Bondarenko, 'Naperedodni prem"ieriady', 10 January 2005, www2. pravda. com.ua/ archive/?50110-3-new.
17. The Russian swearword блядь (*bliad'*) literally means 'whore', but is used indiscriminately, like the English word 'fuck'.
18. J. V. Koshiw, *Beheaded: The Killing of a Journalist*, (Reading: Artemia Press, 2003), pp. 42–3. A slightly different translation can be found in 'New Tape Translation of Kuchma Allegedly Ordering Falsification of Presidential Election Returns', *Kyiv Post*, 14 February, 2001. Mel'nychenko does not date his recordings as precisely as the 2004 'Zoriany' tapes.
19. See the 'Parliamentary Review' for 1999 at www.romyr.com/article_full. php3? article=rewiew_06.
20. Yurii Zushchik, 'Zhenshchina s proshlym', *Korrespondent*, (Ukraine), 19 February 2005, p. 22.
21. Anders Åslund, 'Ukraine's Return to Economic Growth', *Post-Soviet Geography and Economics*, vol. 42, no. 5 (July–August 2001), pp. 313–28. The figures for the electricity industry are on p. 320, and those for subsidy elimination are on p. 318.
22. Oleh Havrysh, 'The Presidential Oil and Gas Scheme: Part Two – Gas', 24 April 2005, www2.pravda.com.ua/en/archive/2005/april/19/3.shtml.
23. *EIU Country Report: Ukraine*, April 2001, p. 17.
24. 'Will Ukraine Abolish Kolkhozes?', *RFE/RL Poland, Belarus and Ukraine Report*, vol. 1, no. 28, 14 December 1999.
25. Åslund, 'Ukraine's Return to Economic Growth', p. 320.

26. Secondhand remarks by Mykola Melnychenko (Ukranian spelling is Mel'nychenko), interviewed by Radio Liberty on 29 December 2000. See www.rferl.org/reports/pbureport/2001/01/1-160101.asp.

27. Koshiw, *Beheaded*, p. 186.

28. Ivan Lozowy, 'Kinakh Appointment Overshadowed by State Secretaries', *The Ukraine Insider*, vol. 1, no. 3, 1 June 2001, via *The Ukraine List*, # 140, reports allegations by the outgoing Yushchenko government that the money was paid to ensure the Communists ensured the appointment of his successor Anatolii Kinakh (by abstaining in the key vote).

29. A full list can be found in the book by the veteran dissident and deputy, Levko Luk''ianenko, *Neznyshchennist'*, (Kiev: Diokor, 2003), pp. 58–62.

30. See the extracted interview dated 3 April 2005 at www2.pravda.com.ua/en/archive/2005/march/25/1.shtml.

## Chapter Four

1. 'Vse pro Oleksandra Volkova', 5 September 2000, www.ukrpravda.com/archive/?0095-4-new.

2. Many useful materials relating to the Gongadze case can be found at a site set up by the British National Union of Journalists, at www.delogongadze.org.

3. This is the underlying thesis in J. V. Koshiw's study of the Gongadze affair, *Beheaded; The Killing of a Journalist*. See also the claims made by ex-KGB man Aleksandr Litvinenko, who had many contacts with Melnychenko in exile, at www.interfax.kiev.ua/eng/go.cgi?31,20050401004.

4. Author's interview with Peter Byrne, 21 February 2005.

5. All extracts are from Koshiw, *Beheaded*, pp. 69–78. See also the alternative transcription at www.s95451559.onlinehome.us/abdymok/conversations.htm.

6. This account relies on the invaluable collection of documents by Leonid Kapeliushnyi, *Zhertovna krov: Daidzhest-doslidzhennia*, (Kiev: Dzerkalo tyzhnia, 2004).

7. 'Was the Prosecutor-General Bribed?', *RFE/RL Organised Crime and Terrorism Watch*, vol. 2, no. 15, 19 April 2002.

8. See Roman Kupchnisky, 'The Gongadze Case', *RFE/RL Organised Crime and Corruption Watch*, vol. 4, no. 16, 6 August 2004 at www.rferl.org/reports/corruption-watch, for a detailed investigation of the Gongadze case and the role of the three procurators. All quotes are taken from this source.

9. The *Independent*'s key article is reproduced, in English, at www2.pravda.com.ua/en/archive/2004/june/20/1.shtml.

10. '"Srazy posle viborov samii zhestokii poriadok. . .". Nove vid maiora Mel'nychenka', 11 February 2001, www.ukrpravda.com/archive/?10211-3-new.

11. Koshiw, *Beheaded*, p. 58.

12. Ibid., p. 68.

13. Nikolai Mel'nichenko [the Russian spelling of Mykola Mel'nychenko], *Kto est' kto. Na divane prezidenta Kuchmy*, (Kiev: 2002), p. 40.

14. Adapted from ibid., p. 10. Compare Koshiw's translation in *Beheaded*, p. 235.

15. Mel'nichenko, pp. 32–3.

16. The author was present at two of the demonstrations in February 2001.

17. Georgii Pocheptsov, *Informatsiia i dezinformatsiia*, (Kiev: Nika-tsentr, 2001), pp. 184–97.

18. 'Ukraine's leaders appeal to the nation', *BBC Monitoring*, 14 February 2001, http://news.bbc.co.uk/1/hi/world/monitoring/media_reports/1168935.stm.

19. As quoted in 'Vice Premier in Charge of European Integration Affairs Oleh Rybachuk. Unofficial Biography', 4 February 2005, www2.pravda.com.ua/en/archive/2005/february/4/ryba.shtml.

20. 'Making Revolution: Q&A with Dmytro Potekhin', *Kyiv Post*, 24 February 2005.
21. 'Lyst Mel'nychenka', 21 October 2004, www.ukrpravda.com/archive/?41021-3-new.
22. *Yabloko* is the Russian for 'apple'. The name came from its original leaders' surnames: Georgii Yavlinskii, Yurii Boldyrev and Vladimir Lukin. But although *Yabluko* is the Ukrainian for 'apple', its leaders were not the same.
23. It was supposed to suggest an image of hardy youth, of a new, meritocratic generation of reluctant politicians.
24. See the detailed analysis of the exit poll at http://www.dif.org.ua/ep/en/.
25. *RFE/RL Newsline*, 16 April 2002.
26. Volodymyr Boiko, 'Vybory po-donets'komu: rozhul zakonnosty ta pravoporiadku', *Ukraïns'ka pravda*, 10 April 2002.
27. Mykola Formazov, 'Ukraine's Local Tycoon Wrestles with Donetsk Group for Control over Port City of Mariupol', *BBC Monitoring Service*, 3 April 2004, translated from the *Ostrov* website, 26 March 2004.
28. Mykola Riabchuk, '"Bezlad" zarady "zlahody"', *Krytyka*, no. 4 (April) 2002, pp. 6–13. For the CVU analysis, see www.cvu.kiev.ua/eng/.
29. Sharon Lafraniere, 'Scare Tactics on the Rise in Ukraine', *Washington Post*, 18 December 2002.
30. 'Pivmil'iona dolariv SShA za vykhid z "Nashoï Ukraïny" – Orobets', www.pravda.com.ua, 20 December 2002.
31. 'The Price of Lytvyn', 20 May 2002, www.unian.net/eng/news/news-14684.html.

## Chapter Five

1. 'Is Yushchenko's Our Ukraine Kuchma's Political Project?', *RFE/RL Poland, Belarus and Ukraine Report*, vol. 3, no. 36, 25 September 2001.
2. Mel'nichenko, *Kto est' kto. Na divane prezidenta Kuchmy*, pp. 108 and 109.
3. Interview with Mykola Martynenko, Zinchenko's deputy responsible for these organisational questions, 20 April 2005, www2.pravda.com.ua/archive/2005/april/20/2.shtml.
4. Oleksandr Solantai, 'Pravda pro PORU ochyma zseredyny', 15 April 2005, www2.pravda.com.ua/archive/2005/april/15/3.shtml.
5. Ivan Haivanovich, 'Peremozhnyi shliakh do PORAzky?', 20 December 2004, www2.pravda.com.ua/archive/2004/december/20/5.shtml.
6. Author's interview with Inna Pidluska, 2 February 2005.
7. 'Making Revolution: Q&A with Dmytro Potekhin', *Kyiv Post*, 24 February 2005.
8. Author's interview with Peter Byrne, 21 February 2005.
9. '"Oranzhevoe" perekrashivanie', 31 January 2005, www.ord.com.ua/categ_1/article_7870.html.
10. Author's interviews with Inna Pidluska, 2 February 2005, and Rostyslav Pavlenko, 22 February 2005.
11. The alleged document 'Ne upustit shans!' was published at www.provokator.com.ua/p/2004/02/26/090819.html, dated 26 February 2004, and was predicated on Moroz's desire to preserve and 'expand his resource base'.
12. Author's interview with Oleksii Haran', 22 February 2005.
13. Author's interview with Rostyslav Pavlenko, 22 February 2005.
14. Oleksii Holobuts'kyi *et al.*, *Kandydat u Prezydenty Ukraïny Oleksandr Moroz: mozhlyvi stsenariï rozvytku sytuatsiï*, (Kiev: AMS, 2004), also available at www.agency.org.ua/index.php?mod=dosl.
15. The document was published in three parts on the *Ukraïns'ka pravda* website. The first part, 'Tretii termin Kuchmy. Yak tse povynno bulo buti', appeared on 25 June

2004, at www2.pravda.com.ua/archive/?40625-4-new; the second, 'Tretii termin Kuchmy. Yak tse povynno bulo buti. Chastyna 2', appeared on 30 June, at www2.pravda.com.ua/archive/?40630-1-new; and the third, 'Tretii termin Kuchmy. Yak tse povynno bulo buti. Chastyna 3, zakliuchna', on 1 July, at www2. pravda.com.ua/ archive/2004/july/1/2.shtml.

16. 'Vytik materialiv v plan Yanukovycha na druhyi tur: teshcha, Fradkov i rukh proty Yushchenka', 8 November 2004, www2.pravda.com.ua/archive/2004/ november/ 8/4.shtml.
17. See the report at www.artukraine.com/buildukraine/const_reform3.htm.
18. Ratushniak was no man of conviction. He was elected as an independent, joined For A United Ukraine in May 2002, People's Power in June, and Democratic Initiatives in October 2002. He became an independent again in September 2003, defected to Yushchenko's Our Ukraine in October and then joined Yanukovych's Regions of Ukraine in December 2003. He became an independent again in May 2004, and ended up in Lytvyn's People's Agrarian Party in December 2004. Source: www.rada.gov.ua:8080/pls/radac_gs09/dep_fr_per?kod=7306.
19. Alexandra Prymachenko, 'Pin-Point Blasting', *Dzerkalo tyzhnia*, no. 35, 4–10 September 2004.
20. Tetiana Nikolaienko, 'Troieshchyna – kashyrs'ke shose Yanukovycha?', 29 August 2004, www.ukrpravda.com/archive/?40828-1-new.
21. 'SBU pidtverdzhuie, shcho UNP ne terorysty', 16 December 2004, www2. pravda. com.ua/archive/?41216-20-77.
22. Author's interview with Rostyslav Pavlenko, 22 February 2005.
23. 'Platyv molodshyi Kliuiev. Tse dokazano telefonnymy rozmovamy. . .', 29 April 2005, www2.pravda.com.ua/archive/2005/april/29/4.shtml. This is a transcript of a pro- gramme on 1+1. See also http://www.1plus1.net/programs/dp_260405.phtml.
24. See Our Ukraine's claims at www.ourukraine.org/newsletter/issue10, and '62% voted for Baloha – Exit Poll', 22 April 2004, www.glavred.info/eng/?news= 106087461.
25. *Nezavisimaia gazeta*, 27 July and 3 August 2004.
26. 'Deputatskaia lapa', *Korrespondent*, (Ukraine), no. 6, 19 February 2005.
27. Yuliia Mostova, 'Tumannist' Yanukovycha', *Dzerkalo tyzhnia*, no. 25, 26 June–2 July 2004.
28. Valerii Khmel'ko, 'Prezidentskie vybory 2004 goda v Ukraine: sotsiologicheskie aspekty'.
29. Author's conversation with Volodymyr Paniotto of KIIS, 16 April 2005.
30. Andrew Wilson, *Virtual Politics: Faking Democracy in the Post-Soviet World*, (New Haven and London: Yale University Press, 2005).
31. Andrei Kurkov, *Penguin Lost*, (London: Harvill, 2002), pp. 65, 53 and 52.
32. Quoted in Caroline McGregor, 'Russia Sending Political Consultants to Ukraine', *Moscow Times*, 21 July 2004.
33. Interview with Pavlovskii, *Nezavisimaia gazeta*, 7 December 2004.
34. Julie Corwin, 'Moscow Ponders How Ukraine was "Lost"', *RFE/RL Belarus and Ukraine Report*, vol. 7, no. 2, 12 January 2005.
35. 'Rosiis'ke lobi Yanukovycha – chy ye kryminal'nyi slid?', 12 November 2004, www2. pravda.com.ua/archive/2004/november/12/6.shtml.
36. Interview with Pavlovskii in *L'vivs'ka hazeta*, 4 February 2005; www.gazeta.lviv.ua/ articles/2005/02/04/2357/. Confirmed by Volodymyr Polokhalo, author's interview, 25 February 2005.
37. Author's interview with Hryhorii Pocheptsov, 25 February 2005.
38. Ibid.
39. Francesca Mereu, 'Spin Doctors Blame Yanukovych', *Moscow Times*, 30 November 2004.

40. Author's interview with Piotr Shchedrovitskii, 3 November 2002.
41. 'Ukraine's Future on the Line', *Jane's Intelligence Digest*, 1 October 2004, at www.janes.com/security/international_security/news/jid/jid041001_1_n.shtml.
42. 'Tretii termin Kuchmy', as note 15 above.
43. 'Vytik materialiv v plan Yanukovycha na druhyi tur.'
44. See the number crunching at www.cidct.org.ua/en/studii/5-6(2002)/3.html.
45. 'Tretii termin Kuchmy', as note 15 above.
46. Andrii Duda, '"Natsyky" z Bankovoï', 17 May 2004, www.tribuna.com.ua/politics/2004/05/17/9843.html.
47. Holobuts'kyi *et al., Segodniashnie lidery Ukrainy: primerka roli prezidenta*, p. 237.
48. *Chysta hazeta*, no. 4 (September) 2004.
49. Originally published in *Postup*, 14 October 2004. See the translation 'An Open Letter from Twelve Apolitical Writers about Choice and the Elections' at www.ukrainianstudies.org/aaus-list/0410/msg00023.html.
50. 'An Open Letter from Representatives of Ukraine's Cultural Intelligentsia', www.ukrainianstudies.org/aaus-list/0410/msg00024.html.
51. Holobuts'kyi *et al., Segodniashnie lidery Ukrainy: primerka roli prezidenta,* pp. 235–6 and 14.
52. Maksim Zharov, 'Ya. stanovitsia Yu.: final'nyi akkord ukrainskikh vyborov', *Russkii zhurnal*, 17 November 2004.
53. Aleksandr Maslak, 'Mify o Yushchenko', 25 November 2004, www.apn.ru/?chapter_name=advert&data_id=257&do=view_single.
54. Oleg Varfolomeyev, 'Yanukovych has Moscow Patriarchate on His Side', *Eurasia Daily Monitor*, vol. 1, no. 127, 15 November 2004.
55. Michael Bourdeaux, 'Independent Churches win new respect', 8 January 2005, www.timesonline.co.uk/printFriendly/0,,1-118-1429937,00.html.
56. Quoted in www.obozrevatel.com/index.php?r=news&id=174586.
57. Remarks to the author, 16 March 2005.
58. 'Chornukha proty Yushchenka', 6 October 2004, www2.pravda.com.ua/archive/?4106-4-new.
59. See the report at www.ukrpravda.com/archive/?4105-32-77.
60. 'Kozak vydav piar Pavlovskoho dlia Yanukovycha', 16 November 2004, www.ukrpravda.com/archive/?41116-4-77.
61. Luba Shara, 'Promoting Yanukovych in Washington DC: Oops, He Did It Again!', 14 November 2004, www2.pravda.com.ua/en/archive/2004/november/10/1.shtml.
62. Vasyl' Yaremenko, 'Yevre_ v Ukra_ni s'ohodni: real'nist' bez mifiv' ('Jews in Ukraine Today: Reality Without Myths'), and 'Mif pro ukra_ns'kyi antysemityzm' ('The Myth of Ukrainian Anti-Semitism'), *Sil's'ki visti*, 30 September and 15 November 2003.
63. From Our Ukraine's version of events at www.razom.org.ua/en/news/1740/.
64. Volodymyr Boiko, 'Taiemnytsi "tainoï vecheri', 1 October 2004, www.pravda.com.ua/archive/2004/october/1/3.shtml.
65. Interviewed in *The Times*, 1 April 2005.
66. Interviewed in R.I. Chyrva *et al.* (eds.), *Viktor Yushchenko: Viriu! Znaiu! Mozhemo!*, (Kiev: In Yure, 2004), p. 149.
67. Interview with Satsiuk in *Stolichnye novosti*, no. 48, 22–28 December 2004, at http://cn.com.ua/N337/events/exclusive/exclusive.html. See also C. J. Chivers, 'A Dinner in Ukraine Made for Agatha Christie', *New York Times*, 20 December 2004.
68. AdReport, 'Zhak Sehela skomprometuvav Yushchenka za zamovlennia Pinchuka?', 7 October 2004, www2.pravda.com.ua/archive/2004/october/7/2.shtml.
69. See www.s95451559.onlinehome.us/test2/archives/2004_09.php, and Yushchenko's reply at www.yuschenko.com.ua/eng/Press_centre/168/1169.

70. The video could be viewed at the *Ukraïns'ka pravda* website, as of the date of access on 4 October 2004, at www.pravda.com.ua/archive/2004/september/24/video.shtml.
71. Interviewed on 'Good Morning America', 12 December 2004; http://abcnews.go.com/GMA/story?id=322922.
72. Adapted from the English translation made at http://eng.maidanua.org/node/137. The transcription of the original programme is at http://5tv.com.ua/pr_archiv/136/0/265/.
73. Author's interview with Rostyslav Pavlenko, 22 February 2005.
74. 'Kerivnyk MVC znaie, yakyi deputat suprovodzhuvav otrutu dlia Yushchenha', 4 February 2005, www.ukrpravda.com/archive/?5024-35-77.
75. Cited in Mereu, 'Spin Doctors Blame Yanukovych'.

## Chapter Six

1. Valerii Khmel'ko, 'Prezidentskie vybory 2004 goda v Ukraine: sotsiologicheskie aspekty'.
2. Author's conversation with Valerii Khmel'ko, 24 February 2005.
3. See also the translations at www.obozrevatel.com/index.php?r=news&id=169474; and www.obozrevatel.com/index.php?r=print&id=169475.
4. Yurii Butusov, 'Ide poliuvannia na "krotiv", ide poliuvannia!', *Dzerkalo tyzhnia*, no. 51, 18–24 December 2004.
5. 'Medvedchuk likviduie svidchennia pro fal'syfikatsiiu vyboriv', 1 December 2004, www2.pravda.com.ua/archive/2004/december/1/news/17.shtml.
6. Holobuts'kyi *et al.*, *Segodniashnie lidery Ukrainy: primerka roli prezidenta: VIII Kandidaty v prezidenty Ukrainy*, pp. 11 and 13; Mykola Velychko, '"Yanukovych? Kozak?" – "Yaka vam riznytsia?"', 27 August 2004, www.ukrpravda.com/archive/2004/august/27/1.shtml.
7. Adrian Karatnycky, 'Ukraine's Orange Revolution', *Foreign Affairs*, vol. 84, no. 2 (March–April) 2005, pp. 35–52, at p. 36.
8. Press release from the Committee of Voters of Ukraine, www.cvu.org.ua, 25 November 2004.
9. See www.ourukraine.org/newsletter/issue58/.
10. 'Yushchenko's Team Found Out How Bilokon Helped Falsify the Election', 20 December 2004, www.ukrpravda.co.uk/archive/2004/december/20/news/18.shtml.
11. 'The Party of Regions and the SDPU(o) Were the Ones that Hired Most of the Additional Trains During the Elections', 14 January 2005, www.razom.org.ua/en/news/5516/.
12. Author's interview with Rostyslav Pavlenko, 22 February 2005.
13. Source: official results at www.cvk.gov.ua.
14. *Ukrainian Weekly,* 7 November 2004.
15. Volodymyr Paniotto, 'Ukraine: Presidential Elections 2004 and the Orange Revolution', www.kiis.com.ua/txt/pdf/president%20election%20in%20ukraine%202004.doc.
16. Serhii Taran, Director of the Institute of Mass Information, 'Sotsiolohichni doslidzhennia staiut' na pokaznykom ob"iektyvnosti vyboriv, a zvychainoiu politychnoiu tekhnolohiieiu', 8 October 2004, http://imi.org.ua/?read=251:2.
17. Tatiana Silana (Tetiana Sylina), 'Exit Poll: Long Ordeal', *Dzerkalo tyzhnia*, no. 45, 6–12 November 2004.
18. See the site www.exitpoll.org.ua and the reporting at www.pravda.com.ua on 31 October and 1 November 2004.
19. 'Ekzyt-pol Pavlovs'koho pokazav peremohu Yushchenka', 18 November 2004, www2.pravda.com.ua/archive/2004/november/18/news/14.shtml.

20. Author's conversation with Valerii Khmel'ko, 24 February 2005.
21. 'Yushchenko zavershyv paralel'nyi pidrakhunok – vin vyhrav 1.3 per cent', 9 November 2004, www2.pravda.com.ua/archive/2004/november/9/news/25.shtml.
22. Vasyl' Koval' and Yurii Butusov, 'Konsul'tant AP Liudmyla Hrebeniuk: "za nashymy danymy, Yushchenko buv uves" chas liderom u khodi pidrakhunku holosiv!', *Dzerkalo tyzhnia*, no. 52, 25–30 December 2004.
23. From the CEC site at http://www1.cvk.gov.ua/wp0011 and from the running score kept at www2.pravda.com.ua/archive/2004/october/31/cvk.shtml.
24. Maksym Vital'chenko, 'Kirovohrad. Epitsentr protystoiannia', 3 November 2004, www2.pravda.com.ua/archive/2004/november/3/1.shtml.
25. 'Shcho narakhuvaly v TsVK?', 2 November 2004, www2.pravda.com.ua/archive/2004/november/2/3.shtml.
26. 'Novosti iz kuluarov Tsentrizbirkoma: kto-to iz komandy Yushchenko slivaet informatsiiu Medvedchuku', 2 November 2004, www.obkom.net.ua/news/2004-11-02/2100.shtml.
27. Author's conversation with Valerii Khmel'ko, 24 February 2005.
28. 'Fal'syfikatsiia bude mizh 1 i 2 hodynoiu nochi. Poroshenko radyt' ne pyty horilku', 19 November 2004, www.ukrpravda.com/archive/?41119-19-77.
29. See www.ourukraine.org/newsletter/issue58, 24 November 2004.
30. 'Fal'sifikatsiia v Zapadnoi Ukraine sostavila dva milliona golosov!', http://zadonbass.org/first/message.html?id=6490.
31. Information provided by OSCE observers.
32. Jackson Diehl, 'Putin's Unchallenged Imperialism', *Washington Post*, 25 October 2004.
33. Mariia Barinova, 'Proekt Rossiia', *Profil'*, no. 43, 22 November 2004, at www.profile.ru/items/?item=10201.
34. Yuliia Stepanenko, 'Komanda Yanukovicha potratit na vtoroi tur vyborov $95 mln', 18 November 2004, www.compromat.ru/main/kuchma/yanukovichdengi.htm.
35. The figures were published in official media such as *Holos Ukraïny*, 14 January 2005.
36. Stephen Velychenko, 'Behind the Scenes in the Provinces (Final Phase)', via *The Ukraine List*, #332, 11 January 2005.
37. Calculation by the Committee of Voters of Ukraine. See www.ourukraine.org/newsletter/issue58, 24 November 2004; author's interview with Rostyslav Pavlenko, 22 February 2005.
38. Author's interview with Rostyslav Pavlenko, 22 February 2005.
39. 'Poperedni resul'taty ekspertnoï otsinky vytrat kandydativ na vyborchu kampaniiu 2004 r.', posted 24 December 2004, http://coalition.org.ua/index. php?option=content&task=view&id=119&Itemid=. See also the analysis at www.irf.kiev.ua/files/eng/news_659_en_doc.doc.
40. Author's interview with Rostyslav Pavlenko, 22 February 2005.
41. Simon Jenkins, 'When is a mob not really a mob? Why, when it's our mob, of course', *The Times*, 1 December 2004.
42. John Laughland, 'The revolution televised', *Guardian*, 27 November 2004.

## Chapter Seven

1. Author's interview with Volodymyr Polokhalo, 25 February 2005.
2. Tet'iana Sylina *et al.*, 'Anatomiia dushi maidany', *Dzerkalo tyzhnia*, no. 50, 11–17 December 2004.
3. Serhii Rakhmanin, 'Ad"iutanty ïkh prevoskhodytelstv-2', *Dzerkalo tyzhnia*, no. 31, 7–13 August 2004.

4. Interview with Martynenko, 20 April 2005, www2.pravda.com.ua/archive/2005/april/20/2.shtml.

5. Ibid.

6. Serhii Sledz', 'Davyd Zhvaniia – ministr MNS', *Dzerkalo tyzhnia*, no. 4, 5–11 February 2005.

7. Interview with Martynenko.

8. Leonid Amchuk, 'Aleksandr Tretiakov: U nas ne bylo amerikanskikh deneg. Na revoliutsiiuperechislili20millionovgriven', 22December2004,www2.pravda.com.ua/archive/?41222-1-new.

9. Author's interview with Valentin Yakushik, 24 February 2005.

10. Sylina *et al.*, 'Anatomiia dushi maidany'.

11. Conversation with author, 31 January 2005.

12. Volodymyr Paniotto, 'Ukraine: Presidential Elections 2004 and the Orange Revolution', www.kiis.com.ua/txt/pdf/president%20election%20in%20ukraine%202004. doc.

13. Peter Byrne, 'SBU officer reveals insurrection plans', *Kyiv Post*, 20 December 2004.

14. Jeffry Groton, 'Living through a revolution', *St Petersburg Times*, 24 December 2004.

15. 'Zakulisnaia istoriia revoliutsii'. See note 34 below.

16. Rostyslav Pavlenko, comments by email, 18 March 2005.

17. Sergei Varshavchik, 'Na Ukraine proizoshla informatsionnaia revoliutsiia', *Nezavisimaia gazeta*, 10 December 2004.

18. Bohdan Klid, 'PORA Coordinator, Vladyslav Kaskiv, Speaks in Edmonton on the Invitation of CIUS', 21 April 2005, via *The Ukraine List*, #345, 22 April 2005.

19. All figures from Andrei Demartino, 'Tainye voiny PR', *Versii i kommentarii*, no. 4 (February) 2005. As of April 2005, the Yanukovych game could still be found at http://pora.org.ua/content/view/707/2/.

20. According to the not particularly reliable Mykhailo Brods'kyi, interviewed in *Ukraïna moloda*, 18 March 2005.

21. To read the lyrics, see www.stanford.edu/~hfilip/Razom_Nas_Bahato.htm, or http://orangeukraine.squarespace.com/journal/2004/11/29/razom-nas-bahato.html; to hear the song see www.pisni.org.ua/.

22. Aleksandar Vasovic, 'Far right flexes during Ukraine "revolution"', http://seattletimes.nwsource.com/html/nationworld/2002138664_ukraine03.html.

23. From the CD prepared by Volodymyr Lytvyn, *Ukraïna-2004: Podiï, dokumenty, fakty*, posted at www2.pravda.com.ua/archive/2005/march/3/3.shtml, and translated by Olga Bogatyrenko for *The Ukraine List*, #340, 9 March 2005.

24. See Chervonenko's interview, dated 29 March 2005, at www2.pravda.com.ua/archive/2005/march/29/3.shtml.

25. Andrei Piontkovskii speaking on Ekho Moskvy, 25 January 2005, www.echo.msk.ru/programs/exit/34180/. Piontkovskii is reporting the words of Viacheslav Nikonov and foreign minister Ivanov.

26. Quoted in C. J. Chivers, 'Back Channels: A Crackdown Averted. How Top Spies in Ukraine Changed the Nation's Path', *New York Times*, 17 January 2005.

27. Mykola Tomenko, 'Sshybka Leonida Kuchmy, abo taiemnytsia avtorstva knyzhky "Ukraïna – ne Rosiia"', *Dzerkalo tyzhnia*, no. 45, 22–28 November 2003.

28. Chivers, 'Back Channels', passim.

29. Konrad Schuller, 'Der Befehl wurde nicht befolgt', *Frankfurter Allgemeine Zeitung*, 20 December 2004, translated as 'The Command was not Obeyed', in *The Ukraine List*, #318, 20 December 2004.

30. 'SBU nakanune bol'shikh peremen', in four parts: 5 January, www.ord.com.ua/categ_1/article_5190.html; 6 January, www.ord.com.ua/categ_1/article_5491.html; 8

January, www.ord.com.ua/categ_1/article_5606.html; and 14 January, www.ord.com.ua/categ_1/article_6183.html.

31. See the interview, dated 12 April 2005, at www2.pravda.com.ua/archive/2005/april/12/3.shtml.
32. Interviewed in *Polityka*, 18 December 2004. An English translation was made available via *The Ukraine List*, #323, 24 December 2004.
33. See also the interview with Kwaśniewski in the *Wall Street Journal*, 17 February 2005.
34. See the story in *Gazeta Wyborcza*, translated as 'Zakulisnaia istoriia revoliutsii', 18 April 2005, www2.pravda.com.ua/archive/2005/april/18/1.shtml.
35. *Le Nouvel Observateur*, 25 November 2004.
36. Daniel McLaughlin, 'Walesa says he averted Ukraine clashes', *Observer*, 1 May 2005.
37. 'Zakulisnaia istoriia revoliutsii'.
38. Ibid.
39. Kwaśniewski, op. cit.
40. Peter Savodnik, 'Ukraine: The Washington Connection', *New York Review of Books*, vol. LII, no. 2, 10 February 2005, p. 42.
41. 'Ukraine on brink of "civil war"', 24 November 2004, http://news.bbc.co.uk/1/hi/world/europe/4040041.stm#startcontent.
42. As note 23 above.
43. An obvious example would be *The Times* editorial on 1 December 2004, 'Kuchma's Moment', which stated that 'he could . . . have tipped his country into open conflict, and his restraint so far should be commended'. See also Peter Finn, 'Old Divisions Resurface in Ukraine', *Washington Post*, 29 November 2004.
44. Yuliia Mostova, 'Ukraïna rozbylasia na shchastia?', *Dzerkalo tyzhnia*, no. 50, 11–17 December 2004.
45. From part 2 of the translation of the Lytvyn material, posted at www2.pravda.com.ua/archive/2005/march/9/4.shtml, via *The Ukraine List*, #341, 19 March 2005.
46. 'Ukrainian paper says "reliable" judges installed before elections', 10 December 2003, republished from the BBC, http://podrobnosti.com.ua/outeropinion/en/2003/12/10/91715.html.
47. 'Disobedient Judge Sentenced to Two Years of Jail', 29 March 2004, www.glavred.info/eng/print.php?news=104022638.
48. Mel'nichenko, *Kto est' kto. Na divane prezidenta Kuchmy*, p. 9. Compare the translation made by *Kyiv Post*, 8 February 2001.
49. The text was published at www2.pravda.com.ua/archive/2004/december/3/5.shtml. A translation can be found at *The Ukraine List*, #298, 3 December 2004.
50. Kuchma's remarks in an interview with the *New York Times*, 6 December 2004.
51. 'Putin Meets Kuchma and Slams A Repeat Vote', *Moscow Times*, 3 December 2004.
52. Isabel Allende, *The House of the Spirits*, (London: Black Swan edition, 1986), p. 350.
53. Poll by the Kiev International Institute of Sociology and the Razumkov Centre, *Gazeta po-kievski*, no. 147, 11 November 2004.
54. Remarks by Volodymyr Paniotto in public and to the author, ASN conference, New York, 15 April 2005.
55. See the press release dated 27 December 2004, and other document links at www.osce.org/item/8841.html.
56. Dominique Arel, Third Annual Cambridge–Stasiuk Program Lecture on Contemporary Ukraine, 'The Orange Revolution: Analysis and Implications of the 2004 Presidential Elections in Ukraine', www.ukrainianstudies.uottawa.ca/pdf/Arel_Cambridge.pdf.

## Chapter Eight

1. 'Kravchenko's suicide note has been shown. He blames Kuchma', 5 March 2005, www2.pravda.com.ua/en/archive/2005/march/5/1.shtml.
2. Volodymyr Tsvil, quoted in Oleg Varfolomeyev, 'Berezovsky Threatens to Open Pandora's Box Created by Fugitive Ukrainian Bodyguard', *Eurasia Daily Monitor*, vol. 2, no. 65, 4 April 2005.
3. See Melnychenko's statement, dated 29 April 2005, at www2.pravda.com.ua/archive/2005/april/29/2.shtml.
4. *RFE/RL Newsline*, vol. 9, no. 9, 14 January 2005.
5. 'Z ostannimy nezakonnymy diiamy uriadu Yanukoycha maie rozbiratysia Hen-prokuratura – Viktor Yushchenko', 30 December 2004, www.razom.org.ua/ua/news/5404/.
6. '7 kryminal'nykh sprav dlia vidomstva Bakaia. Kuchma ne khotiv viddaty dachu Yushchenku', 22 March 2005, www2.pravda.com.ua/archive/2005/march/22/6.shtml.
7. 'Kurochkin is under investigation. The arrests are under way!', 16 March 2005, http://mignews.com.ua/en/categ408/articles/154929.html.
8. See the news report at www2.pravda.com.ua/archive/?41216-10-77.
9. 'Bakai i Kuchma poderybynaly sanatorii sekretnymy ukazymy', 11 February 2005, www.pravda.com.ua.
10. *RFE/RL Newsline*, 15 March 2005.
11. 'Kuchma forever. . .', 4 February 2005, http://eng.imi.org.ua/?id=read&n=41&cy=2005&m=cmnt.
12. 'Bezsmertnyi ne holosuvatyme na "shantazhystku" Tymoshenko', 25 January 2005, www2.pravda.com.ua/archive/2005/january/25/news/25.shtml.
13. Oleksandr Morozov, 'Chotyry zapytannia do Yushchenka. P"iat' zapytan' do Tymoshenka', 26 January 2005, www2.pravda.com.ua/archive/?50126-3-new. The article includes a fax copy of the document, from which all quotes are taken.
14. Kost' Bondarenko, 'Naperedodni prem"ieriady', 10 January 2005; www2.pravda.com.ua/archive/?50110-3-new.
15. Luba Shara, 'Minister Zvarych, Could Be Another Fake Professor?', 18 April 2005, www2.pravda.com.ua/en/archive/2005/april/14/2.shtml.
16. For a strong critique listing such measures, see Serhii Rakhmanin, 'Persha chytan-nia', *Dzerkalo tyzhnia*, no. 9, 12–18 March 2005.
17. '"Pora!" formuie reiestr obitsianok Yushchenka, shchob "havkaty" na n'oho'. 25 January 2005, www2.pravda.com.ua/archive/2005/january/25/news/16.shtml.
18. Author's interview with Rostyslav Pavlenko, 22 February 2005.
19. 'Hard Times for Akhmetov and Pinchuk', 30 April 2005, www2.pravda.com.ua/en/archive/2005/april/21/2.shtml.
20. 'Ukraine economy: Betting on a tax windfall', online analysis by the Economist Intelligence Unit, 30 March 2005, www.viewswire.com/index.asp?layout=display_article&doc_id=208165420.
21. Andrew Wilson, *Ukrainian Nationalism in the 1990s: A Minority Faith*, (Cambridge, UK: Cambridge University Press, 1997).
22. 'Rozhromnyi vystup Yushchenka v Donets'ku', 13 February 2005, www2.pravda.com.ua/archive/2005/february/13/2.shtml.
23. Yuliia Mostova, 'Tumannist' Yanukovycha', *Dzerkalo tyzhnia*, no. 25, 26 June–2 July 2004.
24. Opinion poll by KIIS. See 'Dumky i pohliady naselennia Ukraïny – berezen 2005 r.', www.kiis.com.ua/txt/pdf/press07042005.pdf.
25. Yurii Butusov, 'Donets'k v epokhu fraktsiinoï rozdroblenosti', *Dzerkalo tyzhnia*, no. 15, 23 April–6 May 2005.

## Chapter Nine

1. Pavlovskii interview in *Nezavisimaia gazeta*, 7 December 2004.
2. Francesca Mereu, 'Spin Doctors Blame Yanukovych', *Moscow Times*, 30 November 2004.
3. Gleb Pavlovskii, 'Revoliutsiia, ee vozhdi i ee tekhnologii', 6 December 2004, www.kreml.org/media/72842836.
4. See the interview dated 5 November 2004, www2.yuschenko.com.ua/rus/present/Mass_media/1526.
5. Pavlovskii in *Nezavisimaia gazeta*, 7 December 2004.
6. Julie Corwin, 'Moscow Ponders How Ukraine was "Lost"', *RFE/RL Belarus and Ukraine Report*, vol. 7, no. 2, 12 January 2005.
7. 'O sviaziakh Yushchenka i Berezovskogo', 27 October 2004, www.compromat.ru/main/kuchma/jushenkoberez1.htm.
8. See the linked article by Elena Serebriakova, 'Berezovskii prislal gontsa k Yushchenko', dated 19 October 2004.
9. Dmitrii Sretenskii and Valdimir Sereda, '"Oranzhevaia revoliutsiia": sdelano v Rossii', www.vslux.ru/rubric.phtml?id=244#news4260.
10. 'Ukrainskie oshibki Kremlia', 25 November 2004, www.dni.ru/news/polit/2004/11/25/53489.html.
11. Alexander Militsky, 'Viktor Yushchenko and Britney Spears: Post-Democracy, Ukrainian Fashion', *The Russia Journal* (a Pavlovskii paper), 14 February 2005.
12. Cited in Mereu, 'Spin Doctors Blame Yanukovych'.
13. Pavlovskii interview in *Nezavisimaia gazeta*, 7 December 2004.
14. Author's interview with Peter Byrne, 21 November 2004.
15. Aleksandr Dugin, '"Dve Ukrainy": geopolitika krizisa i karta grazhdanskoi', *Izvestiia*, 29 November 2004.
16. Aleksandr Dugin, 'Rossiia uzhe pobedila na Ukraine, potomu chto ne sdalas' bez boia', *Komsomol'skaia pravda*, 1 December 2004.
17. Konstantin Zatulin, 'Bor'ba za Ukrainu: chto dal'she?', *Vremia novosti*, 3 February 2005.
18. Aleksandr Dugin, *Osnovy geopolitiki. Geopoliticheskoe budushchee Rossii*, (Moscow: Arktogeia, second edition, 1999), pp. 800–1.
19. Interview with Marat Gel'man, 'Ukraina – zerkalo dlia Putina', 23 December 2004, www.dni.ru/news/polit/2004/12/23/55011.html.
20. Varvara Zhlutenko, 'Putin's Energy Maneuver (sic)', *Den'*, 22 April 2005.
21. 'Sovetnik iz Rossii', *Korrespondent*, (Ukraine), no. 6, 19 February 2005.
22. Cited in Vladimir Socor, 'Kremlin Redefining Policy in "Post-Soviet Space"', *Eurasia Daily Monitor*, vol. 2, no. 27, 8 February 2005.
23. Zatulin, 'Bor'ba za Ukrainu: chto dal'she?'
24. Ekaterina Kuznetsova, 'Moskva sleduet podderzhat' evropeiskii vybor Ukrainy: "oranzhevaia revoliutsiia" mozhet priblizit' moment "vozvrashcheniia" Rossii v Evropu', *Nezavisimaia gazeta*, 9 February 2005.
25. *Kyiv Post*, 25 January 2005.
26. Should anyone be interested in reading his speech, it is at http://president.gov.by/rus/president/speech/2005/.
27. Information for the fiscal year 2004, dated 17 August 2004, www.state.gov/p/eur/rls/fs/35990.htm.
28. See www.kabar.kg, 17 March 2005.
29. Ruzanna Stepanian, 'Opposition Vows Another Push For Regime Change', www.armenialiberty.org, 8 April 2005.
30. See the joint statement dated 4 April 2005 at www.whitehouse.gov/news/releases/2005/04/20050404-1.html.

31. 'Why Zimbabwe Is Not Ukraine', *Christian Science Monitor*, 5 April 2005.
32. Jonathan Steele, 'Ukraine's postmodern coup d'etat', *Guardian*, 26 November 2004.
33. Jonathan Steele, 'Not a good way to start a democracy', *Guardian*, 31 December 2004.
34. Ian Traynor, 'US campaign behind the turmoil in Kiev', *Guardian*, 26 November 2004; Nick Paton Walsh, 'Inquiry sought into claims of US funding', idem, 13 December 2004.
35. See the original at www.house.gov/paul/congrec/congrec2004/cr120704.htm.
36. Matt Kelley, 'US Money Helped Opposition in Ukraine', *Associated Press*, 10 December 2004.
37. See www.state.gov/p/eur/rls/rpt/23629.htm, dated January 2003.
38. See www.state.gov/p/eur/rls/rpt/37672.htm, dated January 2004.
39. See www.state.gov/p/eur/rls/fs/36503.htm, dated 13 September 2004. These figures are therefore more provisional. Joel Brinkley, 'Dollars for Democracy? US Aid to Ukraine Challenged', *New York Times*, 21 December 2004, quotes $97 million in the fiscal year that ended on 31 October 2004, including approximately $28 million for democracy-building projects.
40. See www.britemb-ukraine.net.
41. See www.irf.kiev.ua/files/eng/news_659_en_doc.doc.
42. *Chicago Tribune*, 18 March 2005.
43. 'Congressman accuses US Government of supporting Viktor Yushchenko', *ICPS Newsletter*, no. 258, 20 December, 2004, at www.icps.kiev.ua/eng/topics, via UKL #320, 22 December 2004.
44. Brinkley, 'Dollars for Democracy?'.
45. 'Ministry of Economy: America Did Not Finance Yushchenko's Campaign', 30 December 2004, http://hotline.net.ua/content/view/9823/37/, via *The Ukraine List*, #335, 20 January 2005.
46. See the statement by Freedom House, dated 22 November 2004, at www.freedom-house.org/media/pressrel/112204.htm.
47. *Washington Post*, 2 January 2005.
48. Author's conversation with Valerii Khmel'ko, 25 February 2005.
49. Author's interviews with Peter Byrne, 21 February 2005, and Rostyslav Pavlenko, 22 February 2005. Vladyslav Kaskiv, *et al.*, 'PORA – Vanguard of Democracy', at http://pora.org.ua/en/content/view/780/95.
50. Oleksandr Solantai, 'Pravda pro PORU ochyma zseredyny', 15 April 2005, www2.pravda.com.ua/archive/2005/april/15/3.shtml.
51. Jeremy Bransten, 'Ukraine: Part Homegrown Uprising, Part Imported Production?', 20 December 2004, www.rferl.org/featuresarticle/2004/12/BE8E5D97-7EAF-404E-8E91-E21723FF74B6.html; John Simpson and Marcus Tanner, 'Serb Activists Helped Inspire Ukrainian Protests', 26 November 2004, www.iwpr.net/index.pl?archive/bcr3/bcr3_200411_530_1_eng.txt.
52. Roger Cohen, 'Who Really Brought Down Milosevic?', *New York Times Magazine*, 26 November 2000, www.nytimes.com/library/magazine/home/20001126mag-serbia.html.
53. Vital' Silitski, 'Hrantavy skandal', in Valer Bulhakaw (ed.), *Miastsovyia vybary w nainowshai paliitychnai historyi Belarusi*, (Minsk: Arche, 2003), pp. 109–114; *Christian Science Monitor*, 10 September 2001; Ian Traynor, 'Belarussian [sic] foils dictator-buster . . . for now', *Guardian*, 14 September 2001.
54. According to Natalia Antelava, 'How to Stage a Revolution', 4 December 2003, http://news.bbc.co.uk/2/hi/europe/3288547.stm; the US spent $2.4 million in Georgia on democracy support, and the local Renaissance Foundation spent $350,000.

55. The press release at www.rockcreekcreative.com/news/RCC_UKRpress2.pdf, 8 February 2005, implies that the website was closer to the centre of the 'Ukrainian democracy movement' than it actually was.
56. Quoted in Kelley, 'US Money Helped Opposition in Ukraine'.
57. Information provided by Inna Pidluska of the Europe-XXI Foundation, Kiev.
58. Nick Paton Walsh, 'The radicals with vested interest in orange victory', *Guardian*, 30 November 2004.
59. Steele, 'Ukraine's postmodern coup d'etat'; Traynor, 'US campaign behind the turmoil in Kiev'; Mark Almond, 'The price of People Power', *Guardian*, 7 December 2004.
60. 'Rund 180 Millionen Euro aus Kredit der Deutschen Bank verschwunden', 18 March 2005, http://derstandard.at/?url=/?id=1987792.
61. See her remarks to CNN, 20 April 2005, at http://edition.cnn.com/2005/WORLD/europe/04/20/rice.dougherty/index.html.
62. Ira Strauss, 'In Ukraine, Western Media Mirrored Kremlin', *Moscow Times*, 1 February 2005.
63. For web reproductions, see http://zadonbass.org/first/message.html?id=8257; http://zadonbass.org/en/first/message.html?id=7628; and http://zadonbass.org/first/message.html?id=7326. Jonathan Steele's article was reprinted in the government paper *Rossiiskaia gazeta*, and in the Kremlin sounding-board *Komsomolskaia pravda*, 29 November 2004, and in the Luzhkov-backed *Moskovskii komsomolets*, 30 November 2004.
64. *Gazeta Wyborcza*. 5 January 2005.
65. Remarks by senior EU officials to the author, February 2005.
66. R. I. Chyrva *et al.* (eds.), *Viktor Yushchenko: Viriu! Znaiu! Mozhemo!*, (Kiev: In Yure, 2004), p. 176.
67. The official text is at www2.europarl.eu.int/omk/sipade2?PUBREF=-//EP//TEXT+TA+P6-TA-2005-0009+0+DOC+XML+V0//EN&L=EN&LEVEL=3&NAV=S&LSTDOC=Y.
68. Marek Matraszek, 'Ukraine, Poland, and a free world', 2 December 2004, www.opendemocracy.net/themes/article-3-2251.jsp.
69. Interviewed in *Polityka*, 18 December 2004.
70. 'Russian Political Scientist Blames Polish Conspiracy for Ukraine Election Crisis', 25 November 2004, www.mosnews.com/news/2004/11/25/markov.shtml.
71. Cited in Mereu, 'Spin Doctors Blame Yanukovych'.
72. Quoted in Julie Corwin, 'Analysis: A Sign of the Times', www.rferl.org/featuresarticle/2004/12/a3d0fe6e-471b-4ec2-8a7f-fcf38bfcc22f.html.
73. Robert Kagan, *Of Paradise and Power: America and Europe in the New World Order*, (New York: Alfred A. Knopf, 2003).
74. Interview with Radek Sikorski, 15 February 2005, www.aei.org/research/nai/publications/pubID.21979,projectID.11/pub_detail.asp. See also the debate at www.frontpagemag.com/articles/ReadArticle.asp?ID=16715.
75. See his remarks at the National Review Online, dated 26 December 2004, www.nationalreview.com/thecorner/04_12_26_corner-archive.asp#048915.
76. Radek Sikorski, 'Back in the (Former) USSR', 23 December 2004, www.aei.org/publications/pubID.21758/pub_detail.asp.
77. See www.whitehouse.gov/news/releases/2005/01/20050120-1.html.
78. The speech can be found at www.yuschenko.com.ua/eng/Press_centre/168/2894/, dated 6 April 2005.
79. For a prescient view of Ukraine's potential contribution, see Yurii Shcherbak, *Ukraïna: vyklyk i vybir. Perspektyvy Ukraïny v hlobalizovanomu sviti XXI stolittia*, (Kiev: Dukh i litera, 2004).

80. Michael Meacher, 'One for oil and oil for one', *Spectator*, 5 March 2005.
81. Susan B. Glasser and Peter Baker, 'What Comes After Rose, Orange and Tulip?', *Washington Post*, 3 April 2005.
82. Richard Holbrooke, 'From "Tent City" to NATO', *Washington Post*, 14 December 2004.
83. Patrick J. Buchanan, 'What Are We Up to – in Ukraine?', 6 December 2004, www.antiwar.com/pat/?articleid=4114.
84. Leonid Kuchma, *Ukraïna – ne Rosiia*, (Moscow: Vremia, 2003), p. 97.

## Chapter Ten

1. A phrase coined by Anders Åslund, to whom it had the positive connotation of proving Ukraine's 'market' reforms were beginning to develop a real middle class. Cf the PR piece by Kost' Bondarenko, 'Sistema BYUT, ili Blok Yushchenko-Tymoshenko', dated July–August 2004, http://for-ua.com/authcol/2005/01/18/145912.html.
2. Theda Skocpol, *States and Social Revolutions: A Comparative Analysis of France, Russia and China*, (Cambridge, UK: Cambridge University Press, 1979), p. 4.
3. Anders Åslund, 'Ukraine Whole and Free: What I saw at the orange revolution', *Weekly Standard*, 27 December 2004.
4. Author's interview with Volodymyr Polokhalo, 25 February 2005.
5. These points were originally made with greater clarity by Jessica Allina-Pisano, at the ASN conference in New York, 15 April 2005.
6. Wilson, *Virtual Politics*.
7. Author's interview with Volodymyr Polokhalo, 25 February 2005.
8. Ibid.
9. 'Ya ne bazhaiu pani Tymoshenko opynytysia v sytuatsiï pana Zhvaniï', *L'vivs'ka hazeta*, 4 February 2005, www.gazeta.lviv.ua/articles/2005/02/04/2357.
10. See Greg Walters, '100 Days On, Trouble Hits Orange Kingdom', *Moscow Times*, 3 May 2005; Anders Åslund, 'Betraying a Revolution', *Washington Post*, 18 May 2005.

# Bibliographical Note

There are two standard histories of Ukraine currently in English. Orest Subtelny's *Ukraine: A History* (University of Toronto Press) was first published in 1988 and was in its third edition by 2000. Paul Robert Magocsi's *A History of Ukraine* (University of Toronto Press, 1996), is longer, but has more chapter sub-divisions.

There is little in English on the late Kuchma era and its dramatic end, other than the strictly academic. An important exception is J.V. Koshiw, *Beheaded: The Killing of a Journalist* (Artemia Press, 2003), which is a special study of the Gongadze scandal.

Early comment pieces on the Orange Revolution include Adrian Karatnycky, 'Ukraine's Orange Revolution', *Foreign Affairs*, vol. 84, no. 2 March/April 2005, pp. 32–52, and several analyses in academic journals: the special issues of *Problems of Post-Communism*, vol. 52, no. 2, March–April 2005; *Journal of Democracy*, vol. 16, no. 2 April 2005; and *Communist and Post-Communist Studies*, vol. 38, no. 2, pp. 131–292 (June 2005) – the last entitled 'Ukraine: Elections and Democratisation', edited by Taras Kuzio and Paul D'Anieri. There is one eyewitness account in French, by Alain Guillemoles, *Même la neige était orange: La révolution ukrainienne* (Les Petits Matins, 2005). Etienne Thévenin, *L'enjeu ukrainien – Ce que révèle la Révolution orange*, (CLD, 2005) is largely historical. In German there is Ingmar Bredies (ed.), *Zur Anatomie der Orange Revolution in der Ukraine: Wechsel des Elitenregimes oder Triumph des Parlamentarismus?* (Stuttgart: Buchhandel/Ibidem, Soviet and Post-Soviet Politics and Society, 2005). In the pipeline is Michael McFaul and Anders Åslund (eds), *Revolution in Orange: The Origins of Ukraines's Democratic Breakthrough* (Carnegie Endowment, January 2006), as is Askold Krushelnychy, *An Orange Revolution: A Personal Journey Through Ukrainian History* (Harvill Secker, 2006). A history of Pora, 'PORA – Vanguard of Democracy', is available on the web at http://pora. org.ua/en/content/view/780/95/.

The best available source for up-to-date English language news from Ukraine is *The Ukraine List*, which can be obtained via email from Dominique Arel at darel@uottawa.ca, and is being progressively archived at www.ukrainianstudies.uottawa.ca.

# Index